The National Innovation
System of Belgium

Contributions to Economics

continued on page 247

Henri Capron
Wim Meeusen (Editors)

The National Innovation System of Belgium

With 116 Figures
and 33 Tables

Physica-Verlag

A Springer-Verlag Company

Series Editors
Werner A. Müller
Martina Bihn

Editors
Prof. Henri Capron
Free University of Brussels
Department of Applied Economics (DULBEA)
CP 40 – Avenue F.D. Roosevelt
1000 Brussels
Belgium
Email: hcapron@ulb.ac.be

Prof. Wim Meeusen
University of Antwerp – RUCA
Department of Applied Economics
Midelheimlaan 1
2020 Antwerp
Belgium
Email: wmeeusen@ruca.ua.ac.be

ISSN 1431-1933
ISBN 3-7908-1308-7 Physica-Verlag Heidelberg New York

Die Deutsche Bibliothek – CIP-Einheitsaufnahme
The national innovation system of Belgium: with 33 Tables/Henri Capron; Wim Meeusen (ed.). –
Heidelberg; New York: Physica-Verl., 2000
    (Contributions to economics)
    ISBN 3-7908-1308-7

Physica-Verlag Heidelberg New York
a member of BertelsmannSpringer Science+Business Media GmbH

© Physica-Verlag Heidelberg New York 2000
Printed in Germany

Softcover-Design: Erich Kirchner, Heidelberg

SPIN 10769185   88/2202-5 4 3 2 1 0 – Printed on acid-free paper

Preface

This book deals with aspects of the national innovation system of Belgium. It is the result of a study jointly undertaken by teams of the University of Antwerp (RUCA) and the Free University of Brussels (ULB) in the context of the OECD-DSTI Working Group on Innovation and Technology Policy, which brought together specialists from most of the OECD countries in an effort to streamline and co-ordinate research on national innovation systems.

The 'systemic' approach – as opposed to the traditional 'linear causal' approach – has, in recent years, increasingly become the framework for the study of the complex relationships between R&D, innovation, the economic performance of firms and of the economy in which they operate, technological policy, and, finally, the institutional framework of the national economy, including its transnational aspects. Obviously, the systemic approach did not fall out of the blue but has its roots in different schools of economic thought.

The theoretical foundations of the national innovation system approach are therefore first discussed in Chapter 1. Chapters 2 and 3 introduce the reader to some peculiarities of the Belgian economy. Chapter 2 deals with the sources of Belgian prosperity, looked at from a long-term perspective and with particular attention being given to the small-open-economy characteristics of Belgium. Chapter 3 concludes Part I of the book and discusses the very special Belgian institutional setting, with particular reference to the relation of that setting to aspects of science and technology policy. From Chapter 4 to Chapter 7 (Part II of the book), the national innovation system is looked at in function of the inputs in the system. Chapter 4 deals with R&D expenditures and employment. Chapter 5 does the same but focuses on R&D activities at the level of the firm. Chapter 6 is concerned with the international linkages of the Belgian innovation system. The final chapter of this part of the book, Chapter 7, continues this theme by considering more closely the network formed by relations between the different actors in the shape of joint research projects and technological alliances. Part III of the book deals with what can identified as outputs of the national innovation systems. Chapter 8 concentrates on immediate outputs: patents, trademarks, and scientific publications. Chapter 9 looks at more final outputs: export performance and international competitiveness. We conclude in Chapter 10.

The research carried out on the national innovation system of Belgium was made possible by a grant from the Office for Scientific, Technical, and Cultural Affairs (OSTC) of the Belgian federal government. The authors benefited greatly from the comments and help provided by Veerle Lories, Monika Sormann and Greta Vervliet of AWI, Paul Chapelle of DGTRE, Jan Larosse of IWT and Jean Moulin of the OSTC. Special thanks go to Ward Ziarko of the OSTC for the continuous encouragement he gave us, and for his valuable advice. Without him this book would not have been written.

The editors

Table of Contents

PART II   THE INPUTS IN THE NATIONAL INNOVATION SYSTEM

PART III   THE OUTPUTS OF THE NATIONAL INNOVATION SYSTEM AND CONCLUSION

List of Contributors

Henri Capron, Department of Applied Economics (DULBEA), Université Libre de Bruxelles, Brussels (Belgium).

Michele Cincera, Office for Scientific, Technical and Cultural Affairs (OSTC), Brussels and Department of Applied Economics (DULBEA), Université Libre de Bruxelles, Brussels (Belgium).

Michel Dumont, Department of Applied Economics, Universiteit Antwerpen (RUCA), Antwerp (Belgium).

Wim Meeusen, Department of Applied Economics, Universiteit Antwerpen (RUCA), Antwerp (Belgium).

Glenn Rayp, Faculty of Economics, Universiteit Gent, Ghent (Belgium).

Klaus Vandewalle, Study Department, KBC Bank, Brussels (Belgium).

Bruno van Pottelsberghe de la Potterie, Department of Applied Economics (DULBEA), Université Libre de Bruxelles, Brussels (Belgium).

Part I

Introduction and Institutional Setting

Chapter 1. The Theoretical Foundations of the National Innovation Systems Approach

Wim Meeusen

1.1. Introduction

The concept of 'national innovation systems' (NIS) as used by professional economists is fairly recent. According to Edquist (1997) the term made its first appearance in the literature on the relations between technology, innovation, and economic performance in a book published in 1987 by Chris Freeman on the subject of technology policy and economic performance in Japan (Freeman, 1987).

Freeman's definition is still one of the most concise and pertinent. Starting from it and paraphrasing him one could say that a national system of innovation is the network of actors in the public and private sectors whose activities and interactions initiate, modify, and diffuse innovations and implement them in new products, new production processes, and new organisational forms. Clarifying further one might add, first, that, in the Schumpeterian tradition (see Schumpeter, 1939), the systems approach does indeed use a fairly broad definition of the concept of innovation, encompassing product, process and organisational innovations, and, second, that the national dimension does not mean that one must discard globalisation aspects and confine the analysis to the borders of national states. The opposite is true. 'National' (or, for that matter, 'regional') in this context signifies that one stresses differences between the institutions of countries when the issues of international competitiveness, specialisation patterns, directions of trade flows etc., are tackled, rather than assuming, as in the neo-classical tradition, that national production functions are identical and that countries have access to the same technology.

The most salient characteristic of the NIS approach is its emphasis on networks. The obvious reason for the rise of the network, or 'systemic', component of innovation systems is the apparently increasing importance of non-market forms of co-ordination, characteristic of what Dunning (1997) has called 'alliance capitalism'. Researchers, therefore, need to study the behaviour of actors on the system level rather than on the level of individual optimisers. More generally and also as the result of the globalisation process, important strategic decisions in the implementation of new technologies in production and distribution are taken within the context of alliances between firms or between firms and public authorities. Although market co-ordination in the strict sense is probably still effective in the long-run, economists and policy-makers should try in the short and medium

run to understand better the non-market ways of co-ordinating the various interacting components of the network of firms, public-funded research laboratories,
institutes of higher education, and public authorities (Teece, 1992; Galli and
Teubal, 1997; Carlsson and Jacobsson, 1997; Håkansson, 1989). The NIS approach places the role of institutions and their evolution in a central position.

Especially from the policy point of view, the 'systemic' or network aspect of
national innovation systems implies that the old view of technological change with
scientific discovery at one end and new products and processes at the other end of
a linear causal chain should be seriously reconsidered.

The practical importance of the new approach is stressed by its surprisingly
rapid diffusion within organisations like the OECD (cf. its DSTI 'Working Group
on Innovation and Technology Policy') and the European Commission.

Recent as the systems approach to technology and innovation may be, as always in such cases, it did not fall out of the blue. Systems thought was latently
present, and increasingly so, in much that preceded it. Indeed, tracing its origins in
the history of economic thought is revealing. This is what we will set out to do in
Section 1.2 of this chapter. Section 1.3 discusses some early insights and results of
NIS-type research, and Section 1.4 reviews technology policy from this same
doctrinal point of view.

1.2.   A characterisation from the viewpoint of the evolution of economic thought on technological progress and innovation

1.2.1.   The mainstream neo-classical approach

The natural starting point for discussing the neo-classical view of technological
progress and innovation is neo-classical growth theory, since the mainstream view
on economic theory that was prevalent in the post-war period up to the 1970s held
that technological progress was a phenomenon the study of which only made
sense within a long-run context. Some neo-classical economists, however, contributed to the micro-economic analysis of innovation at the firm level under different supply conditions (e.g. Arrow, 1962). We will discuss this literature briefly
in Section 1.3.

In Solow's growth model and its basic variations, the technological level of the
economy was never introduced except as an exogenous variable in the aggregate
production function, growing at a constant rate, and therefore represented as an
exponential time trend appended to one of the primary factors of production or
their combination. Technological progress was 'manna from heaven' and pro-
ceeded at a never varying speed and in a never varying direction.

The main issue in this context was the neutrality of technological progress.
What additional properties – in addition to exogeneity and constant speed – should

aggregate technological progress have in order to be compatible with the existence and stability of a long-run equilibrium growth path upon which the production factors would be kept in balance? It was soon understood that only 'Harrod-neutral' technological progress, i.e. shifts in the production function that would leave the capital-output ratio constant at constant rates of return on capital, could satisfy the requirements of equilibrium in long-run growth. However, Harrod-neutral technological progress is strictly of the labour-augmenting kind. It is difficult to interpret it as resulting from novelties that would be anything other than process or possibly organisational innovations. Product innovations did not enter the picture.

From 1964 onwards, a number of publications by Kennedy (1964), Samuelson (1965), and Drandakis and Phelps (1966) tried to introduce technological progress into the neo-classical growth model in a more satisfactory way. The basic new concept was Kennedy's 'innovation possibility frontier' (IPF). The IPF shows, at a constant R&D budget, the trade-off between the choice of a labour-saving and a capital-saving technology. This choice, in Kennedy's model, is determined by the entrepreneur's tendency to maximise the rate of unit-cost reduction. The Kennedy model is the first instance of an attempt to build a model of endogenous technological change, although, at the end of the day, the model only endogenously explained the factor-saving bias (i.e. movements along the IPF) and not the overall rate of technological progress (i.e. shifts of the IPF). The reason was, of course, that investment in R&D activities remained exogenous. The model came under severe criticism (see, for example, Nordhaus, 1973), and the economics profession soon lost interest in growth theory as such anyway because of the changing economic climate in the 1970s.

When the so-called 'new growth theory', which focused again on endogenous growth, was developed at the end of the 1980s, a long period had elapsed during which technology and innovation had all but disappeared from the agenda of mainstream economics. This period was so long that the older contributions on endogenous or 'induced' technological progress were not even mentioned in the list of references of the seminal papers on 'endogenous growth' of Romer, Lucas, Barro, Rebelo, and others and of the papers by some of these authors discussing its origins (e.g., Romer's otherwise excellent 1994 paper on 'The origins of endogenous growth'; Romer, 1994).

1.2.2. Theories of endogenous growth

The 'new growth theory' emerged mainly as a reaction to three issues. The first one was theoretical. Many economic theorists felt that the nature of technological change and its apparent importance in matters of growth and income distribution had become such that continuing reliance on the traditional assumptions of perfect competition and the free availability and distribution of knowledge could no longer be justified. A new theoretical approach was needed in which the phenomenon of technological progress would be endogenised in a context in which firms operate on imperfectly competitive markets. New theories of this kind would have to make an explicit distinction between rival and non-rival inputs and also between excludable and non-excludable goods. The difference between these two distinctions is important: although scientific knowledge and thus information from discoveries may well be non-rival, this does not mean that economically important discoveries are not often at least partially excludable, so they cannot be considered a public good and treated as such (as in the standard neo-classical growth models).

The other two issues were of a more empirical nature. First, there was the productivity slowdown that apparently occurred in most developed countries from the 1970s onwards, and for which different explanations had been offered, none of them completely satisfactory (see the survey published by the OECD, 1991). In any event, Solow's neo-classical growth model and its variants, all of them treating technological progress as an exogenous variable, seemed not to be relevant to the problem at hand. Second, there was the issue of the apparent absence of economic convergence of income per capita between different countries or groups of countries or at the least the abnormally low speed of that convergence.

It is fair to say that the last issue attracted most of the attention of the 'new growth theorists'. Their basic idea was surprisingly simple; so simple that one may wonder why it took the profession so long to cast it in a formal context. Once the economy experiences a boost in growth for one reason or another, perhaps through a policy-induced increase in the savings rate, then an increase would follow, not only in output and living standards, but also in the rate of human capital formation and innovation, which would again increase output and productivity and so would create a 'virtuous' circle. Unlike as predicted by Solow's model, in which an increase in the savings rate only boosts growth in a transition period and does not influence the long-term rate of growth, the latter is now lastingly affected. In this case, country-specific shocks may easily preclude convergence.

The logical background of this locking-in effect is increasing returns. The increasing returns enter the analysis in different ways, all related to some extent to the nature of technological progress.

One way is by technological spillovers (Romer, 1986). Since new ideas involve the creation of knowledge that is at least partially non-rival and therefore have some characteristics of public goods, constant returns to scale in the standard rival factors of production turn into increasing returns to scale once this non-rival factor is included in the production function. Constant returns to scale do not apply since it is not necessary to replicate the non-rival input. If A is the non-rival (knowledge) input, and X is the vector of normal rival inputs, it therefore holds for the production function that

$$F(A, \lambda X) = \lambda F(A, X) \text{ and } F(\lambda A, \lambda X) > \lambda F(A, X) \text{ for any } \lambda > 0 \ .$$

But non-rival as knowledge inputs may be, technological progress can only occur if the benefits of the use of this knowledge can be conferred to the innovating but self-interested individuals and are at least partly excludable. This is only possible if innovation costs can be recovered by selling the new goods at a price that is above the average cost of production. Therefore, price-setting behaviour must be possible (see Romer, 1990). Thus, most endogenous growth models explicitly abandoned the constraint of perfectly competitive markets.

Another way is through the accumulation of human capital (Lucas, 1988, building on earlier work done by Uzawa, 1965; Rebelo, 1991). Most new growth models that stress the importance of human capital add a specific equation for the education sector to the model that renders explicit the role played by physical and human capital allocated to the education sector in the process of human-capital accumulation. By replacing the employment variable by its equivalent in terms of human capital in the production function for goods and services, the model then allows physical capital to have a marginal return that does not decrease by using more of it.

A very similar result can be obtained by explicitly adding a research sector to the economy that is fuelled by human and physical capital and that has an output that adds to the innovative capacity of the economy. For many authors who consider R&D activities as taking place in a separate sector, R&D adds to the 'stock of designs' (Romer, 1990; Grossman and Helpman, 1991a,b; Barro and Sala-i-Martin, 1995). These models can then be used in a fairly natural way to analyse the implications of technological progress in new products and quality improvements.

Together with a possible explanation for non-convergence of economies, endogenous growth theory now also supplies a possible additional explanation for the observed productivity slowdown. If growth is indeed endogenous (e.g., because of increasing returns to scale), then decreasing growth rates will lower the rate of investment in R&D and thereby adversely influence the rate of increase of productivity. This initial growth contraction can be due to an oil-price shock, to a decrease of government funding of R&D because of budgetary restrictions, or to any number of other adverse shocks. The essential mechanism is that any such temporary shock may produce lasting effects through lock-in by hysteresis.

The new growth theory seems to have integrated into its models an impressive number of aspects of technological progress and innovation that were hitherto ignored: spillover effects of the production of non-rival knowledge goods, the accumulation of human capital, product innovation as well as process and organisational innovation, the aspect of quality improvements, firm behaviour on incompletely competitive markets and, finally, the endogeneity of technological progress itself. Moreover, it gave birth to a promising new line of research in international economics. The Grossman-Helpman-Krugman endogenous trade-and-growth models (e.g., Krugman, 1995), although far from having operational usefulness so far, define a new benchmark for applied analysis, and open the door for more systematic empirical research on what is surely the most important long-term issue in international economics: the growing gap between the rich and the poor countries.

In this process of paradigmatic renewal, the new growth theory thus contributed to the elucidation of a number of nagging paradoxes, among them the non-convergence of economies and the observed productivity slowdown.

Of course, it still remained essentially a macro-economic theory. The conclusion of Metcalfe (1995, p. 426) with respect to the earlier concept of the IPF is equally valid for the policy prescriptions that follow from the new growth theory: 'the scope for technological improvement, the likely productivity of innovative effort, the significance of developments in the underpinning knowledge bases and their location in different institutions, must be understood in some detail if policy is not to collapse into vague generalities.'

If there is no automatic tendency to converge, as the new growth theory predicts, that is, if differences between nations can persist indefinitely, then a detailed understanding of what distinguishes them becomes extremely important if we want them ultimately to converge. Institutions play a first-order role in this. A technology policy for influencing the innovative behaviour of the most important actors in the field, the private firms, must be based on a thorough and detailed understanding of the way in which firms interact between themselves (the network phenomenon) and with the institutions (in the broad sense). This is the hard core of what constitutes the difference between nations.

In the next section, therefore, we will discuss the systems approach to technological progress and innovation as a complement rather than as an alternative to the new growth theory.

1.2.3.   The systems approach

The intellectual origins of the systems approach to technological progress and innovation are markedly different from the origins of the new growth theory, although both were developed out of uneasiness with the reigning approach of neoclassical economics to the subject. While the new growth theory is basically a radical offspring of mainstream thinking, the systems approach stems from a tradition – institutionalist and evolutionist – that has never been mainstream.

The 'pre-history' of the concept of national innovation systems goes back to economists like Kuznets (1930), Schumpeter (1939), Rostow (1952), and Nelson and Winter (1973, 1982), to name only the most important ones. For an even earlier period, one should probably also mention List, the father of the institutional approach to 'political economy' (List, 1883), and of course Marx (see Rosenberg, 1982). More in particular, we owe to Schumpeter the insight that the concept of innovation should not be confined to the technical sphere in the narrow sense, and that technological progress is essentially a discontinuous process. In Schumpeter's view, these discontinuities are intimately related to the process of 'creative destruction' that lies at the heart of his business-cycle theory. Obviously, Schumpeter's approach was basically a historical one whereby, for that matter, institutions play a central role.

Nelson and Winter can rightly be called the originators of the evolutionary approach in economics. Dynamic disequilibrium becomes the key word. Rather than perceiving competition from the perspective of an *equilibrium state* of economic agents and markets, it is perceived as *a process of change* resulting from the differential behaviour of these agents. The open-endedness and path-dependency of evolutionary processes in economics, especially when viewed in terms of the 'rise and fall' – the 'selection' – of firms, regions, and industrial sectors under the influence of technological shocks reminds one, of course, very much of evolutionary processes in biology. Although this analogy seems obvious, some caution is called for. Indeed, it should be clear that many present-day evolutionary biologists, who dominate their field, seem very much to be people who believe that organisms do maximise (e.g. by maximally spreading their genes) and that systems of organisms move to equilibrium positions, very much as in neo-classical economics (see Krugman, 1996).

From the early 1990s on, following the lead of Freeman (1987) and Lundvall (1988), a number of important books appeared that spelled the actual take-off of the systems of innovation approach (Lundvall, 1992; Nelson, 1993; Carlsson, 1995; Edquist, 1997). Around the same time, the Directorate for Science, Technology and Industry (DSTI) of the OECD, by initiating research work within the Working Group on Innovation and Technology Policy, and the European Commission (see the *Green Paper on Innovations* (1995) and the *European Report on S&T Indicators* (1994, 1997a)), gave unmistakable signals that the institutional and 'systemic' view of technology and innovation had become one of the touchstones of their respective views on technology policy. It is probably not an exaggeration to say that the EU Framework Programmes that started in the early 1980s also prefigured in a way this same systems thinking in the policy field.

In order to specify the national systems of innovation approach, we can do no better than to follow the characterisation of Edquist (1997), who distinguishes seven properties, which for our purpose we can synthesise into five.

1) Innovations and learning are at the centre.
The generation of new knowledge and interpretations and combinations of present knowledge lie, in the economic sphere, at the basis of new products and processes. This insight is, of course, not new. However, the vehicle of this knowledge production and transformation is not solely the formal-education sector but increasingly also the informal sector through knowledge-spillover effects. Some use the term 'knowledge economy' to characterise this shift of emphasis. The spillovers occur naturally because of specific characteristics of knowledge production such as appropriability externalities and public-good dimensions. However, these spillovers have in recent decades become more important because of the tendency of firms in high-tech industries to join forces and to set up R&D partnerships and alliances between themselves. The network lines that are implicitly created in this way have unwittingly created additional lines in the form of knowledge spillovers. Of course, this in its turn has reinforced the *network aspects* of the innovation system. In modern 'alliance capitalism', each time new technological collaborations are initiated and new 'primary' network lines are created, a multitude of 'secondary' lines in the form of unintended knowledge transfer or spillovers emerge.

We shall have to come back later to the problem of knowledge spillovers and specifically to the policy implications of the necessary asymmetry in knowledge distribution that lies at its foundation.

2) The approach is interdisciplinary.
In contrast to the traditional philosophy, which deals with all aspects of techno-logical change and innovation within the neo-classical paradigm and so can be called 'reductionist', the systems of innovation approach tries to include institu-tional, social, political, and 'cultural' factors without trying to impose economic rationality on the analysis of these domains. The unifying concept behind this in-terdisciplinary approach, which in a way reflects the interdisciplinary nature of technical change itself, is to treat the whole of this social structure generating, distributing, and operationalising knowledge as a *network* of interacting agents: firms, institutions of higher education, research laboratories, and national and su-pranational governmental agencies.

There is, however, an obvious price to pay. The gain in scope and realism is at least partly offset by a loss of focus and, therefore, of analytical precision. We shall have to come back to this.

3) The perspective is historical, and institutions play a central role.
The interdisciplinary character of the innovation systems approach specifically means that the role of institutions is strongly emphasised. And since the evolution of institutions is characterised by inertia, the analysis is bound to include a histori-cal dimension.

4) The approach is 'systemic', which implies non-linearity and non-optimality.
The 'systemic' quality of the innovation systems approach follows directly from its comprehensive character and from the emphasis put on interdependence and interaction of agents in a network. The range of knowledge required for develop-ing new products and processes is generally beyond the capacity of the individual innovating firm. There must be access to knowledge from similar, if not compet-ing, firms, from suppliers and clients, and from knowledge-intensive actors such as universities and research laboratories. In many cases, the interaction takes place within the framework of R&D co-operation projects with other firms and/or uni-versities or within formalised alliances with other firms.

With respect to the behaviour of individual actors, the network context implies that the concept of rationality loses much of its operational meaning because of the implied loss of autonomy. This does not necessarily mean that individual ac-tors do not behave rationally, but it does mean that their possible rationality is subordinated and, therefore, bounded by the partnerships and alliances of which they are part. Such a diluted form of rationality will most often escape observa-tion.

Non-linearity, on the other hand, is the result of spillovers and feedback ef-fects. Romer (1986) showed that these spillover effects might create a situation of increasing returns to scale. Analogously, feedback effects, arising within the net-work or simply because of the specific and sometimes complex causal paths that are followed in the course of innovating activities, create non-linearities of their own. One might refer to the typical simple case when the seller of a new technol-ogy feeds initial profits back into the innovation process, thereby reinforcing the process that generated the new product in the first place.

Bounded rationality and non-linearity both result, macro-economically, in path dependency and the absence of a well-defined long-run equilibrium. These dynamic disequilibrium properties of innovation systems are often associated with an 'evolutionary' view of economic processes.

The upshot is that, since institutional structures, laws, etc. differ from country to country, and since equilibrium yardsticks are not available, analysis based on direct comparisons between systems becomes more important.

Another consequence of bounded rationality and non-linearity is that the use of optimised situations as points of reference in the micro-economic formulation of policy targets is often no longer possible. Changes occur endogenously without reference to adjustment to some equilibrium state. Moreover, when a long-run equilibrium is no longer uniquely defined, as in traditional post-war Keynesian macro-economics, demand factors and demand-oriented innovation policy become important again, including government technology procurement and the stimulation of 'lead users' (see e.g. Porter, 1990). It is, therefore, a safe guess that the Schmookler hypothesis of demand driven innovation, which in the past did not receive too much support, will once more come into the focus of future research in the context of the innovation systems approach (cf. Schmookler, 1966).

5) The systems approach encompasses process as well as product and organisational innovation.
One of the main reasons why the systems approach was developed in the first place was uneasiness with the neo-classical type of analysis, which consistently limited the scope of technological change to process innovation.

Summing up, we can conclude that the innovation systems approach produced a shift in the analysis of technological progress and innovation and their interaction with the modern society at large, which some will call paradigmatic (see e.g. Galli and Teubal, 1997) but that, in any event, considerably enriches the research calendar. However, it should also be clear that it is a conceptual framework rather than a formal theory. In our view, the concept is still too diffuse to be more than a complement to existing formal theoretical frameworks such as those of endogenous-growth theory and of the new microeconomics of imperfect competition.

1.3.   Some early insights and results from NIS-type studies

The comprehensive studies available to date that compare national innovation systems in different countries – Nelson (1993) being the most prominent – do not follow the tendency of the more traditional literature to argue that a few neatly defined features are the determining factors behind country-performance differences. On the contrary, their analysis leads to a wide-ranging set of different historic and institutional determinants of technological performance of countries.

The search for 'aesthetic' first principles is especially hazardous for two reasons. First, aggregate productivity patterns may give a misleading picture since they may mask large variations between sectors in different countries. Second, the situation does not improve significantly if one steps down from the aggregate level to the level on which one distinguishes high-tech, medium-tech, and low-tech industries in function of the R&D intensity criterion. This distinction is too narrow because of the important difference between knowledge-intensive and R&D-intensive activities: important parts of the services sector, ICT activities, etc. are becoming more and more knowledge-intensive by the employment of highly qualified labour and the use of high-tech equipment (especially computers), but are not necessarily more R&D-intensive.

The first broad result coming from studies based on the NIS approach, therefore, relates to the importance of historic and institutional differences between countries in explaining their innovative performance in terms of factors such as the overall intensity of R&D, the respective weights of the public and the private sector in financing R&D, the role of foreign financing, and the distribution of R&D efforts over industrial sectors.

As an example of the importance of institutional features, the study of the national innovation system of individual countries shows that in the USA the role of antitrust policy has been a determining factor in explaining the typical US paradox: high performance as measured by input and output technology indicators versus relatively poor performance in economic terms, i.e. slow earnings and productivity growth and widening trade deficits. With the legality of price-fixing and market-sharing arrangements coming under attack, firms found themselves bound to resort to horizontal mergers. Antitrust policy was much less effective in this respect and was therefore at least partly responsible for the creation of giant firms. At the same time, corporate reliance on the development of new products became a way to evade antitrust prosecution. Large corporations, for that matter, were better equipped for this (Mowery and Rosenberg, 1993).

Another important institutional factor, which is also applicable to the UK, is the dominant role of large military R&D expenditures. Although they boosted innovation in specific high-tech fields, they also had negative aspects. If R&D in the military sphere did, indeed, have a determining positive influence on innovativeness and growth, why did countries like Germany and Japan fare so well in this respect? Walker (1993) cites three reasons: a) high opportunity costs, given the scarcity of specialised skills (US) or the weak skill base (UK); b) reduced spillover effects because of the sheltered, 'insular' character of military research; and c) the excessive development of 'baroque' product technology, partly because there is no market discipline when major wars are not being fought, but generally also because of the lack of competitive pressure.

Security and secrecy clauses in military procurement contracts, in particular, have an adverse effect of a more systemic nature. Mowery and Rosenberg put it this way: 'proposals to restrict scientific and technological co-operation at the water's edge [because of military strategic reasons] fly in the face of the growing interdependence of national R&D systems' (p. 63). The emphasis on large military procurement contracts may well be a reason why countries like the USA and the UK do not benefit fully from the advantages of technological globalisation.

The UK also suffers on the systemic level from a lack of co-ordination or from co-ordination of the wrong type. Walker (pp. 180-181) cites a) a lack of sufficient bridging institutions strengthening the integration of scientific and technological communities; b) special problems in dealing with high degrees of organisational complexity in R&D and in settling conflicts over technology choice; c) absence of a tradition for close and mutually sustained producer-user relations; d) managerial co-ordination problems (hierarchical rather than participatory); and e) the virtual non-existence of co-ordination between banks and industry in comparison to what takes place countries like Germany and Sweden. The last point is especially significant since it can be interpreted as indicative of a lack of 'collective integration' in conditions where one class of actors is 'myopic': 'Britain's capital markets with their unusual dedication to short-term gain and to trading in rather than developing productive assets' (p. 188).

The case of the national innovation system of the UK contrasts with that of France, where the degree of individualism in society is not less but where there is a 'power elite' of the alumni of the *grandes écoles* that creates a symbiosis between the apparatus of the state and the large French financial and industrial firms (Chesnais, 1993).

Denmark and Sweden (Edquist and Lundvall, 1993) offer another interesting instance in which institutional settings play a major role. Although very similar in many respects, cultural (language, life style, political climate) as well as economic (per capita income, quality of the educational and health services, size of the public sector, long-run growth record), the national innovation systems of these two countries show marked differences. Denmark is characterised by low R&D intensity, the economy being dominated by SMEs centred around the agro-industrial industry. The co-operative movement of the farmers, which dominates the agro-industry, is, for institutional reasons, 'quite myopic' in relation to strategies of innovation (ibid., p. 291). The emphasis is on process innovations. Sweden, on the contrary, has high R&D intensity, and the economy is dominated by large Swedish-based multinationals that often control a sizeable amount of capital abroad. The emphasis is on product innovations.

Considering the contrasts between Denmark and Sweden in terms of the characteristics of their respective system of innovation may lead us to wonder, in the face of their apparent similarities in terms of economic and societal performance, whether the structure of the NIS matters at all. The answer is, of course, that it does. What is important in the case of these two countries is that the future issues and their respective significance are clearly different. The absence of a strong co-ordinating agency makes Denmark increasingly vulnerable to take-overs by foreign multinationals, which would then cream off the results of domestic R&D.

Sweden, according to Edquist and Lundvall, is confronted with a problem of a completely different order. Swedish capital has jumped at the opportunities offered by the process of globalisation. Sweden is an extremely active direct investor abroad. This trend towards internationalisation has put the so-called 'Swedish model', with the important role played by the trade unions, under severe pressure. The strengthening of the position of capital is not a direct threat to the capacity to innovate, but it does oblige the actors on the labour market to reconsider their role.

Belgium represents the case of a small, open, high-income economy that harbours a significant regional imbalance within its borders. We shall show in the remainder of the book that this imbalance is reflected in the regional innovation systems, and is caused at least partly by the differences between these regional systems.

The second broad class of results coming out of NIS studies relates to specific systemic aspects (the role of spillovers; network aspects) of national innovation systems that have surfaced, and that – because of their systemic nature – would have escaped notice if traditional neo-classical lines of approach would have been followed. The Working Group on Innovation and Technology Policy (OECD, 1998a) summarised the main findings, which we now briefly review.

1) Spillover effects knitting the implicit innovation network together can take different forms. Not all of them are easily traceable.

One possibility is by means of patent data. The study of citations of scientific papers in patent applications, for instance, reveals that patents increasingly rely on fundamental, publicly supported research. Patent-science links in the USA measured in this way have tripled from 1987-88 to 1993-94. Of the papers cited in USA patents in 1993-94, nearly three quarters drew on publicly supported research, mainly at universities.

Data on the science linkage of European patents suggest considerable differences across countries. Belgium, together with Denmark and the UK, is one of the countries where science linkages are strongest. This reflects to a certain degree the technological specialisation of these countries (see also European Commission, 1997a). We will deal extensively with patent data for Belgium in Chapter 8 of this book.

Another possibility is through the study of flows of technology embodied in equipment and intermediary goods. Input-output analysis has shown that direct R&D accounts on average for only roughly half of the total of the knowledge flows that are inputs in industrial sectors. Nevertheless, countries differ greatly, especially with respect to the import component of this particular way of indirect knowledge acquisition, which again largely reflects the technological specialisation of the individual countries. The 'technology content' of 'medium-' and 'low-tech' industries is, of course, largely attributable to embodied technology acquisition.

Foreign direct investment is another important 'carrier' of technology. In 1994, only 11% of the total R&D of 12 major OECD countries was carried out in foreign subsidiaries (OECD, 1998a, section 65), but this is an average that masks important differences between large and small countries. Technological transfer through FDI is less of a problem for large countries with a relatively large number of home-based multinationals than for smaller countries like Belgium (see also Chapter 6). For smaller countries, the internationalisation process aggravates their structural vulnerability through the dismantling or expatriation of the results of domestic research laboratories due to foreign take-overs (the main form of FDI) (Krugman, 1991).

2) Mainly as a result of spillover effects but also as a result of more or less for-malised kinds of co-operation, agreements, and alliances between firms, universi-ties, research labs etc., the economy-wide diffusion of technology is at least as important as R&D and innovation at the level of the individual firm.

At this global level 'it is less the invention of new products and processes and their initial commercialisation that generate major economic benefits than their diffusion and use' (OECD, 1998a, p. 7). Another way of putting this is that inno-vative firms do not innovate alone but innovate in the context of a network.

Particularly with respect to formal forms of co-operation, the percentage of in-novating firms that are involved in R&D collaboration with one or more partners ranges, depending on the country, from about half to – in the case of Denmark – 97% (OECD, 1998a, pp. 40-41).

It is a noticeable feature of the evolution of the R&D collaboration networks that internationalisation seems to go hand in hand with a strengthening of national networks. International R&D partnerships act more as a complement than as a substitute for domestic partnerships. Focusing on cross-border collaboration in R&D, Belgium and again Denmark occupy a special place: the propensity of in-novative firms to engage in international technology exchange is in these countries far higher than elsewhere (the Belgian network of collaborative R&D is discussed in detail in Chapter 7).

The results of NIS studies show that the links between the partners in the net-work are selective, durable, and trust-based. Significant product and process inno-vations in a collaborative context in the majority of cases emerge from collabora-tions between partners who were not collaborating for the first time (OECD, 1998a, p. 41).

3) Technological specialisation patterns between countries show little conver-gence.

There is a positive correlation between past and present patterns: technological capabilities obviously accumulate over time. Not surprisingly, the pattern of tech-nological specialisation and the technology clusters that can be detected in this context are reflected in the export specialisation of the respective countries (OECD, 1998a, p. 16). Path dependency seems to hold for export specialisation as well as for trade specialisation. This supports the 'technology gap' hypothesis with respect to the evolution of trade flows.

1.4. Technology policy from the neo-classical and the NIS angle

One of the main motives for designing an adequate technological policy or, in-deed, a technological policy at all is the paradox that, although technological prog-ress would at first sight appear invariably and always to have positive societal effects, in reality it does not. The reason for this, as Metcalfe (1995) points out, is that technological progress involves change and an uneven distribution of the con-sequences of this change: human and other capital are revalued in an often adverse way; countries, regions, towns, and industrial sectors go into decline, and so on. Nevertheless, this particular aspect of 'creative destruction' seems to be essential. It would be difficult to envisage technological progress that would only yield profits for some and losses to none.

Nevertheless, this is what the traditional, i.e. equilibrium, theory of technological policy is about: dealing with market failures that prevent the attainment of Pareto equilibria by violating one or another condition for perfect competition, the most important failures in this context being externalities and missing markets.

Arrow (1962) was the first to address the question of an optimum policy of innovation incentives in a context of equilibrium. He dealt with the polar situations of supply under perfect competition and monopoly. Although pioneering, Arrow's analysis did not deal with the conditions under which innovations are produced or with the relationship between the inputs in the innovation process and the resulting outputs. In other words, some kind of innovation-possibility function (not to be confused with Kennedy's IPF) is missing.

Dasgupta and Stiglitz (1980), in another seminal paper, did include an innovation-possibility function and extended the analysis to a free-entry oligopoly in a Cournot context. The game-theoretical implications are immediate. The Dasgupta-Stiglitz model can feasibly be extended so that process as well as product innovation can be analysed (Levin and Reiss, 1988). The literature that followed in the wake of this literature and of a contribution by d'Aspremont and Jacquemin (1988) is concerned mainly with the issue of R&D co-operation or not. The setting up to now remains however confined to situations of symmetry between the agents in terms of cost.

Useful as equilibrium approaches to technology policy undoubtedly are, especially from a pedagogical point of view, they yield few operational insights as to what a real-life policy could achieve and the ways to achieve it, notwithstanding that in most instances account is taken of most of the economic peculiarities of knowledge and its production. We quote Metcalfe: 'The lifeless nature of the [equilibrium] framework fits uncomfortably with a natural desire to see innovation as a driving dynamic force in the competitive process' (pp. 445-446).

The main reason of this failure of equilibrium analysis is, according to Metcalfe, the emphasis that is put on symmetric behaviour. Spillovers in a world of symmetric actors, i.e. actors with an identical information set, are meaningless since the spillovers would carry no new information. It is the informational asymmetries that create the incentive for, and the possibility of, innovation. They, therefore, drive the dynamics of the competitive selection process. In other words, again quoting Metcalfe, 'much of what appears from the symmetric viewpoint to be inefficient, at the aggregate level *may* [his italics] be a necessary dimension of the competitive [innovation] process' (p. 446). Equilibrium theory has difficulties, for that matter, in determining the rewards for innovational entrepreneurship, which by necessity are transitional. Last but not least, from a policy point of view, the selection of projects, firms, and even industrial sectors that may benefit from subsidies, tax allowances, or public procurement is without meaning in a symmetric world.

This brings us to the evolutionary and innovation systems view on technology policy, since behaviour diversity plays a central role in these approaches. Indeed, rather than perceiving competition in terms of states of equilibrium, competition is interpreted as a decentralised process of change driven by the differential behaviour of firms and other economic agents.

The evolutionary perspective, with its implications of path dependency, has already made clear that there is probably a role for a demand-oriented policy in the field of technology.

It should also be clear that policy prescriptions following from a neo-classical analysis are far from always being beside the point. A typical case for the contrary is a policy promoting the organisation of venture-capital markets, which essentially can be understood as a way of eliminating an obvious case of market failure: credit-rationing as a result of uncertainty and informational asymmetries in an innovation context.

It is probably fair to say that a technology policy inspired by systems of innovation must, first of all, take the process – that is the disequilibrium – character of technological progress seriously and not concentrate too much on what may at first sight appear as 'anti-competitive' market imperfections. Second, in a more positive vein, it should concentrate on those aspects of the network of agents active on the technology and innovation scene that could be strengthened by policy so as to optimise its structure, i.e. to enhance its capacity to process larger amounts of knowledge in function of a higher degree of innovativeness of the system as a whole.

The OECD Working Group on Innovation and Technology Policy (1998b), taking the systems of innovation 'paradigm' as its point of departure, formulates a number of additional policy recommendations in this philosophy and places them under the following headings.

1) Leveraging research and development.
Strengthening the science base of the network is an obvious target for government policy. Apart from the evident need to supply the necessary public funds for fundamental research, this also means flexible funding arrangements for contract-based resources, policy measures to facilitate the mobility of university researchers among universities and between private firms and universities, subsidising patenting costs of universities, and facilitating the development of university spin-off firms. Governments should also encourage interdisciplinarity and lifelong learning.

2) Enhancing technology diffusion.
It is not stretching the argument too far by saying that technology diffusion is an aim in itself. It may prove to be at least as important as the invention of new products and processes. The ways of promoting this diffusion or spillover process are multiple, but they all come down in one way or another to a strengthening of the innovation and technology network: extension services, information clubs, and demonstration and benchmarking schemes. Special attention should in this respect

be given and indeed *is* given (particularly by the European Commission) to technology dissemination in SMEs.

3) Building an innovation culture.

This concerns not only the private sector of the economy but also the fringes of the innovation systems network. The reason is that in the longer run this fringe must feed the network with innovation-prone human actors through an adequate cultural, educational, and family policy. This is of vital importance.

One might call this a typical example of a policy focus that – although it is eminently important – does not follow from a traditional, neo-classical type of analysis. One needs common sense or, what amounts to the same thing, an interdisciplinary analysis at the system level.

4) Promoting networking and clustering.

Innovation policy should join with regulatory and competition policy to remove unnecessary barriers to inter-firm co-operation and alliances. In a more voluntary way, governments may actively intervene to promote the formation of clusters of innovative firms, possibly at the regional level. The example of Silicon Valley springs to the mind.

In smaller countries like Belgium, the promotion of networking and clustering can also be understood as a way to substitute networking for scale. In other words, by creating dense subsystems of firms, laboratories, and universities closely working together on specific technological projects, one may hope to realise scale benefits that would otherwise only be possible through a sufficiently large physical scale.

5) Responding to globalisation.

The international competitiveness of nations is at least partly a function of their ability to link with international innovation networks. There are several ways to promote this, one being to encourage participation in international R&D collaboration such as that which is organised by the European Commission in its Framework programmes or in programmes like EUREKA. Another way is through foreign direct investment, both inward and outward going. An investment climate that places no unnecessary obstacles to outward going FDI and that encourages inward FDI will help to integrate the national innovation network into the global one.

1.5. Conclusion

The systems approach to innovation and technology is not, or not yet, a new paradigm. It still lacks unity and transparency. Nevertheless, it is an illuminating complement to the existing, more formalised, theoretical schools of thought of endogenous-growth theory and the modern micro-economic analysis of imperfect markets. Its synthesis of insights derived from both mainstream economists and from institutionalists and evolutionary economists makes it particularly useful as a framework in which policy issues can be formulated and analysed. The systems approach is here to stay.

Chapter 2.   The Sources of Belgian Prosperity

Henri Capron

2.1. Introduction

As pointed out by Edquist (1997), adopting an historical perspective is natural in an analysis of national systems of innovation. 'To have an historical perspective is not only an advantage when studying processes of innovation, but also necessary if we are to understand them.... History matters very much in processes of innovation as they are often path dependent: small events are reinforced and become crucially important through positive feedback' (Edquist, 1997, p.19). In his retrospective of a survey of some national innovation systems, Nelson (1993) was struck by the institutional continuity in countries with long histories, with many institutions in France, Britain, Germany, and Japan having been in existence for more than a century. In these countries, the behaviour of actors has been 'shaped by a shared historical experience and culture'. Although Belgium changed into a federal state mainly because of major cultural differences, the regions and communities remain linked by strong historical and cultural factors and will certainly so remain for a long time,

In their seminal paper on the science and technology base, David and Foray (1995) put forward a similar argument the significance of which particularly applies to the Belgian case: '...there are strong aspects of complementarity among various features of the institutional landscape observed in any particular society and those complementarities tend to increase institutional stability (inertia), forcing successful institutional innovation to take an incremental form unless the society ... as a whole is disrupted or captured by one that is differently structured. The feasible space for institutional innovations in a given society, thus, is likely to be tightly constrained by its history, which is to say its institutional structure is path dependent' (David and Foray, 1995, pp. 21-22). Even though the Belgian national institutional framework has changed into a federal structure over the last 30 years, the new 'federated' entities have had and still have to manage the historical inheritance of the previous national policy. However, it is also true that the Regions and the Communities are implementing new governance rules in function of their own social and economic context. This new trend in Belgian innovation policy means that it would be virtually fruitless to consider its innovation system from a national perspective without referring to the large areas of competency that have devolved to the federated entities.

Another major issue is geography. 'Industrial agglomerations located in one place, rather some other, create environments in which production experience can be accumulated, exchanged, and preserved in the local workforce and entrepreneurial community' (David and Foray, 1995, p. 18). In her study of the geographic dimension of the innovation process in the United States, Feldman (1994) argues that innovation is in itself a geographic process. Science and technology policies are not spatially neutral. Not only are the spatial structures central in the innovation process, but innovation is a spatial process by its very nature. Innovation appears to be less the product of individual firms than the result of the agglomeration of technological infrastructures in specific places. In this regard, the underlying technological infrastructure of a region strengthens the innovation potential and influences the location of firms. The proximity between industries and academic research centres is also a significant source of productivity benefits. As a matter of fact, spillovers and increasing returns are intrinsically linked to location factors and so cannot be explained without reference to the spatial component, as is the case in classic economic theory. Taking regional and international contexts into account seems essential for understanding the dynamics that underlie the innovation process.

One primary characteristic of the Belgian economy is unequal spatial development. The Walloon region was a first-comer of the Industrial Revolution while the Flemish region was a latecomer. Except for the dimension effect, the Walloon region presently faces problems similar to those of old British industrial areas. After the Second World War, economic growth in Belgium was mainly the result of the accelerated development of Flanders. In fact, the decline of Walloon mining activities combined with a concentration of direct foreign investment in Flanders have accelerated the evolution of regional disparities. In the mid-1970s, the steel crisis further aggravated Walloon industrial decline and the regional divide.

Last but not least, the three Belgian regions have radically different profiles: Brussels is an urban area with a high concentration of administrative centres and little industrial activity; the Flemish region is a highly industrialised area with locational advantages and a very good service infrastructure; the Walloon region is a de-industrialised area with fewer locational advantages and some deficiencies in high-level services.

Before going more deeply into the historical sources of Belgian prosperity, it is worth looking into the dimension factor, which we do in the second section. In order to shed some light on the historical sources of the present position of the regions, we describe their economic evolution of the regions in the 19th and the 20th centuries in the third section. In the fourth section, we continue with an analysis of the present position of the country within the triad. In the fifth section, we will investigate whether the regional innovation systems and their national connections will be sufficiently efficient to cope with the challenge of the knowledge-based economy.

2.2. The strengths and weaknesses of smallness

The conduct of science and technology policy differs radically in small countries from what is done in large ones. As small countries have less money to spend on R&D, they are faced with entry costs in a large number of fields. They are not in a position to master the whole spectrum of R&D activities and, therefore, the efficiency of their science and technology policy is conditioned by their ability

- to identify technological niches in which they can acquire a specialisation in order to be able to compete with large countries;
- to specialise in R&D areas where the barriers to entry are low and economies of scale limited;
- to encourage international co-operation to compensate for their own R&D deficiencies and to promote the networking of indigenous small firms;
- to adopt selective policies aimed at improving the commercial exploitation of R&D results as well as their diffusion to the marketplace.

Furthermore, small industrialised countries are presently faced with the challenge of the newly industrialised countries (NICs) becoming increasingly dominant in mature technologies and the ever-increasing complexity of new technologies shifting upward the minimum R&D efficiency level. Indeed, this competitive threat can be described as follows (Walsh, 1988):

- the markets for simple products based on mature technologies are increasingly dominated by the NICs;
- the markets for complex products based on new technologies are increasingly dominated by the large industrialised countries;
- the fields of influence of large industrialised countries are also increasing since traditional products increasingly embody new technologies;
- therefore, the natural field of small industrialised countries that corresponds to the medium area on the spectrum of products, arranged in accordance with their technological complexity, is being squeezed from two directions.

When we look at the international data on R&D intensity, we observe that small countries, relatively speaking, do not under-invest in R&D relative to large countries. Indeed, to a large extent, the divergences in the R&D intensity among countries can be explained by four other major factors (Capron, 1992):

- the level of wealth: the higher the GDP per capita, the more a country is able to allocate a substantial part of its resources to R&D;
- the size of the domestic market: large countries have at their disposal a very homogenous potential market that allows them to benefit from economies of scale and to make their own R&D investment profitable;
- the openness of the economy: the more exposed to international trade a country is, the more effort it has to make to preserve its technological lead;

- the security focus: defence-procurement-related R&D programmes increase support for technological activities.

Given the high competitive pressure on international markets, small countries have to invest in R&D in order to improve their trade performance. Their wealth level is strongly dependent on their ability to adapt their trade patterns to structural changes. Furthermore, a major difference between relatively closed and relatively open economies is that the latter need to be more flexible, and the more open they are, the greater is the need.

2.3.   Belgium in the world economy

Belgium is a small open economy that is classified among the small economic powers. Table 2.1 gives some general characteristics of the country that show its general positioning. As the regions play a prominent role in the Belgian innovation system, this dimension is taken into account. Once the honeymoon of the Belgian Revolution in 1830 was over, the regional divide of the country began. The entire history of the country has since been deeply influenced by the tensions between the two linguistic communities, French-speaking and Dutch-speaking. Nevertheless, it was only in 1993 that the country became a federal one.

Table 2.1:   Some major Belgian indicators (1995-1996)

	Wallonia	Flanders	Brussels	Belgium	Europe
Area (km^2)	16,844	13,512	161	30,518	3,191,347
Population (thousands)	3,313	5,866	952	10,131	373,607
Density (per km^2)	195	430	5891	329	115
Unemployment rate (%)	12.9	7.1	14.1	9.6	10.9
GDP per capita index	89	115	173	112	100
Activity rate (%)	47.7	50.8	50.4	49.7	55.1
Export rate (%)	-	-	-	74.5	32.3
Productivity	118	135	106	126	100
Investment rate (%)	16.8	18.2	23.2	17.6	18.2
Inflation rate	-	-	-	1.5	1.8

Source: Eurostat, OCDE, World Bank, own calculations.

Belgium has a very high population density on a territory that represents less than 1% of the European territorial area. The large degree of openness of the country makes it one of the European countries whose export/GDP ratio is among the highest of the European Union. The low inflation rate shows that the government policy implemented to reduce the high inflation rates in the beginning of the 1980s has been successful. Unfortunately, the government did not succeed in reducing the structural unemployment rate despite one of the highest GDP per capita of the European Union and a high productivity index and also despite an activity rate that is 10% lower than the European average. This can be attributed to the high labour costs, which accelerated the substitution process of capital to labour in comparison with that of other industrialised countries and adversely affected the Belgium's attractiveness for foreign investment. Another important aspect of the Belgian economy is the weight of the underground economy, which has resulted from onerous fiscal and para-fiscal pressure, the large structural employment deficit, and the generous social security system.

A main challenge for the Belgian economy is to preserve its international competitiveness by moderating labour cost, improving the investment rate, and encouraging SMEs. In order to reduce the public spending deficit, the public R&D support was substantially reduced so the growth of public support for R&D grew at less than 3% over the period 1969-1990. The government budget appropriation for R&D now represents 0.64% of the GDP against 0.70% in the mid-1970s. However, there was a slight improvement in public R&D spending in the last few years.

2.4. Surfing the long waves

The present prosperity of Belgian is rooted in a long-standing tradition of openness to innovations and new ideas. In the background of this prosperity are long waves in economic activity and technology evolution. Indeed, one of the main secrets of Belgian prosperity is its ability to adapt its industrial structure to advances in technology. However, despite the exiguity of its territory, Belgium has a high degree of cultural diversity and very different regional growth trajectories that prohibit a global approach to explaining why and how the country has been in the last two centuries one of the most dynamic regions of the world. The main stylised facts of Belgian economic development over long waves are summarised in Table 2.2. Some historical indicators of the Belgian economic expansion are given in Table 2.3.

On the eve of the Industrial Revolution, Belgium had a very advanced proto-industry with regional specialisation: cotton and linen mills in Ghent, wool in Verviers, coal, metallurgy and zinc in Liège, coal in Mons, and coal, metallurgy, and glass in Charleroi. The take-off of the Belgian Industrial Revolution resulted from a combination of a well-developed rural industry with a good stock of skills, high openness to foreign innovations, a good transport infrastructure, an abundant work force, and high agricultural productivity in a context of significant private and public entrepreneurship. The banking sector was relatively absent from the first phases of the Industrial Revolution and became active mainly in the consolidation phase. As early as 1798, all the ingredients were present for a radical mutation of Belgian society.

The Belgian Industrial Revolution was based mainly on an imitation and diffusion process of British innovations. In the first half of the 19th century, Wallonia was the first place in continental Europe to undergo the Industrial Revolution. Its development came from the exploitation of large coal reserves and the existence of a powerful arms and metalworking industry. The main advantages of Belgian entrepreneurs were their ability to adopt inventions and to adapt them to industrial uses, to invest in incremental innovations, to prospect foreign markets, and to attract foreign entrepreneurs and skilled workers. Another important property of the Belgian Industrial Revolution was the ability of entrepreneurs to reverse-engineer machines produced in England. 'By 1840 the country was highly industrialised, comparable only to Britain, and had relatively the densest rail network in Europe' (Ray, 1984).

At the end of the 19th century, Belgium was certainly the country with the highest GDP per capita. Such a position was the result of the precocity, the speed, and the amplitude of the Industrial Revolution (Lebrun, Bruwier et al., 1979).[1] The propagation of the Industrial Revolution was, in fact, sustained by the support of public authorities, private entrepreneurship being very soon complemented by public entrepreneurship. Large investments in the development of infrastructure (roads, railways, and canals) gave new firms the public amenities necessary for their expansion. The active participation of the financial sector was concentrated mainly in the consolidation phase of the Industrial Revolution. In fact, only five Belgian districts were the main winners of the Belgian Industrial Revolution: a Flemish one, Ghent with the mechanisation of the cotton industry, and four Walloon ones, Mons and Charleroi for the coal, iron, and glass industries and Liège and Verviers for the wool, coal, and metal industries (Lebrun, Bruwier et al., 1979). Thanks to their high industrial specialisation, these Walloon districts were the engines of the Belgian economic growth until the Second World War and the source of Belgian prosperity. It is fair to say that the Belgian Industrial Revolution was mainly a Walloon Industrial Revolution.

During the second long wave, the Walloon districts continued to polarise Belgian growth with the development of the steel industry and the building materials, chemicals, and engineering sectors. In this period, the industrial development was only supplemented by the tertiary development of Brussels and Antwerp. The other Belgian districts remained isolated from the Industrial Revolution and specialised mainly in agricultural products.

This second wave was, therefore, again favourable to the main winners of the Industrial Revolution. Vertical integration in the coal-metal complex continued to intensify in the Liège area, while the Province of Hainaut, especially the district of

---

[1] For example, Belgian enterprises produced 5% to 10% of the world-wide coal production and 27% of the world-wide zinc production in the 19th century Cockerill was the largest steel enterprise in the world. In 1840, the Englishman Tennent wrote that, by comparison with the greatest English steel establishments, Cockerill was like a giant next to a pygmy (cited by Lebrun, Bruwier et al., 1979).

Mons, concentrated further in mining. A development of the tertiary sector in Brussels and Antwerp occurred in this period due to the choice of Brussels as the capital of the Kingdom and the locational advantage of Antwerp. Brussels quickly became the financial and administrative centre of the country. Its population increased fourfold between 1830 and 1900, while the population of Belgium as a whole multiplied by only 1.8. In the 16th century, Antwerp had been one the most important economic centres of the world, but its economy was destroyed by the blockade of the Scheldt River by the Netherlands in the middle of the 17th century. It was only during the second half of the 19th century that all the constraints affecting its economic development were removed. For the Walloon metal, steel, glass, and cement industries, the Port of Antwerp was the door to international trade.

The third long wave was marked by the slowing-down of the effects of the two preceding waves in the Walloon districts. Given their specialisation patterns, they had developed adverse attractiveness for the development of the new types of activities. Nevertheless, their industrial dynamism allowed them to expect a renewal of the Walloon industry by means of diversification. This period was characterised by the industrial take-off in Flanders. For instance, the maritime position of Antwerp attracted large-scale foreign investment. The discovery of coal in the Province of Limburg gave another impulse to the development of the region.

At the end of the 19th century and the beginning of the 20th, new industrial structures were indeed emerging in the Flemish region: Gevaert launched the photography industry, a group of investors founded Petrofina, a Belgian subsidiary of the Bell Telephone Company was created, and Ford and General Motors established assembly plants (Baudhuin, 1945). In this period, the coal and steel industries continued to sustain the economic expansion of Wallonia thanks to a large amount of support form the banking system. These years were associated with the highest stage of the Belgian capitalist expansion abroad.

With the fourth long wave, the decline of the Walloon economy set in. The development of alternative energy sources and the exhaustion of the coal pits caused the coal mines to be gradually closed down. During the 1950s, the steel industry improved its production processes and increased productivity but continued to specialise mainly in products with low added value. A major cause of the Walloon decline was the defensive investment policy of the large holding companies in Brussels. At the same time, a boom in the industry and the availability of alternative sources of energy stimulated the creation of new plants for which the coastal areas in the Flemish region were chosen. Multinational companies, during the ongoing wave of foreign investment, preferred to build new plants in new industrial areas near the port of Antwerp and in other Flemish areas rather than in Wallonia, where the demography as well as the environment was less favourable. In order to avoid major social unrest, the government took initiatives in support of the economic reconversion of Wallonia in the mid-1960s. In the 1970s, the economic crisis struck severely the Walloon steel sites, the equipment of which was older than those of the coastal (Flemish) sites.

Table 2.2:   Belgian economic growth over long waves

Kondratieff waves	Phases	Annual industrial growth rate	Stylised facts of the Belgian prosperity

Industrial revolution
 	
Leading sectors:
  Cotton
  Textile
  Iron
	Upswing:
	1792-1825
	
	Downswing:
	1826-1847
		-
		
		2.2
			1799: Cockerill starts making spinning machines.
			1801: Bauwens builds the first mechanised spinning mill.
			1807: Huart-Chapel invents a reverberatory furnace for melting down scrap iron.
			1819: Brussels is the first continental town to be equipped with gaslight.
			1835: Creation of the first railroad line on the European continent.

Construction of railroads
 	
Leading sectors:
  Railroads
  Chemicals
  Steel
	Upswing:
	1847-1873
	
	Downswing:
	1874-1893
		4.0
		
		1.7
			1851: Coppée builds the first coke furnace.
			1861: Solvay invents the ammonia process to separate soda from salt.
			1871: Gramme builds a ring dynamo to produce steady continuous current without overheating.
			1878: Dulait creates an electrical product company that will become the ACEC.
			1882: Creation of the Bell Telephone subsidiary.
			1885: Empain builds the local railroads, in 1900 the Paris metro, and in 1906, Heliopolis near Cairo.
			1889: Creation of FN, a metalworking company.

Neo-Mercantilism
 	
Leading sectors:
  Motor vehicles
  Electricity
	Upswing:
	1893-1913
	
	Downswing:
	1914-1939
		3.4
		
		2.2^1
			1894: Gevaert creates a photography company and makes incremental innovations.
			1901: Discovery of the coal basin in the Province of Limburg.
			1915: Meurice creates a pharmaceutical company that will be sold to UCB in 1928.
			1920: Creation of Petrofina.
			1922-1924: Ford and General Motors build assembly lines.
			1927: Creation of the National Fund for Scientific Research.

Table 2.2 (continued)

| Mass production

Leading sectors:
  Chemicals
  Electronics
  Aerospace | Upswing:
1940-1974

Downswing:
1975- ? | 3.8^2

1.6^3 | 1947: The government stimulates the development of the petroleum industry.
1947: Creation of the Institute for the Encouragement of Scientific Research in Industry and Agriculture.
1956: Commencement of the closing-down process of the Walloon coal mines.
1959: Creation of the European Community and the development of the industrial policy.
1959: Creation of the Science Policy Office (OSTC).
1964-1975: Direct foreign investment boom.
1974: Creation of the first technology parks.
1976-1985: Restructuring of the Walloon steel industry. |
| Information society

Leading sectors:
  Electronics
  New materials
  Biotechnology | ? | ? | 1986: Creation of Ion Beam Applications, a world leader in accelerator-based systems.
1987: Creation of Lernout & Hauspie, a world leader in the field of advanced speech and language technologies.
1991: Belgium becomes a federal state with a high degree of regional autonomy as regards the economic, scientific, and technological policy. |

Notes: (^{1}) Excluding 1914-1920 period (First Word War).
        (^{2}) Excluding 1940-1946 period (Second World War).
        (^{3}) Until 1998.

Table 2.3:   Historical indicators of the Belgian expansion

Foreign patent share in the US	1.59 (1883)	1.35 (1900)	1.23 (1973)	1.00 (1998)
Productivity level (US = 100)	106 (1870)	96 (1890)	75 (1973)	109 (1996)
Manufacturing OECD export share	5.5 (1899)	5.0 (1913)	5.9 (1971)	5.0 (1996)

Source: Maddison (1982), OECD and USPTO.

As a consequence, the Walloon steel industry has been faced with the need for major restructuring over the past 20 years. The combined effects of the crises in both the coal and the steel industry involved the Walloon economy in a vicious cycle of decline.

In summary, the beginning of the 20th century marked the slowing down of Walloon economic expansion despite the development of new activities linked to key technologies characterising the third Kondratieff wave. Although Wallonia remained the dominant region until World War II, its industrial structure was very dependent on activities developed during the Industrial Revolution. Conversely, the development of new industrial activities in growing sectors allowed the Flemish economy to take off. The growth process of the Flemish economy was accelerated by the profound modification of the economic environment. The wave of foreign investments in Europe combined with the preference of multinational companies for 'green fields' rather than for 'brown fields' greatly benefited Flanders. In the absence of a regional industrial policy, the central government was not in a position to reverse the process of decline of the Walloon economy.

To a large extent, what one may call the Belgian industrial miracle would not have been so miraculous without the active participation of several successive kings. During the Dutch period, King Willem I stimulated the start of the Industrial Revolution and founded the first Belgian bank that played an important role in the development of the coal and metal industry. After the Belgian Revolution in 1830, Leopold I sustained the acceleration of the Industrial Revolution. Over the end of the 19th century and the beginning of the 20th century, Leopold II, known as the 'Builder King', was an very active artisan of the economic development of the country. Among other things, he purchased what would later become the Belgian Congo, launched large infrastructure investment projects that contributed considerably to the modernisation of the economic environment and the promotion of industrial growth, and actively supported Belgian industrial expansion abroad.

After the Second World War, the priority was the reorganisation of the economy and reparation of war damages. A first step was the improvement of infrastructure: the railways were electrified, motorways were constructed, the telegraph and telephone networks were modernised, and the capacity of the waterways was increased. A major event of the period was the launching of the petrochemical industry. This project was implemented by the Belgian government, which took two important measures: first, it built a petroleum port in the area of Antwerp, and, second, it provided important public support to attract multinational petroleum companies.

Although the introduction of contingency rules and the obligation to use Belgian components constrained the automobile constructors to develop assembly lines in the country, it induced the start-up of Belgian subcontracting firms and attracted new foreign firms for the production of sophisticated components.

Despite the efforts of the government to maintain coal mining, the exhaustion of the Walloon pits forced them to close.

In 1959, the implementation of economic expansion laws led to a foreign-investment boom and the development of industrial areas.

These last observations explain why the share of the chemical industry in manufacturing employment is 13% in Flanders against 10% in Wallonia, in the automobile industry 10% and 1%, respectively, and in the textile industry, 12% and 5%, respectively. The food industry is equally represented in the industrial structure of both regions with 12 to 13% of the employment. Conversely, the metal industry has a predominant weight in Wallonia with 21% of the industrial employment against 13% in Flanders.

Nevertheless, as in other industrialised countries, some very prominent industrial failures also characterised the economic development of the country. Thus, as early as 1898, initiatives were taken by industrialists to launch the automobile industry. Very rapidly, Belgian cars profited internationally from a good reputation as luxury products. In the 1920s, the development of mass production, however, led Belgian producers to adopt large production programmes in order to boost the production of high quality cars. This was a radical strategic error for a small open economy whose market was not large enough to absorb a large part of the initial production and sustain the development of the industry. The failure of the indigenous car industry in the 1930s was the logical consequence, the more so because, in the 1920s, American companies had already built assembly lines with the support of the Belgian government. Another failure was the unsuccessful launching of an aeronautics industry. In 1920, an aeronautics company was created but it was unable to profit from the expansion of this new type of activity. It remained a small company confined to the assembly of foreign aircraft.

Another important failure in the Walloon region was the inability of ACEC, an electrical and electronic company, to maintain its high level of technological and business know-how. The company was severely affected by the economic crisis of 1900 and was purchased by Empain in 1904. Over the years, it became an important company specialised in high-tech products. At the end of the 1950s, it employed 15,000 workers in five plants in Belgium and had two Belgian subsidiaries, seven foreign subsidiaries and 80 foreign business agencies in 70 countries (Baudhuin, 1970). The company had all the constituents needed to become a large multinational. Unfortunately, the company's accumulation of strategic errors led to its disintegration into several small companies under foreign control in the nineties. In a nutshell, it was unable to valorise its high technological level commercially.

Fabrique Nationale (FN) specialised in arms manufacture, was confronted with the same phenomenon. Founded in 1889, the company diversified its activities by producing motorcycles and automobiles. An R&D laboratory was very soon created. In the 1950s, it started to produce jet engines and the number of its employees exceeded 10,000. However, despite its good technological level, depressed economic conditions forced it to restructure its activities. It is now under foreign control and specialises, among other things, in aerospace engines.

2.5. The present economic structure

Table 2.4 summarises the economic evolution of the regions after the Second World War. Wallonia, the dominant region whose GDP was higher than the European average, lost its economic leadership at the mid-1960s. Since then, the

Flemish region has increasingly strengthened its position while the Walloon economy has continued to decline. The Brussels GDP per capita is considerably higher than that of the two other regions. The region concentrates a high activity level in a small geographic area, and commuters represent around 50% of the working population.

These data show that Belgian history is a very impressive illustration of the theory of unequal spatial development: Wallonia was the engine of growth until the mid-1960s, when Flanders took over the old industrial tradition region. Given the industrial profile of the regions, which industrial sectors are emerging as new engines of growth and to what extent will Wallonia be able to assure long-term economic recovery?

Table 2.4:   Index of GDP per capita (EUR 15 = 100)

	Wallonia	Flanders	Brussels	Belgium
1955	103	92	155	103
1965	93	93	163	100
1975	90	106	161	107
1985	87	106	167	106
1996[1]	90	116	174	113

Note: ([1]) European data include the new German *Länder.*

Table 2.5 shows the regional economic bases of Belgium with respect to the European and the triad averages. The bases are calculated as the indexes of sectoral employment per capita in comparison with the European and the triad averages. In the manufacturing industries, employment has been distributed among the four technology groups according to the classification suggested by the OECD. Obviously, the Belgian economic base is under the average, and the technological profiles of regions vary considerably. Thanks to the concentration of activity in Brussels, its economic base is very high, which is explained by the high commuting rate from the neighbouring regions. Indeed, the number of commuters is equivalent to the Brussels active population. Given the high productivity level of the employed active population, Belgium can be classified among the most industrialised countries.

Nevertheless, the manufacturing structure of the Belgian economy is mainly oriented to medium low- and low-tech industries. Although Flanders has a higher technological base than the two other regions, it is under the average except in sectors like pharmaceuticals, chemicals, motor vehicles, and transport equipment. Flanders is specialised mainly in medium low- and low-tech industries. Except for pharmaceuticals, other transports, iron and steel, non-mineral and metal products, the manufacturing base of the Walloon economy is relatively weaker than that of the two other regions and the European and the triad averages. As a whole, the Belgian base in high-tech industries is very limited. Although Flanders has a significant industrial base in electronics at the European level, its relative weight is very weak in comparison with the average for industrialised countries. Drugs appear to be the most prominent Belgian industrial base in the high-tech sectors. In this field, all three regions benefit from a comfortable position.

The development of S&T institutions has been the result of several impulses. First, the major universities have been in existence for more than a century. The oldest is the University of Louvain, which traces its history to 1425 and which was split into two separate entities in 1971, the French-speaking university at Louvain-La-Neuve in Walloon Brabant and the Dutch-speaking one in Leuven in Flemish Brabant. The Universities of Ghent and Liège date from 1817. The University of Brussels was founded in 1835 and split into two linguistic entities in 1981. The other university institutions also originated in the 19th century. They are the backbone of the Belgian innovation system and receive the major part of the publicly-financed R&D. They are also the only scientific institutions in Belgium that cover a large spectrum of research activities. In the 1980s, the universities were dramatically affected by the government budget restrictions. This will lead to a considerable imbalance between teaching and research that will be accentuated by the growth in the number of university students. As experts observed in the mid-1980s, there are three main clear weaknesses in the Belgian science system: the very low level of employment, the instability of that employment, and the ageing of the research staff (Fondation Roi Baudouin, 1985). A new challenge for Belgian universities is to become real partners in regional development and to leave their ivory towers to translate their research output into products and new enterprises as well as to forge closer and more fruitful ties with industry.

During the 19th century, scientific research was to a large extent supported by private funds. In the first part of the 20th century, some major institutions were created: the University Foundation in 1919 and the National Science Research Fund in 1928. But it is only after the Second World War that the Belgian S&T policy was structured. In 1947, the collective research centres were launched by an act of Parliament known as the De Groote Law. In the subsequent years, 10 Collective Research Centres were constituted, mainly by enterprise federations, to form sectoral research groups for applied research for industry, technology transfers, and fundamental research. The functioning of the centres is financed jointly by the government and by enterprises. This financing is completed by research contracts with enterprises, which amounts to around 40% of their overall budget.

In the same period, the Institute for the Encouragement of Scientific Research in Industry and Agriculture as well as the Prototype Fund were created. In 1959, the organisation of the scientific policy was improved by the creation of central consultative organs and by the inclusion of science policy in the Prime Minister's portfolio. In 1968, the post of Minister for Science Policy was finally created.

Table 2.5:   The regional economic basis (1997) – indexes of sectoral employment per capita in terms of European and Triad averages

	EUR15 = 100				TRIAD = 100			
	Brussels	Flanders	Wall.	Belgium	Brussels	Flanders	Wall.	Belgium
Whole economy	149	89	73	90	136	81	67	82
Agriculture	3	57	38	46	4	58	39	47
Extraction	5	11	79	33	4	9	67	28
Manufacturing industry	57	96	56	80	57	96	56	79
High-technology industries	71	84	65	77	49	59	45	54
Electronics	27	96	22	65	17	58	13	40
Aircraft	75	31	69	48	59	24	54	38
Pharmaceuticals	158	97	153	121	203	124	197	156
Computer and office machines	0	9	5	7	0	5	3	4
Medium-high-tech industries	54	81	39	65	59	88	42	70
Chemicals	54	111	45	84	87	179	72	136
Instruments	43	36	34	36	35	29	28	29
Electrical machinery	30	49	35	43	27	43	31	38
Motor vehicles	118	138	12	95	119	139	12	96
Non-electrical machines	31	50	46	47	32	52	48	49
Other transports	48	99	155	113	70	142	223	163
Medium-low-tech industries	42	100	85	90	46	109	93	98
Rubber and plastics	11	83	46	65	14	103	58	80
Shipbuilding	0	40	10	27	0	32	8	22
Metal products	58	108	74	93	61	114	78	98
Iron and steel, non-ferrous metals	12	98	117	97	14	121	145	119
Stone, clay and glass	32	84	121	92	40	105	151	114
Petroleum refineries and products	16	166	2	99	8	83	1	50
Other manufacturing	192	179	109	157	124	116	71	101
Low-tech industries	66	108	51	86	66	108	51	86
Paper and printing	130	88	54	81	108	73	44	67
Textiles	33	105	25	72	34	109	26	76
Food & tobacco	74	127	73	105	79	135	77	111
Wood products	36	107	52	83	39	114	55	88
Construction	90	93	81	89	80	84	73	80
Utilities	169	70	87	85	167	70	85	84
Services	208	96	86	104	184	85	76	92
Wholesales and retail	146	102	77	98	127	88	67	85
Finance	382	110	78	126	301	86	62	99
Transports	186	100	72	100	190	102	73	102
Other services	221	97	110	114	200	88	100	103

Source: own calculations based on OECD and Belgian data.

In fact, the Ministry for Science Policy directly managed only a small part of the publicly-financed R&D budget, the support programmes being administered by *ad hoc* ministries, mainly the Ministry of Education (e.g., general university funds and science research funds) and the Ministry of Economic Affairs (e.g., IRSIA and Prototype Funds). Nevertheless, the Science Policy Office came to play a major role in the orientation and the co-ordination of the Belgian S&T policy. While the Science Policy Office still remains a major actor of the Belgian S&T policy, the competencies transferred to the regions in 1980 set off new trends in the S&T policy based on regional technological choices. The present S&T policies of the regions continue the specific and diversified actions implemented in the field of technology policy in the beginning of the 1980s.

2.6. The challenge of the 21st century

The acceleration of technological change, the trend toward globalisation, the modification of the economic context, and the emergence of new technologies and markets place the Belgian innovation system, like that of other countries, at a crossroad. Given the profound institutional change of the country, its very high degree of dependence on multinationals, its budgetary constraints, and its smallness, the way Belgium can and will be able to take up the challenge of the 21st century is largely an open question.

For a small country like Belgium, international co-operation in R&D is vital. As the country is not focussed on items like national sovereignty and defence matters, all the public effort is put on the promotion of civilian R&D. According to the taxonomy suggested by Ergas (1987), the technology policy can be classified as diffusion-oriented, the main purpose being to diffuse technological capabilities throughout the industrial structure and to stimulate adaptation to change. The university system is able to keep up with the advances of science, although it cannot necessarily do pioneering exploration, except in some specific scientific niches like health research. Moreover, the role played by joint research centres, which are partly financed by each industry and whose tasks are to facilitate technology transfers and assist firms to identify new technological opportunities, is very important.

In the Walloon Region, the technology policy implemented in the 1980s was structured under the denomination of the Athena operation and based on three technological fields: biotechnology, composite materials, and robotics. Nevertheless, the policy was developed without any clear strategic framework as regards the structure of the innovation system. In the 1990s, the Region launched mobilisation programmes in new materials, environmental technologies, and multimedia technologies. More recently, a new mobilisation programme has been implemented in biotechnology.

The Flemish Region has structured its technology policy under the appellation of the Third Flanders Industrial Revolution on the three following technological fields: microelectronics, biotechnology, and new materials. These technological choices led the region to create three inter-university centres: the Interuniversity Microelectronic Centre (IMEC), the Flemish Institute for Biotechnology (VIB), and the Flemish Institute for Technology and Research (VITO) with the environment, energy, and metal products being its main fields of research. Presently, the focus is on the emergence of two major poles of excellence: the Flemish biotechnology valley in the Ghent area and the Flemish language valley in the area of Ieper.

In the Brussels-Capital Region, the actions are implemented mainly in the framework of Brussels Technopole and are centred on four strategic poles: communications, agro-food, precision industries, and health.

More globally, both the regional and the federal authorities have targeted their S&T policies in order to provide an impulse to move the structural adjustment process of the Belgian economy into the new technological and economic environment with a special focus on space programmes, microelectronics, and biotechnology.

What about the position of Belgium and its regions in biotechnology, a major Belgian specialisation? There are 52 firms active in the biotech industry. In 1997, the biotechnology market grew by 24% and R&D expenses by 20% for a total of 8.6 billion Belgian francs. Human health science represents a major part with 89%. As shown at Table 2.6, around 4470 people are presently employed by the biotech industry. While the biotech industry is mainly located at present in the Walloon Region, as pointed out above, the Flemish Region has also decided to promote it more actively. Nevertheless, the Flemish policy was only reinforced relatively recently with the creation of VIB in 1993 while IMEC was created in 1984. The data on the regional public support to biotechnology presented in Tables 2.7 and 2.8 illustrate the stress placed by the regional governments on this technological field.

Table 2.6:   **The biotech industry in Belgium by region – 1997 (millions of BEF)**

	Revenues	Revenues (%)	Employees	Employees (%)
Brussels	1763	3.0	244	5.5
Flanders	15180	25.9	1193	26.7
Wallonia	41731	71.1	3034	67.8

Source: Belgian Bioindustries Association, 1998.

While at first, i.e. in the 1980s, the Flemish Region was marked by higher involvement in microelectronics and environment technologies than in biotechnology, recent years have been marked by the intention of the Flemish government to promote actively the biotech sector.

Table 2.9 shows the more positive trend of the number of researchers in Flanders than in the two other regions.

Table 2.7: **Walloon public support to biotechnology (millions of BEF)**

	Enterprises	Universities	Total
1994	312	340	652
1995	225	255	480
1996	240	834	1074
1997	398	730	1105
1998	412	526	938

Source: DGTRE.

The number of researchers was multiplied by 3.3 in the Walloon Region and only by 1.3 in the Brussels-Capital Region, while it was multiplied by 4.5 in Flanders. Consequently, the Flemish Region has developed its potential R&D human resources more rapidly than have the other regions and now has a higher relative R&D potential than does the Walloon Region. Nevertheless, the most striking thing is that the number of researchers in the Brussels-Capital Region did not grow as rapidly as it did in the two other regions so that it is no longer the Belgian region with the most R&D investment as was the case in the 1960s.

Table 2.8: **Flemish public support to main R&D institutions (millions of BEF)**

	1994	1995	1996	1997	1998	1999
Micro-electronics	935	981	981	1082	1106	1115
Biotechnology	-	200	1120	1148	1176	976
Environment, energy and new materials	980	1041	1124	1173	1115	1108

Source: Vlaams Indicatorenboek, 1999.

Table 2.9: **Regional distribution of scientific personnel**

	Wallonia	Flanders	Brussels	Belgium
1963	1,926	2,647	3,660	8,264
1971	2,809	4,906	4,245	11,960
1995	6,400	12,260	4,600	23,260

Source: Own estimates based on official data.

It is certainly of importance to examine Belgian participation to international R&D programmes. The Belgian participation to the two main European research programmes are reviewed below. The participation of Belgium to the European Space Agency is very substantial. As shown in Table 2.10, this participation also represents three quarters of the public budget devoted to international collaboration. Table 2.11 gives a view of the financial contributions of the main participating countries over the period 1997-1999. Given that approximately 21% of the total was devoted to the Agency's 'Mandatory Programme' and 76% to the 'Optional Programmes', and 3% to other programmes, in absolute terms, Belgium is positioned just behind the large countries with a participation equal to 5.9%. Nev-

ertheless, the measure of the participation index as given by the ratio of the financial contribution per capita to the European average shows that Belgium is the
country that is the most involved, in relative terms, in ESA.

As pointed out by Müller (1989) in his analysis of the ESA programmes, small
countries are dependent on their collaborative partners but large countries are not,
which prevents participation in an interdependent system. Indeed, small countries
often implement government funding of international programmes only through
the collaborative option, without prior or parallel national activities. Furthermore,
they only manage to secure partial system capability, which large countries are
able to cover with their national programmes. According to Müller, "one might
argue that these countries essentially contributed financially to the establishment
of a technology capability in the larger, advanced countries; they contributed to a
widening of the technology gap which already existed prior to the collaborative
programme. Their dependence on United States technology prior the joint effort
was not extended to dependence on their collaborative partners... In fact, one can
hardly expect to close a technology gap with a financial contribution of only ... 4
percent for Belgium...." This pessimistic diagnosis shows how difficult it is for a
small country to develop an efficient policy to cope with the technological challenge and to become a leading-edge partner in international programmes.

Table 2.10:   **Main financial contribution to international**
                collaborations – 1999 (billions of BEF)

	Budget
Office of Scientific, Technical & Cultural Affairs	
European Space Agency	5933
European Organisation for the Exploitation of Meteorological Satellites	302
European Southern Observatory	161
Airbus Programme	115
European Laboratory for Particle Physics	725
Others	821
Economic Affairs	
UEO Satellite	131
Airbus Programme	115

Source: OSTC.

The participation to the European Laboratory for Particle Physics (CERN) is
the second main involvement of Belgian authorities to European co-operation programmes. As the Belgian financial contribution is calculated on the basis of the
national revenue, the amount does not necessary reflect the scientific real use of
facilities. In 1999, the share of the Belgian contribution was 3% of the CERN
budget, while the number of Belgian users was only 1.4%, which represents a very
low use rate of the research potential available in this European research organisation.

A critical challenge for the Belgian authorities is to develop new incentives in order to valorise economically its scientific potential and to stimulate its endogenous sources of growth. An alternative way to classical technology transfers is the direct creation of new enterprises from university spin-offs (Silicon Valley, Route 128, and the Cambridge Science Park are well-known major examples of these particular forms of knowledge-based local development originating in technology transfers from universities[2]). University spin-offs may be the most striking form of university technology transfer, but there are other channels equally important for transferring technological knowledge: R&D co-operation between industry and university, university consulting, scientific publications and seminars, industrial incubators and science parks, professional associations, and technology licensing.

The number of university spin-offs (around 100) is presently rather meagre in Belgium. Nevertheless, the increasing involvement of universities in regional and local development and the growing availability of venture capital from regional authorities and private investors lead one to expect an increase of university spin-offs in the years to come.

Table 2.11: Distribution of contributions to ESA (%) - 1997

| | Programmes | | | Participation |
	Mandatory	Optional	Total	Index
France	17.41	30.92	28.00	1.76
Germany	25.00	23.20	23.59	1.05
Italy	14.67	13.78	13.97	0.90
UK	13.80	7.30	8.71	0.54
Belgium	3.22	6.62	5.88	2.11
Spain	7.13	4.31	4.92	0.46
Netherlands	4.56	4.05	4.16	0.98
Switzerland	3.94	3.14	3.31	1.41
Sweden	2.65	2.53	2.56	1.05
Austria	2.53	1.26	1.53	0.69
Denmark	1.74	1.11	1.25	0.87
Norway	1.56	0.97	1.10	0.94
Finland	1.14	0.55	0.68	0.48
Ireland	0.61	0.25	0.33	0.33

Note: The participation index is equal to the Belgian contribution per capita
           divided by the European total contribution per capita.
Source: European Space Agency.

Thus far, the University of Liège and the University of Leuven have the most spin-offs with totals of around 25 and 32, respectively. The experience of other universities in this field is more limited. Some Belgian successful university spin-

---

[2] For a survey of technopoles, see Castells and Hall (1994).

offs deserve mention here. In 1986, Ion Beam Applications (IBA) was created in the science park of Louvain-La-Neuve. This firm rapidly acquired a dominant position in accelerator-based systems for medical and industrial applications. IBA started with the invention of a new type of cyclotron, the first ever designed for the industrial-scale production of medical radioisotopes. Revolutionising the market, it took the new cyclotron only two years to jump to its leadership position where it has since remained with 80% of the world market share. In the first half year of 1998, IBA's turnover was BEF 741 million, which represents growth of 53%. The number of people employed by the firm at Louvain-La-Neuve is presently around 150. In 1998, it acquired the Swedish firm Scanditronix, with around 70 employees, and the German company Wellhöfer, with 60 employees. Recently, it purchased three American companies: RDI (50 employees), Griffith (450 employees) and Steregenics (300 employees).

Another successful spin-off is ICOS, which was founded in 1982 and specialises in visual application systems. It is a spin-off of the Leuven University and has around 180 employees for a turnover of BEF 1.3 billion. The firm has several subsidiaries abroad and acquired Qtec in 1998, a German company specialised in industrial vision systems. Its R&D ratio is around 15%. It is one of the top three suppliers of computer vision systems for the worldwide semi-conductor industry. The enterprise is now listed on both the NASDAQ and EASDAQ stock markets.

Devgen is the first university spin-off of the Flemish biotechnology institute. It is a spin-off of the University of Ghent. Founded in 1997, it is a functional genomics and drug-discovery company employing 47 people. Located in the technology park of the university, the enterprise has strong links with the Flanders Interuniversity Institute for Biotechnology and collaborates with Janssen Pharmaceutica, a Flemish subsidiary of Johnson & Johnson.

A last major university spin-off is Eurogentec, which was founded by scientists from the Genetic Engineering Laboratory and Biochemistry Laboratory of the University of Liège. Recently, the firm split into two different companies: Eurogentec-Bel for the manufacture and sale of reagents for molecular biology and Pharos for the research and development, production, and sale of pharmaceuticals for fish health. The group counts now around 120 people and plans to extend its sale activities in the US to counterbalance the present technology flow and allow European scientists to stay in Europe, work with European companies, and have the possibility of seeing their discoveries developed in Europe.

Although it is not a university spin-off, a major Flemish success story is worth citing: it is the case of Lernout & Hauspie company. Founded in 1987, the firm has become a world leader in the field of advanced speech and language technologies. It now employs more than 1700 employees worldwide and is considered by the Flemish government as the backbone of the Flanders language valley project. In the same high-tech field, some competencies are emerging in the Walloon Region with the creation of Babel Technologies in 1997, a spin-off of the Mons Polytechnic Faculty, which has successfully developed a high level of expertise in speech and image processing.

2.7. Conclusion

Historical and geographic factors have deeply influenced the evolution as well as the present structure of the Belgian innovation system. Up until the country was federalised, the differences between the regional components were maintained at a latent level. The recent regional focus makes them apparent and provides an opportunity for the regions to target the S&T policy according to their own needs and choices. However, some of the primary institutions have long existed in Belgium. Thus far, the federalisation of these institutions has not led to large transformations of their rules of operation.

The present economic performance as well as the technology policy choices of countries are directly influenced by the trajectory of their historical development. The restructuring of mature industrial complexes and the transition to new industrial clusters based on emerging technologies make the policy choices more difficult in depressed regions or countries than in the ones benefiting from more recent growth poles. Economic specialisation, the learning process, and R&D activities imply a policy mix to manage the social costs (among other things, for unemployment) of the gradual disappearance of declining sectors and the soft transition (labour market adjustments, etc.) to new, emerging activities.

Presently, Belgium can be considered to be a high technology country classified just behind the countries falling into the category of technological leaders. Nevertheless, although apparently favourable, this present position emphasises a kind of breathlessness of the Belgian technological dynamism in comparison with its prestigious contribution to technological change and economic growth in the 19th century and the beginning of the 20th century. The post-war economic growth was largely sustained by foreign investments. Given its high technological level, a large number of foreign companies established R&D laboratories in the country or maintained them when Belgian companies were acquired by multinationals. The Belgian industrial structure and its industrial R&D system are strongly integrated to the international networks of technology development. The phenomenon of increasingly transnationalisation of the industrial process has been a reality in Belgium for 40 years. The recent process of decentralisation of industrial R&D centres at the international level is favourable to the country, which has been able to attract new R&D laboratories from foreign sources over the last years. One major challenge here is the implementation of efficient policies that can internalise the R&D outputs and materialise them in economic performance.

Chapter 3.   The Institutional Profile

Henri Capron, Michele Cincera and Michel Dumont

3.1. Introduction

If the present-day institutional profile of the Belgian innovation system can be characterised in one word, 'complexity' seems — as the reader who manages to struggle through this chapter will probably agree — the most obvious candidate.[1] However, this chapter is essential if one wants to understand the specific situation of a country like Belgium that, in a period of internationalisation and European integration, initiated a far-reaching process of regionalisation. This process has probably yet not reached its final conclusion. The major transformation with regard to science, technology and innovation occurred during the various state reforms initiated since 1980. They remodelled Belgium from a unitary national state to a federal state with a high degree of autonomy and a large number of competencies having been transferred to the regions and the 'communities'.

Although the regions now have the primary authority in science and technology (S&T) policy and possess a substantial number of competencies, some regionalists argue for a further transfer of competencies to the regional level because of what they perceive as a lack of coherence and homogeneity in the attribution of authority. Others, on the other hand, contend that the need for co-operation and co-ordination in a number of matters related to joint initiatives and institutions, international activities, and the implementation and maintenance of inventories, argue for a restitution of a number of competencies to the federal authority for reasons of efficiency and effectiveness.

In Section 3.2 we will describe the complex legal framework of the Belgian innovation system and its regional aspects. Section 3.3 gives an overview of the institutional structure of the federal authority as well as of the 'federated' entities with regard to S&T policy. Sections 3.4 to 3.6 cover the most important public S&T institutions and other organisations with significant links to S&T activities. Section 3.7 considers the main aspects of the Belgian federal and regional S&T policy. We conclude in Section 3.8.

---

[1] Some material presented in this chapter is based on or updates the COPOL report prepared by the Belgian science policy authorities (COPOL, 1993).

3.2. The legal framework

Belgian scientific policy was given its first impulse in 1928 with the creation of the National Fund for Scientific Research (NFSR). The second important stage was entered in 1947 with the creation of the Institute for the Promotion of Scientific Research in Industry and Agriculture (ISRIA), which laid the foundations for a technology policy. In 1959, the organisation of scientific policy was given a new co-ordinating and consultative structure by the creation of a number of central consultative organs, i.e. the National Science Policy Committee and the Inter-ministerial Science Policy Committee. These new structures for the political and administrative co-ordination of science policy were included in the Prime Minister's portfolio. In 1968, a State Secretary, later on a Science Policy Minister, was appointed whose actions were supported by a specific agency, the Science Policy Office (SPO), which was in charge of the Scientific Policy Planning Services. This office was established as a state administrative agency, and one of its main tasks was to compile an inventory of the country's scientific and technical potential. In 1969, a special science-policy section was added to the budgets of the different ministerial departments with a view to develop an interdepartmental budgetary programme for science policy.

From 1830 to 1970, Belgium was a centralised unitary state. The question of relations between the 'communities' played however a very important role throughout the whole of Belgian history. The start of the federalisation of the country is found in several institutional reforms that began in 1970. With four consecutive state reforms, Belgium was transformed into a federal state. The 'federated' entities presently have their own legislative bodies and governments. In fact, Belgium can be seen as the result of the overlapping of different cultural and regional specificities that often transcend regional geographical frontiers. First, there are three regions: Brussels-Capital, Flanders, and Wallonia. The regionalisation of the country was to a large extent inspired by economic concerns and is based on a territorial concept. Second, there are three communities: the Flemish Community which covers the Flemish Region and the Brussels-Capital Region, the French Community which covers the main part of the Walloon Region and again the Brussels-Capital Region, and, finally, the small German-speaking Community, which is located along the German border and is part of the Walloon Region. Language and cultural differences are the source of this 'communitarisation' of the country. Map 3.1 presents the different 'federated' entities of the Belgian State. To some extent, the Belgian regions are similar to the American states and the German *Länder*. A major problem in the analysis of the Belgian innovation system is disentangling the extent to which it is still national, and to which extent it is regional, perhaps increasingly and irreversibly so.

The state reform in 1970 was the first major step in the transition of Belgium towards a federal state. In this first step, the existence of three cultural communities was recognised. It is also in this framework that the creation of three regions was planned. During the 10 subsequent years, emphasis was placed on the devolution of responsibilities to be assigned to the new 'federated' entities. In this period, the competencies of the communities were, for the time being, limited to cultural matters, while the existence of regions was only recognised in principle, and their institutional framework was still to be developed.

Map 3.1: The structure of the Belgian State

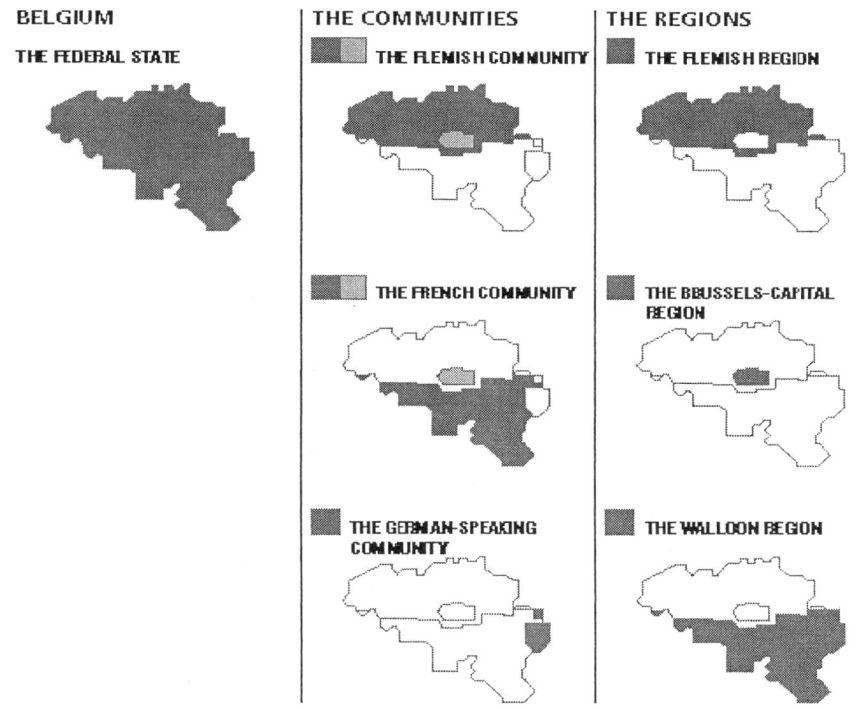

Source: Federal Information Services (1999).

With the second state reform in 1980, both the Flemish and Walloon regions were institutionalised and some competencies in economic policy were transferred to the regions and the communities, among them being grants to firms, investment incentives, economic expansion schemes, public industrial initiatives, education and training programmes, and applied scientific research. Each 'federated' entity henceforth had its own parliament and government. Only about 10% of the public R&D budget, however, came under the responsibility of the regions. Nevertheless, although the national state kept the main competencies in the fields of higher education, fundamental research, and the financing of research by the major ministries (mainly Education, Economy, Agriculture, and Health), the regions acquired responsibility for technology policy, while the communities became competent for science policy (the philosophy behind it being that all matters related to persons fell under the authority of the communities while economic matters fell under that of the regions). The years following this second stage in the reform of the Belgian State saw the start of regional technology policy in Flanders and Wallonia. The technological choices made by the regions during this period have to a large extent defined the general framework of the present regional S&T policies. However, the question of the legal status of the Brussels-Capital Region was postponed until the next state reform, the technology policy for this region remaining under the responsibility of the federal state.

It is in the framework of the third state reform in 1988-1989 that the two (French and Dutch-speaking) Ministries for National Education were transferred to their respective communities and that the Region of Brussels-Capital was officially institutionalised with its own parliament and government. The regions and the communities also saw an extension of their authority in S&T policy. A special law in 1988 abolished the policy distinction between fundamental and applied research.

Henceforth, each authority was allowed to arrange every aspect of scientific research for the matters for which they were qualified. The Federal Government had, and still has, some authority to manage and take initiatives for scientific research in support of federal policies and international agreements (like participation in the European Space Agency and the European Organisation for Nuclear Research) and those topics that are beyond the concerns of a single region or community (such as health research and research on transportation and mobility). Following this institutional reform, the EUREKA projects were to be managed by the regions, with the SPO playing a national co-ordinating role and acting as spokesman within international bodies. In 1991, co-operation agreements between the federal state, the communities, and the regions were implemented and led to the creation of the International Co-operation and Federal Co-operation Committees of the Inter-Ministerial Science Policy Conference (IMSPC). These agreements also covered the involvement of the different authorities within the activities carried out by the European Communities in the field of science policy. The SPO provides the secretariat for these two committees.

It is worth noting that the parliaments and governments of the Flemish Region and the Dutch-speaking Community have merged, but the other 'federated' entities did not. Consequently, the parliaments and governments of the Flemish Region and the Dutch-speaking Community have now formed a single Flemish Parliament and Government. This merged entity is called the Flemish Community.

The fourth state reform in 1993 led to a modification of the Belgian constitution to define Belgium as a federal state composed of three communities and three regions with real institutional autonomy. It confirmed that applied-research policy was a matter for the regions while both education and fundamental research policies came under the responsibility of the communities. With regard to the federal state, there were no substantial modifications. However, it is fair to say that, basically, scientific research have as a matter of principle been allocated to the regions and the communities since 1993, while the competencies of the federal authority with respect to S&T policy are explicitly listed.

The transfer to the SPO of some activities, among them educational national matters and federal scientific institutes, has led to its transformation into a new entity called the federal Office for Scientific, Technical and Cultural Affairs (OSTC). This office now forms an administrative part of the Prime Minister's Services and comes under the authority of the federal Minister for Science Policy.

Each 'federated' entity now has its own political, administrative, and consultative structure. The management of the Belgian S&T policy is, therefore, conducted by these actors in function of their respective areas of authority. The general support for industrial and technological research falls within the authority of the regions, while the communities support fundamental research, in particular the research carried out by the universities. The Federal Government remains responsible for the research needed to support its own functions, i.e. data-exchange networks operating between scientific institutions at the national and international levels, research and public service activities of the remaining federal scientific and cultural institutions, space research, nuclear and agricultural research and — according to the rules laid down by co-operation agreements with the federated entities — all programmes and activities requiring a uniform implementation at the national or international level, including the permanent inventory of the scientific potential of the country and Belgium's participation in the activities of international research bodies. The Federal Government can also take initiatives, create structures, and provide funding for scientific research in matters that fall within the authority of the federated entities, if it acts on the basis of a recommendation given by the Federal Council for Science Policy (FCSP). These matters are either covered by international or supranational acts or agreements or relate to activities and programmes that transcend the interests of a community or a region. Each federated entity may decide not to participate to a federal initiative of this kind. Finally and more generally, the law allows the federal state, the regions, and the communities to sign co-operation agreements with each other relating to the creation and management of joint services or institutions, the joint exercise of their own powers, and the development of joint initiatives.

Finally, it should be mentioned that, although Belgian S&T policy is now mainly outlined at both the regional and 'community' levels, not all the corresponding instruments to carry out this policy are integrally under the complete control of the federated entities. For instance, most of the funds needed for an innovation policy are still collected by the federal Ministry of Finance, and, for that matter, most fiscal instruments still fall under the authority of the federal state.

The regionalisation of most competencies produced important shifts in the percentage of R&D allocations from the federal to the regional level. This is illustrated in Figure 3.1, which shows the evolution of the relative contribution of the different authorities to the total Belgian R&D budget in 1998 compared to that in 1994 and 1989. By now, the Flemish Community, with 41.7%, controls a bigger part of the global Belgian R&D budget than do the federal authorities (32.3%). A

more detailed analysis of this evolution and other aspects of R&D budget allocations is given in Section 4.7 of the next chapter.

**Figure 3.1:   Contribution of the federal and regional authorities to public R&D
allocations in 1989, 1994, and 1998**

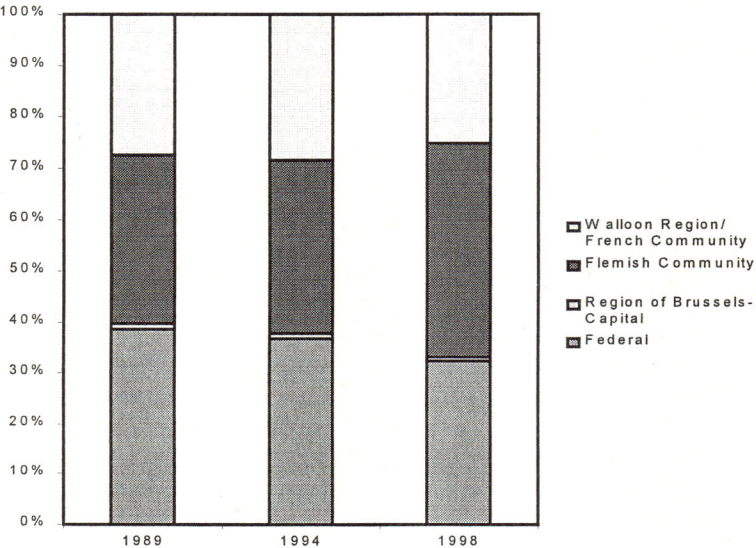

Source: OSTC, 1999.

In Belgium, most of the basic scientific research is performed by the higher
education institutions (HEIs), 21 of which are universities and university centres,
and by some public or non-profit-making S&T institutes.

As stated by the OECD (1998a), the institutional set-up of the innovation system of countries is an important explanatory factor for cross-country differences in
innovativeness. In Belgium, both the federal and the federated governments have
their own administrative organs for the design, financing, and co-ordination of
S&T activities. Apart from the fiscal policy that favours innovation, for which the
federal authorities are responsible, the regional authorities are competent for the
direct support of business R&D activities and for subsidies and refundable loans.

The Belgian S&T institutional profile is outlined in Figure 3.2. Four groups of
actors are involved in this figure: the administrative organisations that formulate
and co-ordinate the S&T policy and that control public-financing organisations,
the private research sector, the higher education institutions, and the research and
bridging institutions that act as intermediaries among the other actors. The dia-

gramme has been substantially simplified. A more detailed diagram for the federal and regional entities is presented by Capron, Meeusen *et al.* (1998).[2]

Figure 3.2:   The Belgian institutional profile

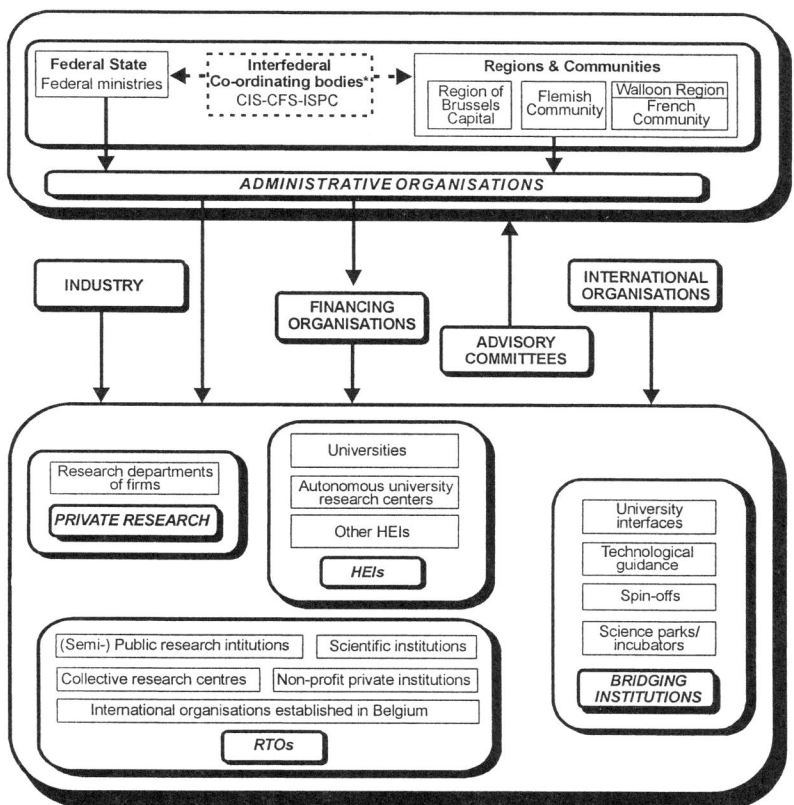

Note: (*) For a description of the inter-federal co-ordinating bodies see Section 3.3.

In the following sections of this chapter, we will focus on the public institutes relevant to the Belgian innovation system and the way these organisations fit within the Belgian S&T policy framework. A description of the industrial structure of the Belgian economy in general and the innovation system in particular is given in Chapter 4.

---

[2] For a more detailed analysis of the Flemish innovation system, see Capron and Cincera (1999).

3.3. The institutional structure

3.3.1.   The federal state

The Council of Ministers is the highest authority for deciding on the major options of the Federal Government as regards science policy. In addition to the activities for which he or she is directly responsible, the Minister for Science Policy also has a co-ordinating role with respect to the general guidelines and the implementation of the science policy of the Federal Government. The functions of various other ministers may also include activities relating to research and scientific public services connected with matters falling within their competence.

As an administrative part of the Prime Minister's services but under the control of the Minister for Science Policy, the Office for Scientific, Technical, and Cultural Affairs (OSTC) carries out horizontal co-ordination and programming tasks at the federal level. It also prepares and conducts research activities that fall within the competence of the federal state. The other federal departments managing major research budgets are Economic Affairs, Agriculture, Development Co-operation, National Defence, Public Health, and Environment.[3]

The Inter-ministerial Science Policy Committee (ISPC), following ministerial instructions, co-ordinates the preparation and implementation of governmental decisions requiring concerted action by two or more federal departments. The ISPC consists of senior civil servants from those federal ministerial departments that include scientific activities among their functions. It is chaired by the Secretary-General of the OSTC, and its secretariat is run by this office. An important task of the ISPC is to prepare the annual outline of the Interdepartmental Science Policy Budgetary Programme, which centralises and co-ordinates the proposed budgetary allocations to the various federal ministries of research and scientific public service.

An advisory body, the Federal Council for Science Policy (FCSP) is responsible for advising the government on the broad lines of science policy. It is assisted by the OSTC, which provides the secretariat and consists of prominent persons from the scientific, university, economic, and social sectors. The communities and the regions are represented on this council.

Traditionally, Belgian authorities have used a wide range of methods for the allocation of public-research appropriations. Nowadays, however, most of the funds used in the S&T domain are made directly available to independent funds and financial institutions that have been regionalised.

---

[3] In 1998, the budget allocated by the federal authority to R&D amounted to 19.2 billion BEF. In this amount, the OSTC has a part of 64.3% and the Departments for Economic Affairs, Agriculture, and Development Co-operation and other departments of 13.5%, 6.9%, 6.4%, and 8.9%, respectively (OSTC, 1999).

For example, in the area of basic research, the National Fund for Scientific Research (NFSR) has been financed for the greater part by the communities since 1988. In 1992, NFSR adopted a regionalised structure. Following this modification, the NFSR remains a national institution, but its two main parts, the Flemish part (FWO-Vlaanderen) and the French-speaking part (which continues to use the old French denomination FNRS), are administered independently by two separate boards. These boards manage and allocate the resources released by their communities together with resources allocated by the federal authority and transferred by the National Fund.

Because of the obvious need for co-ordination, a number of inter-federal institutions were created in which the regional authorities and national authorities are represented. In 1989, the Inter-Ministerial Science Policy Conference (IMSPC) was created with representatives of the federal, community, and regional governments. IMSPC is an instrument for consultation between the authorities and is the place where co-operation agreements are formulated and various procedures for collaboration and exchange of information are implemented. In 1991, IMSPC established two committees: the Federal Co-operation Committee (CFS) and the International Co-operation Committee (CIS). In the same year, CFS set up a specialised group on inventory and statistics in experimental research and development (CFS/STAT) to prepare the decisions on the creation and updating of the federal review of public R&D expenditures and the federal review of the Belgian R&D effort. CIS concentrates on the preparation of the Belgian position within the science-policy bodies of the European Union. The two committees are alternately chaired by a representative of a regional or a national authority. The secretariat is again provided by the OSTC.

3.3.2.   The federated entities

3.3.2.1. The Flemish Community

The activities falling directly within the competence of the Flemish Minister for Science Policy are co-ordination and co-operation activities, multi-sectoral activities (in conjunction with other ministers), and activities in support of sectoral scientific policy. Moreover, each member of the Flemish Government has authority over the sectoral science policy activities associated with the matters assigned to him or her.

The Administration for Science and Innovation (AWI) has general co-ordination as one of its functions, both at the level of the Flemish Community and in the context of federal and international co-operation (European in particular). Tasks relating to studies, analyses, and research inventories also belong to the domain of AWI.

IWT is a new institution. It was established in 1991 to manage all government support for industrial R&D. It is not part of the administration but has an autonomous board composed of representatives of business, universities, and social organisations and of individuals mandated by the government.

An advisory body on matters of science and technology, the Flemish Council for Science Policy (VRWB) gives advice to, and formulates proposals for, the Flemish Government at the request of the latter or on its own initiative. VRWB consists of representatives of institutions and scientific research bodies as well as the socio-economic world.

3.3.2.2. The French Community

While the Flemish Region and the Flemish Community have merged politically and administratively into what is now called the Flemish Community, the French Community and the Walloon Region remain distinct as regards government, parliament, and administration. It is worth noting however that the French Community and the Walloon Region have recently taken steps to integrate the political responsibilities for scientific research and S&T policy. The Walloon Minister for Research and Technological Development, Sports, and International Relations is presently also in charge of the same matters in the government of the French Community.

Within the government of the French Community, the minister in charge of higher education is also responsible for scientific research. The community exercises its authority essentially as regards university and basic research. The other ministers also have authority over science policy activities associated with their particular competencies, such as health, socio-cultural matters, sports, and tourism.

The Directorate-General for Non-compulsory Education and Scientific Research (DGENORS) is responsible for implementing the science policy of the community. It handles, for example, the financing of the university institutions, the 'generic' scientific research funds (FNRS and associated funds), and the so-called 'concerted' research activities. DGENORS also performs all the coordination and co-operation tasks in the conduct of science policy, both for the community itself and at the federal and international levels.

3.3.2.3. The Walloon Region

The main responsibility for research within the Walloon Government lies with the Minister for Research, Technological Development, Sports and International Relations. He or she manages the most important item of regional R&D policy, that of research with technological objectives. The other ministers, however, are also able to finance research and studies within their own spheres of competence.

The Directorate-General for Technologies, Research and Energy (DGTRE) is responsible for supervising and financing projects and for monitoring work in the research field. DGTRE also has the task of overseeing Walloon participation in European and international research programmes and co-ordinating all data relating to the research activities supported by the different administrations of the

Walloon Region. DGTRE consists of two divisions, the Research Division and the Division for Company Assistance and Energy. The Research Division has the task of handling all problems connected with the funds allocated to universities and research centres, initiating and managing regional programmes, promoting trans-regional and transnational scientific co-operation and managing interventions to promote innovation in Walloon SMEs and in support of individual inventors. The Division for Company Assistance and Energy is also responsible for various activities intended to promote technological development, namely the management of programmes relating to the monitoring, re-use and saving of energy and of requests for intervention from companies for projects involving basic industrial research, applied research, or development.

The Council for Science Policy (CPS) in the Walloon Region advises the Walloon Government on the preparation of the science policy of the region. It consists of representatives of universities and non-university institutions of higher education, research centres, and social interlocutors. CPS is integrated into the Walloon Regional Social and Economic Council (CESRW).

3.3.2.4. The Brussels-Capital Region

Within the government of the Brussels-Capital Region, one minister is in charge of scientific research with both economic and non-economic objectives.

The research is administered by the Research and Innovation Service (RIS). RIS provides assistance to research and innovation activities of companies, in particular SMEs (subsidies for basic industrial research, aid to prototyping related to industrial R&D, subsidies for participation in European research programmes).

3.4. Institutions of higher education

In Belgium, science has traditionally been associated with educational establishments. Since 1874, basic research has been to a large extent performed at universities. Today, a considerable number of Belgian university departments and research institutes are poles of scientific excellence in fields like biotechnology, new materials, microelectronics, and space research.

Belgium has 21 universities and university centres, among which six institutions cover the full range of academic fields.[4] All the universities are engaged in research. The universities are now directly financed by the communities. In 1996, higher education received 18.3 billion BEF or 35% of the total of Belgian public

---

[4] The six institutions that cover the full range of academic fields are: KULeuven, UG, UCL, ULB, ULG, and VUB. More than 80% of the university students are concentrated in these universities.

allocations to R&D activities of 52.2 billion BEF. The number of students by university is given in Table 3.1.

Table 3.1:   Number of students in Belgian universities (academic year 1997-98)

French-speaking universities	# of students	Dutch-speaking universities	# of students
Université Catholique de Louvain (UCL)	19566	Katholieke Universiteit Leuven (KULeuven)	23659
Université Libre de Bruxelles (ULB)	16708	Universiteit Gent (UG)	19920
Université de Liège (Ulg)	12814	Universiteit Antwerpen (UA)	8053
Facultés Universitaires Notre-Dame de la	4026	Vrije Universiteit Brussel (VUB)	7607
Université de Mons Hainaut (UMH)	2393	Limburgs Universitair Centrum (LUC)	2040
Facultés Universitaires Catholiques de Mons	1374	Katholieke Universiteit Brussel (KUB)	750
Facultés Universitaires Saint-Louis (FUSL)	1361		
Faculté des Sciences Agronom. de Gembloux	1038		
Faculté Polytechnique de Mons (FPMs)	903		
Fondation Universitaire Luxembourgeoise	129		
Total	60312	Total	62029

Source: CRef (1998), VLIR (1999).

Universities have been facing, and in the French-speaking part of the country continue to face, drastic reductions in governmental support. The reduced amount of public resources allocated to research has led Belgian universities to increase their participation in research programs financed by external contracts. One important effect of this is the instability of research teams and high rotation of the academic research personnel (due to short-term financing). The size of the most important universities and university centres in function of personnel is given in Table 3.2. There are 24 university and inter-university autonomous research centres in Belgium active in different scientific fields. Some of these centres carry out applied research in fields related to the development of new products or processes by spin-offs or interested firms. Some of the 84 Belgian non-university HEIs also provide a significant amount of the training for applied scientists and engineers and conduct applied research, often in collaboration with private firms, universities and RTOs.[5]

---

[5] The non-university HEIs have around 171,000 students.

Table 3.2: **Personnel in Belgian universities (in full-time equivalents - 1997)**

	Permanent staff			Contractual staff			
	Aca-demic	Scien-tific	Other	Aca-demic	Scien-tific	Other	Total
French-speaking universities							
UCL	605	461	1156	676	301	297	3496
ULB	413	526	1068	520	231	216	2973
Ulg	362	622	923	651	253	346	3157
FUNDP	134	170	280	131	54	22	791
UMH	61	112	192	81	17	19	482
FUCAM	36	33	52	11		3	135
FUSL	36	30	44	8		1	119
FPMs	53	54	134	77	10	17	346
FUSAGx	34	49	140	93	22	74	411
FUL	4	11	20	12	9	10	66
TOTAL	1738	2068	4009	2260	897	1005	11976
Dutch-speaking universities							
KUL	1580		1442		1891	807	5720
UG	1067		1017		734	744	3562
UA	594		514		508	351	1967
VUB	563		493		292	380	1728
LUC	171		97		108	62	438
KUB	52		25		12	14	103
TOTAL	4027		3588		3545	2358	13518

Note: For the Flemish universities the complete teaching and assisting staff as well as permanent researchers are classified as academic personnel. The scientific personnel are the contractual researchers who are paid from funds or as stipends. Therefore, none of the permanent staff are classified as scientific personnel and none of the contractual staff are classified as academic personnel.

Source: CRef (1998), VLIR (1999).

3.5. Research and Technology Organisations (RTOs)

With the federalisation of most competencies related to S&T, new research and technology organisations (RTOs) were established at the regional level. These new institutes are increasingly oriented towards knowledge and technology diffusion. At the federal level, their tasks consist of scientific research in specific fields, classification and registration of available knowledge, and promotion of scientific knowledge among the population at large. Some of these institutes play an important role in the Belgian innovation system. Here are some of the most important:

- The Belgian Nuclear Research Centre (SCK-CEN), with over 600 researchers and technicians, carries out research in nuclear safety, radioactive waste disposal, and radiation protection;
- The Belgian Institute of Space Aeronomy (BISA), as part of the international programmes of the EU and ESA or bilateral agreements (e.g. with NASA), is engaged in research on the monitoring of the ozone layer, solar radiation, atmospheric modelling, and interactions of solar wind, the magnetosphere, and the ionosphere;
- The Belgian Royal Institute of Natural Sciences (RINS) focuses on biology and palaeontology and, with the creation of the Mathematical Model of the North Sea and the Scheldt Estuary (MUMM), also on the management of marine ecosystems;
- The Louis Pasteur Scientific Institute of Public Health (IPH), performs specific tasks like epidemiological surveillance, quality assessment, risk evaluation and monitoring;
- The Royal Meteorological Institute (RMI) engages in research in meteorology, climatology, hydrology, geomagnetism, and terrestrial and atmospheric electricity.

The Flemish Community established and finances three research institutes. IMEC is an inter-university research institute for advanced research in microelectronics and has been operational since 1984. VITO, created in 1991 by the Flemish Government, is a multidisciplinary research centre, active in the fields of environment, non-nuclear energy, new materials, and raw materials. VIB was created in 1995 to co-ordinate scientific research in biotechnology. This institute consists of nine biotechnology departments from four Flemish universities.

The Scientific Institute of Public Service (ISSeP), financed by DGTRE of the Walloon Region, also conducts research and development and is a centre of industrial projects and an expertise, testing, and analysis laboratory. ISSeP is mainly active in three areas: mineral resources and energetic minerals, the environment and the counteracting of the effects of pollution, and technical and industrial security. Similar to the Flemish Region, the Walloon Region has developed a policy of centres of excellence in specific fields such as biotechnology (BCR), information technology (CEDITI and MULTITEL), and new materials (MATERIA NOVA).

The 'sectoral collective research centres' and other similar centres[6] occupy a separate place in the Belgian S&T landscape. Their objective is to meet the specific scientific and technological research requirements of generally medium-sized private companies in specific sectors. Basic technological research (pre-competitive and pre-normative) and the introduction of new technologies in industry constitute their main field of activity. This joint research also promotes the

---

[6] The difference between the 'sectoral collective research centres' and other similar centres is that the former were created by a specific law and are also known as 'De Groote Centres' while the latter emerged from private initiatives.

exploitation of the results of basic research, thus allowing companies, especially SMEs, to keep in contact with the world of research. The 12 largest of these sectoral centres are the ones connected with the wood, ceramics, cement, building, electricity, metallic constructions, gas, metallurgy, paints and coatings, roads, textile, and glass industries. They represent a potential of some 1200 specialists. Most of the income of these centres derives from compulsory contributions from companies in the industry and from the authorities as far as exploratory research is concerned. The third source of income is the provision, funded by the regions, of technological assistance to companies. Under a co-operation agreement signed in 1991 between the Federal Government and the regions, half of the public support for research at these centres comes from the federal state (Ministry of Economic Affairs) and the other half from the three regions. The scientific personnel and R&D expenses of the most important collective research centres are shown in Table 3.3. The Belgian authorities allocated 590 million BEF in 1995 and 540 million in 1996 to the R&D budget of the sectoral collective research centres,.

Table 3.3: **Scientific personnel and R&D expenses of the major Belgian Collective Research Centres (1995)**

	Scientific Personnel	R&D expenses (Mio BEF)
Total for all Collective Research Centres	684.4	2619.5
Among which:		
Metallurgical Research Centre (CRM)	22.4%	28.5%
Belgian Building Research Institute (BBRI)	12.4%	14.6%
Scientific and Technical Research Centre of the Metalworking Industry (CRIF/WTCM)	16.9%	11.9%
Scientific and Technical Centre of the Belgian Textile Industry (CENTEXBEL)	12.5%	11.9%

3.6. Bridging institutions

Both in innovation theory and in policy, a shift occurred from a focus on knowledge and technology creation towards diffusion and absorption. Bridging institutions emerged to facilitate the interactive aspects of the innovation process and to resolve mismatches, potential and otherwise, between different types of actors in the innovation system. Interfaces, science parks, incubators, and other types of bridging institutions were created to exploit the results of research performed by HEIs and RTOs, to reinforce the absorption power of existing firms, and to promote the creation of new-venture firms and university spin-offs.

3.6.1. Business-university/HEI interfaces

The business-university/HEI interfaces directly assist companies in solving technical problems, developing new products and processes, integrating new technologies and training by bringing the company into direct contact with the laboratory or the research unit best placed to respond to the company's needs. Their work consists of various forms of co-operation between companies and research centres, such as *ad hoc* services, consultancy assignments, joint research programs, and license transfers.

By means of publications, seminars, technological demonstrations, and the like, the interface cells also provide private firms with information on the prospects offered by the most recent technological developments and on the help they can receive in implementing them. The promotion and benefits that can be derived from the technological potential of universities and other institutions of higher education can lead to partnerships with existing companies and to the creation of new industrial activities. Recently, a number of universities have created their own funds to provide venture capital to university spin-off activities.

3.6.2. Science parks and incubators

One of the main purposes of science or research parks is to encourage the formation of technology-based firms and to promote the transfer of technology from the academic institution on site to the firms housed in the park.

As can be seen in Table 3.4, the main Belgian universities with a faculty of applied sciences (KUL, LUC, UG, UCL, ULB, ULG, and VUB) have created or have actively participated in the creation of these parks.

More recently, most of the university-related science or research parks took up the role of innovation and incubation centres, the main objective being to stimulate and support spin-off activities and to assist in the start-up of high-tech companies.

Table 3.4:   Belgian science and research parks

	Creation date	Location (region)	surface (ha)	# firms	Main technological fields	University
Louvain-la-Neuve	1969	Louvain-la-Neuve (W)	227	100	Chemicals, biotechnology	UCL
Haasrode Research Park	1972	Haasrode (F)	120	45	DSP, ICT, materials and software	KUL
Da Vinci Park	1974	Evere (B)	25	40	Information technologies	ULB
Sart Tilman	1975	Liège (W)	50	40	Aeronautics, health, optics	ULG
Research Park	Begin 1980s	Neder-Over-Heembeek (F)	17	14	Software, mechanics, hydraulics	VUB
Research Park		Zellik (F)	19	14	Measuring instruments, software	
Nivelles Science Park	1980	Nivelles (W)	n.a.	n.a.	Industrial research	ULB
Erasmus Science Park	1981	Anderlecht (B)	16	n.a.	Health	ULB
Vesalius Science Park	1985	Woluwé (B)	n.a.	n.a.	Audiovisual technology, biotechnology, pharmaceuticals	UCL
Science Park	1986	Zwijnaarde (F)	13.6	8	Biotechnology	UG
Wetenschapspark Limburg	1989	Diepenbeek (F)	11	8	Multimedia, telematics	LUC
Parc Scientifique des Isnes	1990	Gembloux (W)	50	12	Biotechnology, food	FUNDP FSAGx
UBCA (Antwerp Incubation Centre)	1992	Antwerp (F)	n.a.	8	Software, medical and pharmaceutical technologies	UA
Aéropôle	1996	Charleroi (W)	n.a.	n.a.	Biotechnology, information technologies	UCL-ULB-FUNDP
Research Park Kortrijk	1996	Kortrijk (F)	10	n.a.	New materials, electronics, IT/biotechnology	KULAK
Initialis	1998	Mons (W)	43	12	Information technologies & new materials	FPMs, UMH
Seneffe	1998	Seneffe (W)	4	n.a.	Chemicals	UCL

3.7. Science and technology policies

This section reviews some of the policies and instruments used in the field of S&T activities at the various governmental levels. As mentioned above, in Belgium most areas of competencies and decision-making power as regards S&T policies, particularly the financing and support of both fundamental and applied R&D activities, have – starting with the institutional reform of 1980 – gradually been devolved to sub-national authorities. We will, therefore, pay specific attention to policy measures at the regional level.

3.7.1.   The Federal Government

The OSTC, in addition to its policy, co-ordinating and programming activities, finances both basic and applied research by non-business institutions and R&D projects by private firms. Following the institutional reforms, which transferred competency for industrial policy and research to the regions, the OSTC retained a co-ordination and stimulating role at the national level and an interface role at the European level.

The OSTC finances the participation of Belgian partners in EUREKA projects and actively promotes Belgian participation to the EU Framework Programmes. It allocates a large part of its budget to space research and participation in international space programmes. The OSTC participates in the definition of ESA activities and negotiates the participation of Belgian scientific or industrial partners in ESA programmes. The contribution of Belgium to the different optional ESA programmes is determined by the federal Minister for Science Policy.

The OSTC is also responsible for the management of the participation and the representation in the pan-European Airbus programme and finances Belgian participation in European intergovernmental organisations like the European Southern Observatory (ESO), the European Synchrotron Radiation Facility (ESRF), and the European Molecular Biology Laboratory (EMBL).

3.7.2.   The Flemish Community

Confronted with the need to adapt Flemish industry to new knowledge intensive activities, priority in Flemish S&T policy is given to the stimulation of the development and diffusion of new technologies (ICT, biotechnology). The relative dominance of low R&D-intensive sectors and the relative retardation of SMEs argued for a policy of technology diffusion to improve the innovativeness and competitiveness of Flemish firms. The focus was very much on SMEs.

In 1991, the Flemish Government created IWT, a semi-autonomous institute. IWT was established as a one-stop institution for the implementation of industrial R&D policy and for dealing with all R&D programmes and activities with an economic impact in which the Flemish Government is involved. The shift from technology policy towards a more broadly defined innovation policy made IWT a central agent in stimulating technological innovation. It not only provides financial support for R&D programmes but it also deals with the development of new initiatives to provide information and expertise. It must also enhance networking, support related non-technological issues, and co-ordinate the government policy with regard to bridging institutions and to cluster development.

Three Flemish research institutes (IMEC, VITO and VIB) were created to transfer technological knowledge and exploit the results of their own fundamental and applied research through co-operation or the creation of spin-off companies. As will be documented in Chapter 7, the Inter-university Microelectronics Centre (IMEC) participates intensively in international R&D projects and often assumes the role of project leader. The Flemish Institute for Technological Research (VITO), although created only in 1991, also occupies a central position in the Belgian R&D network, especially in its fields of activity (environment, energy, and materials technology). Because of its recent creation (1995), it was as yet not possible to evaluate the role played by the Flanders Inter-university Institute for Biotechnology (VIB) in international R&D co-operation.

The most important policy areas in which the Flemish Community acts, and the channels through which it acts are the following.

- *Financing R&D*: IWT promotes and finances pre-competitive as well as more applied R&D in industry. In 1998, its total budget amounted to 3.2 billion BEF. It has specific programmes aimed at SMEs (Flemish SMEs with an 11% share of R&D business expenditures obtain 24% of the financial R&D support), and impulse programmes in some high-tech disciplines.
- *Cluster policy*: In the framework of its cluster policy the Flemish Government promotes co-operation between firms in specific technological disciplines. Technology diffusion from research institutions and large firms to SMEs is a prerequisite for financial support in the start-up phase. A distinction is made between 'clusters' and 'technology valleys'. While the former relate to more traditional activities, the latter are defined as geographical concentrations of activities of high-tech firms, research centres, and educational and training institutions in the same technological domain. The Flemish Government distinguishes some ten 'technology valleys' in Flanders ('Flanders Language Valley', 'Digital Signal Processing Valley' and 'Biotech Valley' being the most prominent). It is however not clear whether all these 'valleys' satisfy any serious cluster criterion.
- *Research centres*: IMEC, VITO, and VIB are the three Flemish research centres that receive financial support from the Flemish Government. In 1998, this amounted to 1.1 billion BEF, 1 billion BEF, and 975 million BEF, respectively. In addition to performing basic research of their own, a main part of their mission is to valorise research results and diffusing technological knowledge and know-how among Flemish firms in general and Flemish SMEs in particular. They are expected to foster the start-up of spin-offs (so far, 17 spin-off firms have originated from IMEC; VIB, despite the recentness of its creation, has already engendered two spin-offs).
- *The policy of encouraging new-venture industries*: Flemish authorities have set as a priority objective the alteration of the specialisation pattern of Flemish firms into more knowledge-intensive products and services with high value added. Therefore, R&D efforts will be oriented to knowledge-intensive sectors and disciplines. The Flemish cluster policy can, to some extent, be seen as an expression of this concern. Apart from this, a number of spearhead actions focus on specific disciplines that are thought to be essential for future

competitiveness, like information technology, multimedia, new materials, and environmental and energy technology.

- *The promotion of highly skilled labour in SMEs*: To reinforce the absorption ability of firms, SMEs can receive a wage subsidy to reduce labour costs if they employ a highly skilled person. This employee must develop an innovation plan for the SME. In doing this they are supported by researchers of a sectoral centre of collective research or by one of the clusters. Fiscal policy however remains largely a federal competence and fiscal measures to promote innovation are therefore limited at the regional level.
- *The Flemish Regional Investment Company (GIMV)*: GIMV is a Flemish public investment and holding company that was established in 1980. In 1998, its investment portfolio amounted to 19.3 billion BEF. One of its main objectives is to increase the pace of the technological renewal of the Flemish economy. For this purpose, GIMV assumes the role of major Flemish venture capitalist (4.8 billion Belgian francs in 1998). GIMV participates in various leading-edge companies, mostly related to ICT and biotechnology, and participates in public and private risk funds. It supports the introduction of Flemish companies on EASDAQ and NASDAQ. GIMV has a specific scheme for financing innovation in SMEs and manages a take-off fund for starting firms.
- *Regional Development Agencies (GOM)*: In Flanders, each province has its Regional Development Agency to promote the socio-economic development of the region. They promote new investments and innovation projects and support starting companies. They play an important role in technology diffusion, especially towards SMEs. The five Flemish Regional Development Agencies have created a common 'Technological Innovation Cell' (TIV) to track the potential of new products, processes and services in companies.
- *Regional Technology Advisory Centres (RTAC)*: The RTACs support companies with technological advice and play a role in the diffusion of information. They focus, again, on SMEs. A large number of sectoral centres of collective research act as a RTAC, as do most Regional Development Agencies.

3.7.3.   The Walloon Region

The actions taken by the Walloon Region in support of research mainly relate to R&D with industrial purposes: basic research, applied research and development, and contextual research. In the Walloon Region, the competence with regard to S&T remains under the direct control of the regional administration (DGTRE). DGTRE allocated about 4.3 billion BEF in 1996 to R&D support (see Table 3.6 for a breakdown of this budget). More than half of this budget concerns direct R&D financing of industrial firms through subsidises for all R&D costs related to basic research performed by firms or by universities and research centres in collaboration with firms. For applied research, firms can apply for reimbursable grants and support for (environmental) R&D. The rest of the budget covers other

S&T activities, such as technological guidance of, and assistance to (mainly) SMEs, sectoral analyses, and a 'technology watch'. The Walloon Region assists firms – essentially SMEs – with specific aspects of R&D projects. It finances personnel for project development and technological co-operation with other European firms and technological and economic feasibility studies for new products, processes, and software. It supports the evaluation of potential collaborators and assists firms in aspects related to technology transfer and legal matters. Through HORIZON-EUROPE, the Walloon Region finances R&D projects submitted in the framework of international R&D programmes.

The main other policy channels are the following:

- *The Walloon Regional Investment Society (SRIW)*: SRIW, a public utility corporation, contributes through its financial interventions, to the reorganisation, modernisation, and development of the industrial structure of the region. By participating in the registered capital of over 1200 companies, it, along with its subsidiaries, has gradually acquired a portfolio valued at some 69 billion BEF. Both a development bank and a public holding company, it constitutes the financial arm of the industrial policy of the Walloon authorities. In addition to its main general activity, SRIW supervises a number of specialised subsidiaries, among them being the Walloon Investment Management Society (SOWAGEP[7]). This society mainly aims at co-ordinating the actions and financing of local investment societies (INVESTS). The mission of the INVESTS is to promote the creation and the development of SMEs by means of financial support. SRIW and its subsidiaries also administer programmes that provide venture capital to small businesses.

- *Regional development agencies*: In Wallonia, there are nine regional development agencies, which manage 130 industrial zones, fully equipped and linked to the major railway and motorway network. Each province has its regional development agency, except the Province of Hainaut, where there are five '*intercommunales*'. They play a major role in the promotion of the socio-economic development of their geographical area. They are also increasingly active in the implementation of technology initiatives at the local level, such as technology guidance, promotion of regional S&T instruments, and networking.

- *The Economic and Social Council of the Walloon Region (CESRW)*: Created in 1983, CESRW is a regional consulting and negotiating organisation, composed of representatives of the main Walloon economic and social actors (employers' federations, trade unions). An important function of the organisation is to transmit recommendations to the Walloon Government. These recommendations are formulated by *ad hoc* commissions, among them the Science Policy Commission. This commission is a mixed commission that in-

---

[7] This subsidiary was recently renamed SOGEPA.

cludes representatives from the higher education sector as well as from research centres.

- *Research centres*: Apart from ISSeP (Institut Scientifique de Service Public),
  Wallonia has so far no autonomous research institutes aimed at diffusing
  technological know-how, similar to the three Flemish research institutes mentioned above. However, some science parks of the Walloon Region (Namur
  Province Scientific Park and Sart Tilman Science Park) actively promote syn-
  ergy and co-operation between universities and firms (mostly high-tech
  SMEs). As will be shown in Chapter 7, Walloon universities have relatively
  central positions in the R&D network. Unfortunately, the same does not hold
  for Walloon firms, which, with some exceptions, do not actively participate in
  international R&D activities. Moreover, co-operation between Walloon firms,
  universities, and research institutes seems meagre in comparison with what
  occurs in the Flemish part of the country. Undoubtedly, a more active diffusion policy could increase the valorisation of the scientific and technological
  potential in the Walloon Region.
- *Walloon Innovation Relay Centre (CRIW)*: Created on the initiative of
  DGTRE in collaboration with the six Walloon EURO-Info-Centres and the
  five Walloon European Business and Innovation Centres, CRIW promotes innovative projects, technology transfer, European partnerships, and 'technology watch'. The main beneficiaries are, again, SMEs, research centres, and
  universities.
- *Technology diffusion*: Several specific measures have been implemented in
  the Walloon Region to stimulate technology transfer. The FIRST programme
  is one of the most important. It promotes the mobility of researchers from the
  higher education sector to enterprises by paying for part of the corresponding
  wage cost.

3.7.4.   The French Community

The French Community finances research activities linked to higher education
(mainly research performed in French-speaking universities). The S&T budget of
the French Community in 1996 amounted to 6.9 billions BEF. This amount relates
primarily to the part of the general university funds allocated to research, the
grants to the special funds for research in universities, the grants to the *Fonds National de la Recherche Scientifique* (FNRS), and the financing of the actions of
so-called 'concerted' research.

3.7.5.   The Brussels-Capital Region

The Research and Innovation Service (RIS) of the Brussels-Capital Region subsidises and supports R&D programmes and projects in which regional firms are
involved. Special attention is given to SMEs. Basic industrial research is subsidised, and refundable loans are granted to prototype projects resulting from indus-

trial research. Participation in European research programmes can also be subsidised.

In the Region of Brussels-Capital, Brussels Technopol was established as a bridging institution to promote technological diffusion to, and R&D co-operation with, firms and institutes. It promotes access and integration of innovation within companies on the basis of a systematic methodology: identifying needs, guiding a firm to the technological source, promoting co-operation between firms, and encouraging the participation in European programmes.

Due to its small size, the resources of this region are not substantial. For 1996, the total R&D and S&T budget of Brussels-Capital Region amounted to only 395 million BEF.

Table 3.5 summarises the different types of public support for Belgian actors involved in S&T activities. The table shows that a substantial amount of authority has devolved to the regions with regard to S&T policy. Table 3.6 gives an overview of the financial support to S&T activities of the different regional authorities in 1996. The regional distributions of public support to S&T activities show that regions have developed different S&T policies. The Walloon Region has a more diffuse policy, while the Flemish Region concentrates a portion of its resources in selected technology fields.

3.8. Conclusion

In a recent paper, the OSTC raises the question 'Does Belgium still need a federal science policy?' (DWTC, 1999). In fact, the new Belgian institutional system is still in a transitional phase, and it is difficult to predict in which direction it will evolve. As shown in this chapter, the large degree of autonomy of the regions with regard to the science and technology policy makes any institutional analysis of the Belgian Innovation System very complex. Each region has implemented S&T instruments that are supposedly adapted to their own socio-economic environment. The regional dimension today is, therefore, a major aspect of the Belgian Innovation System. Although the specific competencies of the federal authority in the S&T field are now rather limited, this level of political decision-making still remains very important because it is a main channel through which the regions try to cope with the intensification of techno-globalisation.

Table 3.5:   Public support for industrial research

Measure		Federal	Brussels	Wallonia	Flanders	European Union
						Authorities
FINANCIAL INCENTIVES						
Tax advantages	Multinational/managers established in Belgium	X				
Fiscal exemption	Additional R&D personnel	X				
Capital allowances	Advantageous treatment for R&D investments	X				
Grants/subsidies	Agriculture	X				
	R&D Investment		X	X	X	X
	Project preparation & submission for a participation in European R&D actions, EUREKA (Horizon Europe)			X	X	
Refundable loans	R&D investment		X	X	X	
	EUREKA projects		X	X	X	X
Subordinated loans	(SRIB)	X				
Minority interests participation	(SRIB)	X				
Awards	Yearly competition for best technological innovation			X		
MISSION-ORIENTED CONTRACTS AND PROCUREMENTS						
Implementation of research actions & programmes	On themes and issues of regional/national/ international interest	X	X	X	X	X
S&T INFRASTRUCTURE						
Industrial R&D institutes	Technical diffusion, training, technical advises (sectoral collective research centres)	X	X	X	X	
Assistance (costs intervention)	• Wages + contributions for unemployed engaged in R&D activities in the private sector		X	X	X	
	• Training of unemployed engaged in R&D activities (ORBEM)		X			
	• Consulting studies linked to investments and training		X			
	• Study & materalisation of innovations by SMEs and isolated inventors			X		
	• Consultency studies: sectoral analysis, technical & commercial risks of R&D projects, acquisition/transfer of new technologies, techn. collaborations			X		
	• Knowledge diffusion (FIRST): apprenticeship for a researcher in a HEI or RTO			X		
	• RIT Europe: complementary personnel			X		
	• Partners seeking for European R&D actions, submission of RTD projects, transfer of technological results (CIRW, VIA)			X	X	

Table 3.6: **Public financial assistance to S&T activities by the regional authorities (millions of BEF, 1996)**

Actors (total)		%	R&D financing		%	Other S&T activities		%
Brussels-Capital Region								
Enterprises	258	0.7	R&D subsidies	140	0.5			
			Refundable loans	118	0.4			
RTOs	3	0.0				Operating costs and investment	3	0.0
Total	261	0.7		258	0.9		3	0.0
Flemish Community								
Enterprises	2627	7.5	IWT financial assistance	1197	4.3	Other IWT activities	179	2.4
			FIOV financing	1051	3.8			
			Biotech fund	200	0.7			
University and non-university HEIs	13145	37.6	General university funds	4536	16.4	Other funds	3141	42.7
			Research funds	4317	15.6			
			Other funds	1051	3.8			
			Industrial research at high-schools	100	0.4			
RTOs	3025	8.6	VITO	645	2.3	Other VITO activities	479	6.5
			IMEC	981	3.5			
			VIB	920	3.3			
STV	64	0.2		64	0.2			
Scientific institut.	1614	4.6		906	3.3		708	9.6
Policy initiatives	807	2.3		655	2.4		152	2.1
Sectoral initiatives	1119	3.2		697	2.5		422	5.7
Total	22401	64.0		17320	62.6		5081	69.1
French Community								
University and non-university HEIs	7913	22.6	General university funds	5230	18.9	Support credits	166	2.3
			Research funds	1846	6.7			
			Research projects	671	2.4			
RTOs	109	0.3	R&D projects	55	0.2	Operating costs and investment	54	0.7
Total	8022	22.9		7802	28.2		220	3.0
Walloon Region								
Enterprises	1372	3.9	R&D subsidies	247	0.9	Complementary assistance to R&D of SMEs	73	1.0
			Refundable loans	1009	3.6			
			FIRST	43	0.2			
University and non-university HEIs	2035	5.8	R&D projects	683	2.5	Invest	1109	15.1
			FIRST	181	0.7	Interfaces	62	0.8
RTOs	907	2.6	R&D projects	103	0.4	Operating costs investment	330	4.5
						Sectoral analyses, techn. support & techn. watch	155	2.1
						Technological guidance	50	0.7
						Complementary personnel	46	0.6
						Trade & industry chambers interfaces	36	0.5
						Scientific parks	116	1.6
						Others	71	1.0
Total	4314	13.3		2266	8.2		2048	27.9
TOTAL	34998	100		27646	100		7352	100

Source: OSTC (1997), own calculations.

Appendix: List of abbreviations[8]

AWI (D): Administration for Science and Innovation
BBRI: Belgian Building Research Institute   **WTCB** (D) - **CSTC** (F)
BISA: Belgian Institute of Space Aeronomy   **BIRA** (D) - **IASB** (F)
CENTEXBEL: Scientific and Technical Centre of the Belgian Textile Industry
CESRW (F): Walloon Regional Social and Economic Council
CFS: 'Federal Co-operation' Committee of the IMSPC
CIS: 'International Co-operation' Committee of the IMSPC
CPS (F): Council for Science Policy
CRIF/WTCM: Scientific and Technical Research Centre of the Metalworking Industry
CRIW (F): Walloon Innovation Relay Centre
CRM: Centre for Metallurgical Research
DGENORS (F): General Directorate for Non-obligatory Education and Scientific Research
DGTRE (F): General Directorate for Technologies, Research and Energy
FCSP: Federal Council for Science Policy   **FRWB** (D) - **CFPS** (F)
FIOV (D): Fund for Industrial Research
FPMs (F): Faculté Polytechnique de Mons
FUCAM (F): Facultés Universitaires Catholiques de Mons
FUL (F): Fondation Universitaire Luxembourgeoise
FUNDP (F): Facultés Universitaires Notre-Dame de la Paix
FUSAGx (F): Faculté des Sciences Agronomiques de Gembloux
FUSL (F): Facultés Universitaires Saint-Louis
GIMV (D): Flemish Regional Investment Company
GOM (D): Regional Development Agency
IMEC (D): Interuniversity Microelectronics Centre
IMSPC: Inter-ministerial Science Policy Conference   **IMCWB** (D) - **CIMPS** (F)
INVEST (F): Local Investment Company
IPH: Scientific Institute of Public Health Louis Pasteur   **WIV** (D) - **ISP** (F)
ISPC: Inter-ministerial Science Policy Committee   **ICWB** (D) - **CIPS** (F)
ISRIA: Institute for the Promotion of Scientific Research in Industry and Agriculture
                                                                                                IWONL (D) - **IRSIA** (F)
ISSeP (F): Scientific Institute of Public Services
IWT (D): Flemish Institute for the Promotion of Research in Industry
KUB (D): Katholieke Universiteit Brussel
KULAK (D): Katholieke Universiteit Leuven Afdeling Kortrijk
KULeuven (D): Katholieke Universiteit Leuven
LUC (D): Limburgs Universitair Centrum
NFSR: National Fund for Scientific Research   **FWO-Vlaanderen** (D) - **FNRS** (F)

---

[8] For all federal institutions the English denomination is used, as it is throughout the text, with the Dutch (D) and French (F) denomination following. For regional institutions the original denomination is used.

MUMM: Mathematical Model of the North Sea and Scheldt Estuary   **BMM** (D) - **MMMN** (F)

OSTC: Federal Office for Scientific, Technical and Cultural Affairs   **DWTC** (D) - **SSTC** (F)

RINS: Royal Institute of Natural Sciences   **KBIN** (D) - **IRSNB** (F)

RMI: Royal Meteorological Institute   **KMI** (D) - **IRM** (F)

RTAC (D): Regional Technology Advisory Centres

RIS: Research and Innovation Service   **DOI** (D) - **SRI** (F)

SCK-CEN: Belgian Nuclear Research Centre

SOWAGEP (F): Walloon Investment Management Company (now SOGEPA)

SPO: Science Policy Office   **DPWB** (D) - **SPPS** (F)

SRIW (F): Walloon Regional Investment Company

STCB: Scientific and Technical Centre for the Building Industry   **WTCB** (D) - **CSTC** (F)

STCM: Scientific and Technical Centre for the Metalworking Industry   **WTCM** (D) - **CRIF** (F)

UA (D): Universiteit Antwerpen (confederation of RUCA, UFSIA and UIA)

UCL (F): Université Catholique de Louvain

UG (D): Universiteit Gent

ULB (F): Université Libre de Bruxelles

ULG (F): Université de Liège

UMH (F): Université de Mons Hainaut

VIB (D): Flanders Interuniversity Institute for Biotechnology

VITO (D): Flemish Institute for Technological Research

VRWB (D): Flemish Council for Science Policy

VUB (D): Vrije Universiteit Brussel.

Part II

The Inputs in the National Innovation System

Chapter 4.   R&D Expenditures and the National Innovation System

Henri Capron and Michele Cincera

4.1. Introduction

The conduct of science and technology policy differs radically in small countries from what occurs in large ones. Johnson (1988, p. 297) rightly pointed out that "the need for an institutional system is relatively strong for small countries. The possible benefits of such a system are considerable, and so are the potential costs of institutional rigidity". He added that the coherence and the consensus-generating capacity of the institutional system are vital elements for its efficiency. As implied in the previous chapter, there is at least the suspicion that the Belgian innovation system has problems more with the volatility of its institutional setting rather than with its rigidity. High volatility leads to high uncertainty and adverse effects on the propensity to invest in technology.

In order to compensate for their limited market, small countries have to turn to the international market. Stabilising, let alone improving, trade performance in the face of high competitive pressure on world markets requires small countries to invest in R&D. Indeed, their market share of international trade depends greatly on their ability to apply trade patterns to structural changes. The 'squeeze' on small industrialised countries by large countries as well as by the newly industri-alised countries (Walsh, 1988) makes the implementation of an efficient S&T system more necessary than ever.

As shown in Chapter 3, the present Belgian prosperity is rooted in a long-standing tradition of openness to innovations and new ideas, which is witnessed by an early, in historical terms, development of the government authorities and institutions needed to monitor this openness.

In this chapter, we will limit the analysis to the present structure of Belgian R&D expenditures. After a comparison in Section 4.2 of the distribution of R&D activities in Belgium to that observed in other main industrialised countries, we will focus on the analysis of the structure of Belgian R&D expenditures in Section 4.3. Section 4.4 examines the distribution of R&D employment by type of qualifi-cation across industries and firm size and also the share of this kind of personnel in total employment. The relative importance of the several sources for financing intramural business R&D activities is discussed in Section 4.5. As shown in the previous chapter, regional entities are becoming increasingly self-governing.

Therefore, it is worthwhile to analyse regional patterns of R&D expenditures whenever regional data are available.

In order to appreciate better the role of both the federal government and the regional authorities in the support of R&D activities, the main budget allocations with respect to functional destinations and type of institution are considered in Section 4.7. One important feature of innovation systems is the capacity of the education and training system to provide competitive and innovative organisations with the required knowledge and skills (Nelson, 1993). Consequently, it is worth examining the performance of the Belgian education system. Two main aspects are studied in Sections 4.8 and 4.9: the number and the mobility of graduates and the characteristics of the workforce. The chapter concludes in Section 4.10 with a brief presentation of joint research activities and other forms of technological collaboration between Belgian firms and other national and foreign actors. These kinds of technological linkages are major channels of technology transfer and are further investigated in Chapters 6 and 7.

4.2. Financing and performing sectors

In order to obtain a global overview of efforts devoted to innovative activities, the two most commonly used indicators are R&D intensity measured as R&D expenditures as a percentage of GDP or those expenditures *per capita*. A closer look at the distribution of R&D expenditures allows one to appreciate quantitatively the institutional structure of R&D activities. First, firms, research organisations, government, and higher education are the main actors of the innovation system. Second, the analysis of R&D expenditure levels both by area of performance and origin of funding shows how closely the actors are interconnected as far as financial flows are concerned. The international openness of Belgium makes a positioning in comparison with its main trading partners very relevant to this discussion.

Table 4.1 compares Belgium with other industrialised countries with respect to the relative efforts devoted to research activities and to government subsidisation rates over the 1981-1995 period. The international comparison of gross domestic expenditures on R&D (GERD) is done with two different scaling factors: population and GDP. GERD *per capita* has apparently increased in all countries over the last fifteen years except in the USA, Germany, the UK, France, and Italy, where it has slightly decreased over the last decade. The US has the highest level of R&D expenditure *per capita* (index 595 at US PPP exchange rates in 1995), and it is closely followed by Japan (561), France (416), and Germany (389). Belgian R&D investments *per capita* (296) were in 1995 almost as high as those of Canada (305). In terms of R&D expenditures related to GDP – the usual R&D intensity measure – the evolution during the 1990s is quite different, however. In general, R&D intensities with respect to GDP have shown a more stable pattern and have increased from 1990 to 1995 only in Canada. In 1995, Belgium (1.9%) comes out

above the Canadian and Italian levels but below the levels of the other main industrialised countries. Japan (3.0%) and the US (2.5%) have the highest R&D
intensities.

The share of government R&D in GERD has decreased from 1981 to 1995 in
all countries, except Japan and Italy. Japan and Belgium are associated with the
lowest degree of government interventionism measured as a proportion of total
R&D expenditures (32.2% and 26.4%, respectively, in 1995). Furthermore, Belgium is characterised by a very important decrease of this share. The reason is, of
course, the adverse snowball effect on government debt that developed in the beginning of the 1980s and the subsequent budgetary squeeze.

**Table 4.1:   International comparison of total R&D intensities and government
subsidisation rates (1981, 1985, 1990 and 1995)[1]**

		USA	CAN	JAP	BE	FR	DE	UK	NL	IT
Total R&D per capita[2]	1981	375	174	241	169	221	274	240	205	90
	1985	485	210	334	181	264	368	261	244	131
	1990	618	269	542	294	419	403	346	343	211
	1995	595	305	561	296	416	389	339	356	177
Total R&D / GDP (%)	1981	2.4	1.2	2.3	1.6	2.0	2.4	2.4	1.9	0.9
	1985	2.9	1.4	2.8	1.7	2.3	2.7	2.3	2.1	1.1
	1990	2.8	1.5	3.0	1.7	2.4	2.6	2.2	2.2	1.3
	1995	2.5	1.6	3.0	1.9	2.3	2.3	2.0	2.1	1.0
Higher Education	1981	0.4	0.3	0.6	0.4	0.3	0.4	0.3	0.5	0.2
R&D / GDP (%)	1985	0.4	0.3	0.6	0.4	0.3	0.4	0.3	0.5	0.2
	1990	0.4	0.4	0.5	0.4	0.4	0.4	0.3	0.6	0.3
	1995	0.4	0.4	0.6	0.4	0.4	0.4	0.4	0.6	0.3
Private R&D / GDP	1981	1.2	0.5	1.4	1.0	0.8	1.4	1.0	0.9	0.4
(%)	1985	1.4	0.6	1.9	1.1	0.9	1.7	1.1	1.1	0.5
	1990	2.0	0.8	2.2	1.2	1.5	1.8	1.5	1.1	0.8
	1995	1.8	1.0	1.9	1.2	1.4	1.5	1.3	1.1	0.6
Government R&D /	1981	1.2	0.6	0.6	0.5	1.1	1.0	1.2	0.9	0.4
GDP (%)	1985	1.4	0.7	0.6	0.5	1.2	1.0	1.0	0.9	0.6
	1990	1.1	0.7	0.5	0.5	1.2	0.9	0.8	1.0	0.7
	1995	0.9	0.6	0.7	0.4	1.0	0.9	0.7	0.9	0.5
Government share in	1981	49.3	49.6	26.9	33.4	53.4	40.7	49.0	47.2	47.2
total R&D (higher	1985	48.3	47.6	21.0	31.6	52.9	36.7	42.8	44.2	51.7
education incl.) (%)	1990	42.7	46.4	26.2	30.2	49.1	35.8	35.8	48.7	49.6
	1995	38.3	38.0	32.2	26.4	43.1	37.4	34.2	42.3	51.2

Notes: (1) 1991 instead of 1990 for Belgium and Germany.
            (2) Total R&D investment in constant prices and US PPPs of 1990.
Sources: BSTS/OECD; own calculations.

In a large number of countries, government R&D includes a high part of the
financing of R&D within the higher education sector. This has to be taken into
account in cross-country comparisons. At the European level, while Belgium is in
a medium position for business and higher education R&D, it is in the last place
regarding government R&D infrastructure (Capron, 1997). Although the absence
of defence-oriented R&D in Belgium can partly explain this, the relatively weak
contribution of Belgian authorities to R&D efforts in *per capita* terms remains

largely inferior to that which is observed in diffusion-oriented countries like Germany and Japan (the Belgian government debt imbroglio is also a factor here).

Figure 4.1 provides a more precise illustration of the importance of the various financing and performing sectors in Belgium during the early 1990s. The private business sector is by far the largest R&D performing sector with nearly 70% of GERD. The higher-education and government sectors are responsible for 25% and 4%, respectively. Funding by the government is the largest source of financing for the higher education sector (74%) and is fairly weak in the business sector (4%).

Figure 4.1:   Belgian R&D in 1995, by source of funds and sector of performance

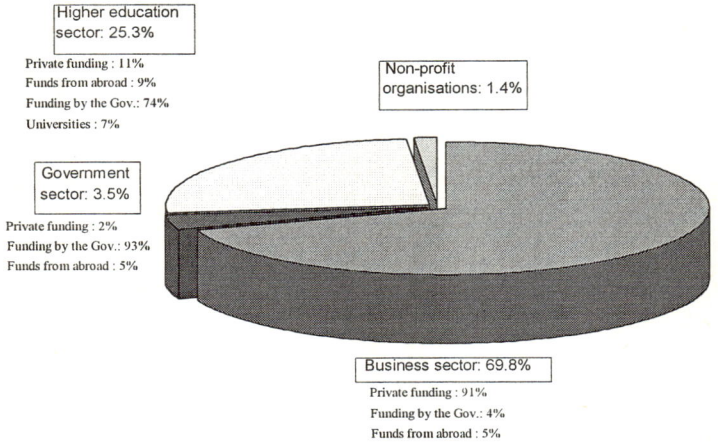

Sources: BSTS/OECD, own calculations.

4.3.   General structure of the industry: R&D and value added

The distribution of value added and R&D expenditures across the Belgian manufacturing and services industries is presented in Table 4.2 for 1995. For the manufacturing industries, Figures 4.2 and 4.3 show the industrial distribution of value-added and R&D expenditures in function of four classes of technology intensity. High-tech industries account for about 8% of the total manufacturing value added; medium high-tech industries account for 32%, medium low-tech industries for 14%, and, finally, low-tech industries for 46%. The largest industries in terms of value added are food and beverages (14%), chemicals (13%), and motor vehicles (10%).

Table 4.2: **Value added and intramural R&D in Belgian industries in 1995**

NACE-Bel		Value added (BEF Mio)	R&D (BEF Mio)	R&D Intensity (%)	VA shares (%)	R&D shares (%)
1	Agriculture	114790	595	0.5	1.6	0.6
14	Mining	1007	66	6.6	0.0	0.1
	High-tech industries	**115251**	**32966**	**28.6**	**1.6**	**34.6**
24.4	Drugs[a]	45447	12422	27.3	0.6	13.0
32	Electronic equipment[a]	33003	14101	42.7	0.5	14.8
32.1	Electronic components[a]	18564	2161	11.6	0.3	2.3
35.3	Aerospace[a]	6743	1431	21.2	0.1	1.5
33	Instruments and Office machines	11493	2850	24.8	0.2	3.0
	Medium high-tech industries	**491421**	**29996**	**6.1**	**6.6**	**31.5**
24	Chemicals (exclusive of drugs) [a]	193749	18798	9.7	2.6	19.7
29	Non-electrical machines	93119	5187	5.6	1.3	5.4
31	Electrical machines[a]	60536	4370	7.2	0.8	4.6
34	Motor vehicles	144018	1642	1.1	1.9	1.7
	Medium low-tech industries	**213739**	**7460**	**3.5**	**2.9**	**7.8**
23	Refineries	20860	2343	11.2	0.3	2.5
25	Rubber and plastic products	74101	2363	3.2	1.0	2.5
26	Stone, clay, & glass	96497	1708	1.8	1.3	1.8
35	Other transport[a]	8472	656	7.7	0.1	0.7
35.1	Shipbuilding[a]	2075	91	4.4	0.0	0.1
36	Other manufacturing[a]	11734	299	2.5	0.2	0.3
	Low-tech industries	**703168**	**9453**	**1.3**	**9.5**	**9.9**
15	Food and beverage	207082	2256	1.1	2.8	2.4
16	Tobacco	11148	14	0.1	0.2	0.0
17	Textile	69091	914	1.3	0.9	1.0
18	Clothing	31706	14	0.0	0.4	0.0
19	Leather and shoes	1923	34	1.7	0.0	0.0
20	Wood and wood product	36518	63	0.2	0.5	0.1
21	Paper	13182	235	1.8	0.2	0.2
22	Printing	92155	391	0.4	1.2	0.4
27	Iron and steel and non-ferrous metals	121566	4256	3.5	1.6	4.5
28	Metal products	87690	1114	1.3	1.2	1.2
36.1	Furniture[a]	31108	161	0.5	0.4	0.2
	Total manufacturing industry	**1523579**	**79874**	**5.2**	**20.6**	**83.9**
40	Utilities	160302	338	0.2	2.2	0.4
45	Construction	405517	2328	0.6	5.5	2.4
50	Wholesale and retail trade	1121442	954	0.1	15.1	1.0
55	Hotels and restaurants	250561	0	0.0	3.4	0.0
60	Transportation and storage	595945	89	0.0	8.0	0.1
64	Telecommunications	158906	541	0.3	2.1	0.6
65	Financial intermediates	371558	632	0.2	5.0	0.7
72	Computer services[a]	27237	1651	6.1	0.4	1.7
72.2	Software production[a]	15365	3115	20.3	0.2	3.3
73	Research and development[a]	23047	222	1.0	0.3	0.2
74	Other services to firms[a]	628556	4603	0.7	8.5	4.8
90	Other services	2013085	191	0.0	27.2	0.2
	Total services	**5771521**	**14663**	**0.3**	**77.9**	**15.4**
	Total	**7410897**	**95198**	**1.3**	**100.0**	**100.0**

Notes: 'a' denotes the industries belonging to a more aggregated industry for value-added figures, the desegregation has been made according to employment figures; own calculations.

Sources: R&D figures: OSTC, 1997, provisional data; value-added figures: BNB, 1997.

The distribution of R&D expenditures across manufacturing industries differs substantially from the distribution of value added. The high-tech and medium high-tech industries account for more than 79% of the R&D expenditures in manufacturing industries, whereas this ratio was under 40% in terms of value-added. The low-tech and medium low-tech industries accounted for 20% of R&D in investments in manufacturing, and produced more than 60% of manufacturing value-added.

A similar distortion occurs when the services industries are compared to the manufacturing sector. Table 4.2 indicates that the services industries and the construction sector are the main source of value-added creation in Belgium by accounting for 83% of it. However, in terms of research activities, the manufacturing industries invest 84% of the total R&D outlays.

In the service industry, three sectors account for a major part of the R&D activities: computing services, software production, and engineering services. Although these sectors have an R&D intensity comparable to the one observed in some medium high-tech and high-tech industries, their share in BERD remains weak relative to that of other industrialised countries like the US, Canada, Denmark, and Norway (OECD, 1996).

This asymmetry between value-added creation and R&D performance finds its expression in the different R&D intensities of each industry. The ratio of R&D investments to value added is 29% for the high-tech industries, 6% for medium high-tech, 4% for medium low-tech, 1.3% for low-tech, and about 0.3% for services industries. In addition, Table 4.2 clearly shows that there are strong variations within each subgroup of industries. In Figure 4.2, the share of each industry in total R&D is shown ranked according to their share in value added. There is apparently no clear relationship between an industry's share in value added and its share in R&D. This is due to the high heterogeneity in R&D intensities, as can be seen in Figure 4.3.

The evolution of R&D outlays in the Belgian industries from 1981 to 1995 is presented in Table 4.3. For the average manufacturing industry, intramural R&D investments have increased by 40% from 1981 to 1991. In 1995, there has been a slight increase in total R&D expenditures as compared to 1991 (the index raises from 140 to 142). The services industry has followed a different trend. During the early 1980s, R&D investment in services has sharply fallen from an index of 100 in 1981 to 47 in 1985.[1] The late 1980s and early 1990s are characterised by a reverse trend, with R&D expenditures rising by 125% in 1995 as compared to 1981. On average, the yearly growth rate of total intramural R&D investments in Belgium has been around 4%. The services industry and the high-tech and medium high-tech manufacturing industries exhibit the highest growth rates.

---

[1] This might be due to a measurement problem resulting from a change in the survey method in 1992 (see Capron, Meeusen *et al.*, 1999).

Figure 4.2:   Value-added shares and R&D shares in Belgian industry, 1995

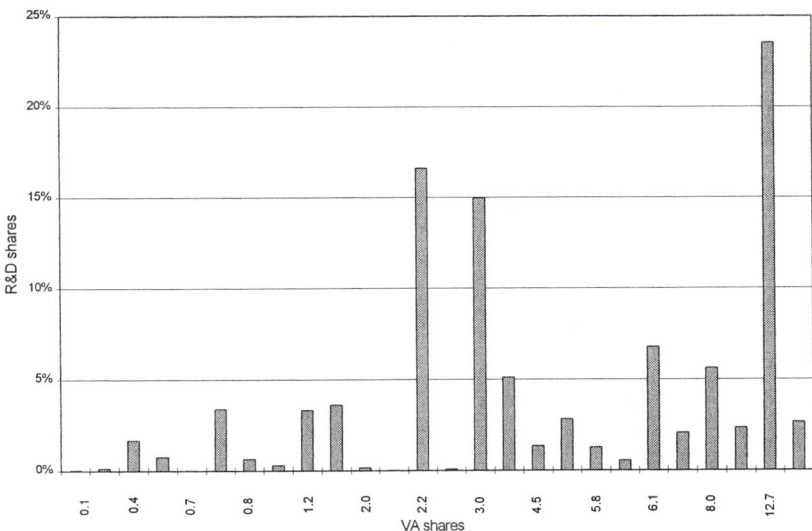

Note: The industries are ranked from the lowest to the largest share in total industrial value added.
Source: Table 4.2.

Figure 4.3:   Value-added shares and R&D intensities in the Belgian industry, 1995

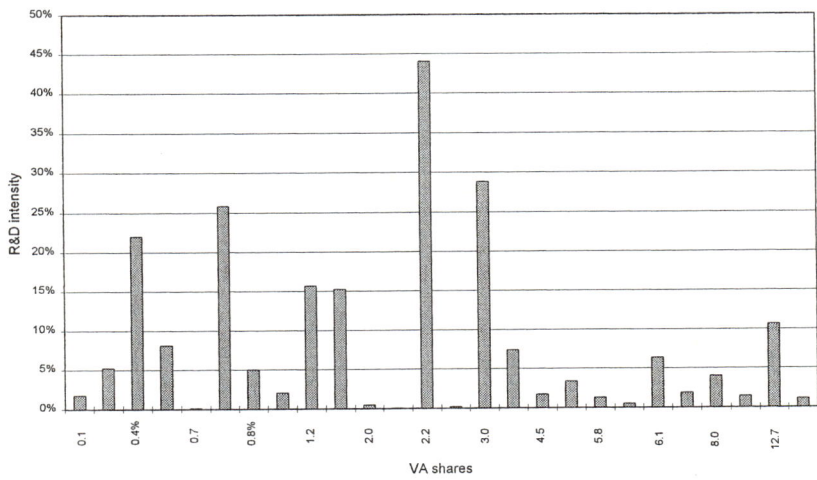

Note: The industries are ranked from the lowest to the largest share in total industrial value added.
Source: Table 4.2.

Table 4.3: Evolution of intramural R&D investments of firms, by industrial sectors, 1981-1995 (constant 1981 prices: GDP deflator)

	1985	1991	1995	1995
Index, 1981=100				Millions of BEF
Agriculture	212	209	244	
Mining	46	412	223	
High- and medium high-tech industries				
Drugs	117	141	171	10727
Chemicals (excluding drugs)	104	120	123	18256
Non electrical machines	152	212	194	4480
Electrical machines, electronics, instruments, office machines.	160	140	141	20278
Motor vehicles and other transport	233	269	261	3299
Medium-low- and low-tech industries				
Rubber and plastic products	177	1056	925	2040
Stone, clay, and glass	44	53	66	1475
Other manufacturing	198	254	214	242
Food, beverage, and tobacco	139	307	256	1960
Textile, clothing, and leather	130	192	135	830
Wood, paper, and furniture	146	166	187	735
Iron and steel and non-ferrous metals	108	92	90	3676
Metal products	156	105	93	962
Total manufacturing industry	128	140	142	68960
Construction	101	190	199	2318
Total services	47	123	225	10360
Total	121	140	149	82209

Notes: Provisional data for 1995. A different census methodology was used for 1985; extrapolated data for 1991. GDP deflator: OECD; own calculations.
Sources: OSTC, 1997.

4.4.   Employment in R&D activities

The qualification of human capital devoted to research activities in all industries is presented in Table 4.4. R&D personnel can be divided into three classes: university (or university-equivalent higher education), other non-university higher education, and others. There is a sharp contrast between manufacturing and services industries. In the former, less than half of the R&D personnel possess a university or university-equivalent diploma while in the latter more than 70% do.

Table 4.4:   **R&D employment by level of qualification, by industry, and as a share of total employment, 1995 (full time equivalents)**

NACE-Bel		University (%)	Short term higher educ.(%)	Others (%)	Total R&D Personnel	Total Employment	Share of R&D pers. in total(%)
01	Agriculture	70.8	25.7	3.5	203	112408	0.2
14	Mining	66.7	33.3	0.0	28	6153	0.5
	High-tech industries	58.6	17.6	23.8	7561	60745	12.4
24.4	Drugs	38.4	26.2	35.4	2442	13737	17.8
32	Electronic equipment and components	72.1	10.0	17.9	3371	13023	25.9
32.1	Electronic components	70.7	19.5	9.7	443	7189	6.2
33	Instruments and office machines	70.1	18.9	11.0	380	19746	1.9
35.3	Aerospace	42.2	14.7	43.1	738	6459	11.4
	Medium high-tech industries	39.7	27.3	33.0	8410	177859	4.7
24	Chemicals (excl. drugs)	37.7	31.0	31.3	5009	57033	8.8
29	Non-electrical machines	47.2	22.7	30.0	1495	43187	3.5
31	Electrical machines	51.7	22.1	26.3	1418	23880	5.9
34	Motor vehicles	27.5	18.3	54.2	506	53759	0.9
	Medium low-tech	40.4	24.8	34.9	2046	82223	2.5
23	Refineries	56.4	43.6	0.0	781	4854	16.1
25	Rubber and plastic products	39.4	26.4	34.3	678	23224	2.9
26	Stone, clay, and glass	42.6	24.5	32.9	473	34714	1.4
35	Other transport	25.5	32.7	41.8	154	8106	1.9
35.1	Shipbuilding	2.7	0.0	97.3	224	1846	12.1
36	Other manufacturing	98.1	1.9	0.0	49	9479	0.5
	Low-tech industries	44.9	25.5	29.6	3046	403822	0.8
15	Food and beverage	42.3	37.0	20.7	1019	112408	0.9
16	Tobacco				0	3115	0.0
17	Textile	72.2	14.7	13.1	219	50825	0.4
18	Clothing	0.0	100.0	0.0	14	22090	0.1
19	Leather and shoes	100.0	0.0	0.0	18	5362	0.3
20	Wood and wood product	84.6	11.5	3.9	16	25659	0.1
21	Paper	51.5	23.6	24.8	103	16621	0.6
22	Printing	72.0	21.6	6.5	54	35123	0.2
27	Iron and steel, non-ferrous metals	38.0	11.7	50.3	1024	49334	2.1
28	Metal products	45.3	27.9	26.9	384	61636	0.6
36.1	Furniture	32.4	14.7	52.9	80	21649	0.4
	Total manufacturing industry	47.8	23.1	29.1	20992	724649	2.9
40	Utilities	100.0	0.0	0.0	676	28252	2.4
41	Construction	51.4	28.2	20.5	670	243188	0.3
50	Wholesale and retail trade	37.1	2.9	60.1	568	575776	0.1
55	Hotels and restaurants				0	142473	0.0
60	Transportation and storage	42.9	57.1	0.0	38	243566	0.0
64	Telecommunications	80.4	19.6	0.0	109	75881	0.1
65	Financial intermediates	89.4	8.1	2.5	135	149271	0.1

Table 4.4 (continued)

NACE-Bel		University (%)	Short term higher educ.(%)	Others (%)	Total R&D Personnel	Total employment	Share of R&D pers. in total(%)
72	Computing services	42.1	53.8	4.2	434	11385	3.8
72.2	Software production	76.1	21.7	2.2	920	6485	14.2
73+74	Other services to firms	85.5	10.0	4.5	1279	283685	0.5
90	Other services	83.9	16.1	0.0	85	207928	0.0
	Total services	**73.9**	**21.6**	**4.5**	**4309**	**1706195**	**0.3**
	Total	**51.4**	**23.0**	**25.7**	**25410**	**2820845**	**0.9**

Sources: OSTC, 1997; ONSS and INASTI databases, and own calculations.

On average, manufacturing industries use a larger share of relatively less quali-fied than average R&D personnel ('others' (29%) versus 'other non-university higher education' (23%)). In the services industry, only 5% of R&D personnel are less qualified employees. However, it is worth noting that the share of total R&D personnel in the total employment in the manufacturing industry (2.9%) is much higher than in the services industry (0.3%). The only service industry that uses a relatively large number of employees for R&D activities (14.2%) is the software-production industry.

Table 4.5:   Intramural R&D investment in the Belgian industry by firm size, 1995

Firm size (employment)	Intramural R&D investment			R&D employees		
	1995 (millions of BEF)	1995 1994=100	Share	1995 (FTE)	1995 1994=100	Share
0-9	1560	131.6	1.6	911	116.5	3.6
10-19	1847	105.3	1.9	744	93.2	2.9
20-49	6625	105.1	7.0	2490	104.8	9.8
50-99	8084	105.9	8.5	2386	101.4	9.4
100-199	6133	101.4	6.4	1918	97.4	7.6
200-499	10333	114.7	10.9	2647	104.9	10.4
500-999	11684	112.5	12.3	2665	107.5	10.5
more than 1000	48932	104.6	51.4	11652	103.4	45.9
TOTAL	95198	106.8	100.0	25410	103.5	100.0

Source: OSTC, 1997, and own calculations.

As can be seen in Table 4.5 from the official firm-level business R&D survey, large firms with more than 1000 employees accounted for more than half of the total intramural R&D investments in 1995. In contrast, the smallest firms, with fewer than 20 employees, accounted for only 3.6% of BERD. However, as compared to 1994, the largest increase in BERD was by the smallest firms. The analysis of the number of R&D employees by firm size emphasises that, with respect to R&D investment, the smallest firms use relatively more R&D employees than do the largest. Indeed, the firms with fewer than 20 employees accounted for 6.5% of total R&D employees in the business sector, against a 3.5% share in BERD. This suggests that small firms rely relatively more on human capital than do the largest ones.

4.5.   Financing sources by industry

The five potential financing sources for intramural research activities in business firms are their own funds, funds of other firms, government subsidies, other funds (e.g. from non-profit organisations), and funds from abroad. Table 4.6 presents the relative importance of each of these financing sources in the manufacturing and the services industries. The manufacturing and services industries finance their R&D projects from notably different sources. On average, firms in the manufacturing sector finance the lion's share of their R&D investments with their own funds (91%). Next come other firms, government subsidies, and funds from abroad. Each of these three sources accounts for about 3% of the total intramural R&D outlays by firms. The services industries rely much more than the manufacturing industries on outside funding. Although the largest share of their R&D activities is also financed by their own funds (72%), they use funds from abroad (13%) and government subsidies (12%) more than do the manufacturing industries.

Interestingly, the share of R&D subsidies in total intramural R&D expenditures is more important in low-tech (6%) and medium low-tech manufacturing industries than in high-tech (2.5%) and medium high-tech industries. Nevertheless, the most subsidised industries in relative terms are electronic components, aerospace, computing services, and R&D services.

Another feature that distinguishes the services from the manufacturing industries is the extent to which they finance extramural R&D projects. Firms in the manufacturing industry invest about 11% of their total R&D expenditures in projects realised in other organisations. For firms in the services industry, this share is 22%.

4.6.   Regional R&D intensities

Given that Belgium is characterised by strong regional and cultural identities, any analysis of its innovation system cannot escape the issue of the regional design that underlies the Belgian innovation performance. More than in other countries,

Table 4.6:   **Intra- and extramural R&D expenditures: Financing sources by industries, 1995 (% and millions of BEF)**

NACE-Bel		Intramural (%)					Total Extra-muros	extra muros /total	(%)
		Own funds	Other firms	Govern ment	Others	From abroad			
1	Agriculture	**95.5**	**0.0**	**2.7**	**0.0**	**1.8**	**595**	**84**	**12.3**
14	Mining	**100.0**	**0.0**	**0.0**	**0.0**	**0.0**	**66**	**9**	**12.5**
	High-tech industries	**86.1**	**4.2**	**2.5**	**0.0**	**7.2**	**32966**	**3870**	**10.5**
24.4	Drugs	98.9	0.0	1.1	0.0	0.0	12422	2225	15.2
32	Electronic equipment (excl. components)	74.6	8.8	1.7	0.0	14.9	14101	929	6.2
32.1	Electronic components	72.8	0.0	18.5	0.0	8.8	2161	193	8.2
35.3	Aerospace	63.1	0.0	16.6	0.0	20.3	1431	272	16.0
33	Instruments and office machines	87.3	5.3	6.1	0.0	1.3	2850	155	5.1
	Medium high-tech industries	**95.1**	**1.6**	**1.6**	**1.1**	**0.6**	**29996**	**4198**	**12.3**
24	Chemicals (excluding. drugs)	98.5	0.2	1.0	0.0	0.3	18798	3043	13.9
29	Non-electrical machines	84.0	2.1	4.1	8.8	1.0	5187	477	8.4
31	Electrical machines	84.2	10.0	3.4	0.0	2.4	4370	227	4.9
34	Motor vehicles	99.6	0.0	0.4	0.0	0.0	1642	264	13.8
	Medium low-tech industries	**93.0**	**0.1**	**3.7**	**0.4**	**2.9**	**7460**	**596**	**7.4**
23	Refineries	100.0	0.0	0.0	0.0	0.0	2343	1171	33.3
25	Rubber and plastic Products	90.8	0.0	3.3	0.8	5.1	2363	174	6.8
26	Stone, clay, and glass	94.5	0.1	5.3	0.0	0.1	1708	243	12.5
35	Other transport	98.3	0.0	1.6	0.0	0.1	656	26	3.8
35.1	Shipbuilding	100.0	0.0	0.0	0.0	0.0	91	0	0.0
36	Other manufacturing	93.0	0.0	5.4	0.0	1.6	299	0	0.0
	Low-tech industries	**93.6**	**0.6**	**5.5**	**0.1**	**0.2**	**9453**	**1460**	**13.4**
15	Food and beverage	92.7	0.0	7.1	0.0	0.3	2256	345	13.3
16	Tobacco	0.0	0.0	0.0	0.0	0.0	14	0	
17	Textiles	95.7	0.0	4.3	0.0	0.0	914	183	16.7
18	Clothing	100.0	0.0	0.0	0.0	0.0	14	0	0.0
19	Leather and shoes	100.0	0.0	0.0	0.0	0.0	34	0	0.0
20	Wood product	100.0	0.0	0.0	0.0	0.0	63	3	4.9
21	Paper	100.0	0.0	0.0	0.0	0.0	235	16	6.3
22	Printing	100.0	0.0	0.0	0.0	0.0	391	4	1.0
27	Iron and steel and non-ferrous metals	94.8	1.2	3.8	0.0	0.1	4256	566	11.7
28	Metal products	90.1	0.7	8.5	0.2	0.6	1114	225	16.8
36.1	Furniture	100.0	0.0	0.0	0.0	0.0	161	0	0.0
	Total manufacturing industry	**90.8**	**2.5**	**2.6**	**0.4**	**3.6**	**79874**	**10226**	**11.4**
40	Utilities	**100.0**	**0.0**	**0.0**	**0.0**	**0.0**	**338**	**0**	**0.0**
45	Construction	**90.1**	**0.0**	**9.9**	**0.0**	**0.0**	**2328**	**403**	**14.8**
50	Wholesale and retail trade	95.1	0.0	4.9	0.0	0.0	954	173	15.3
55	Hotels and restaurants	0.0	0.0	0.0	0.0	0.0	0	0	0.0
60	Transportation and storage	100.0	0.0	0.0	0.0	0.0	89	13	12.5
64	Telecommunications	97.6	0.0	0.1	0.5	1.8	541	911	62.8

Table 4.6 (continued)

NACE-Bel		Intramural (%)					Total Extra-muros	Extra muros /total	(%)
		Own funds	Other firms	Govern ment	Others	from Abroad			
65	Financial intermediates	88.3	0.0	11.8	0.0	0.0	632	280	30.7
72	Computing services	73.1	0.0	22.9	0.0	4.0	1651	111	6.3
72.2	Software production	82.9	0.6	8.7	0.0	7.9	3115	725	18.9
73	Research and develop-ment	37.9	2.1	22.7	0.0	37.3	222	57	20.4
74	Other services to firms	58.7	9.8	5.6	0.0	25.9	4603	1190	20.5
90	Other services	91.0	2.6	0.0	0.0	6.4	191	85	30.8
	Total services	**72.3**	**3.0**	**11.3**	**0.0**	**13.4**	**14663**	**4119**	**21.9**
	Total	**88.6**	**2.6**	**3.7**	**0.4**	**4.8**	**95198**	**13949**	**12.8**

Sources: OSTC,1997, provisional data, and own calculations.

geography does matter in Belgium, and it is a question whether, besides the economic gap, there is also a technology gap between the regions. A further look at the regional technological profiles could help indicate if this is indeed the case and if a technology gap is forming as a consequence of the economic gap, or, alternatively, if the regions are increasingly following autonomous technological trajectories.

A global view of the technological performances of the regions is given in Table 4.7. A main drawback of the Belgian NIS as a whole is the relative weakness of the governmental infrastructure (Government R&D indexes in 1994/95 of 50, 16 and 10 for Brussels, Flanders and Wallonia respectively, as compared to the EU average of 100).

Apart from government R&D, Flanders is characterised by high technological indexes, especially for the indicators of the degree of innovativeness. Nevertheless, compared to the richest European regions, higher education R&D is not as high as could be expected. Although the *per capita* total R&D index in this case is slightly above the European average, the intensity index points to some degree of fragility. The recent emphasis of the Flemish government on the development of inter-university research centres could partly close the gap.

Nevertheless, all in all, the indicators for business R&D lead one to conclude that the Flemish industrial R&D system performs well. Not only are its industrial R&D indexes high but the indexes relative to the number of patent applications and R&D productivity are considerably above the European average (see also Teirlinck and Meeusen, 1999).

Largely thanks to its central position, the Brussels Region is also characterised by good indexes on business R&D. Nevertheless, the output indexes are globally very weak, which could be due to the high commuting rate of the active population. Indeed, many of the researchers who work in the Brussels Region live in the Flemish and Walloon peripheral districts.

The indexes obtained for the Walloon Region are not very favourable. To a large extent, this low performance is not due to a lower propensity of Walloon enterprises to invest in R&D but rather to its insufficient industrial base. As can be observed in Table 4.7, both the productivity and patent indexes suggest a lower degree of inventiveness for Walloon R&D, a phenomenon that might be explained by the industrial specialisation pattern as well as by the research orientation of the enterprises.

Table 4.7:   R&D investment indexes, 1994/95 (EUR15 = 100)

	Brussels	Flanders	Wallonia	Belgium
R&D intensity				
Business R&D	99	102	81	96
Government R&D	50	16	10	19
Higher education R&D	180	96	109	111
Total R&D	107	87	75	87
R&D per capita				
Business R&D	180	124	77	114
Government R&D	90	19	9	23
Higher education R&D	324	115	103	131
Total R&D	196	106	72	103
R&D per active				
Business R&D	108	143	100	125
Total R&D	116	120	92	112
Patent applications				
per capita	114	123	61	102
per active	68	141	78	111
R&D productivity				
Business R&D	67	105	84	95
Total R&D	62	124	91	105

Notes: The R&D productivity as measured by the ratio of patents
            on R&D expenditures. Patents are allocated to the residence
            of inventors.
Source: Capron and Cincera (1999).

While regions perform very differently in their R&D activities, it cannot be concluded that there is a significant technological gap that is as important as the economic one in terms of the R&D intensity. Although it cannot be denied that the Flemish Region invests more in R&D and exhibits better output indicators than the Walloon Region, historical factors must be kept in mind when making any comparisons between them. Thanks to its more recent industrial structure and geographic advantages, it is easier for the Flemish Region to take up the challenge of the present change of technological regime than for the Walloon Region, which must simultaneously manage its heritage from the Industrial Revolution and ensure the transition to the knowledge-based economy. Nevertheless, efforts should still be devoted in the Walloon Region to boost its R&D intensity. Flanders, on the contrary, is on its way to becoming one of the most innovative regions of Europe. Although the R&D indicators are still very high in the Brussels Region, the high concentration of industrial R&D expenses in the Brussels Region has substantially decreased over time. Thus, the federalisation of the country has led to a more balanced distribution of R&D expenditures among the regions.

4.7. The role of the federal government and the emergence of regional authorities

Figures 4.4 and 4.5 show the main public budget allocations with respect to functional destination by institution and provide further information on the regional distribution of public support to R&D (cf. the previous section). Three main conclusions emerge. First, there is a clear tendency towards the regionalisation of S&T policies. In 1989, the federal authority had the highest share of budget allocations (39%) as compared to the Flemish Region (33%)[2] and the French Community and the Walloon Region (28%). In 1996, the Flemish Region accounted for 39% of the total amount spent by all Belgian authorities, while the federal budget allocations fell to 34% and those of the French Community and Walloon Region dropped to 27%. Second, the federal authority devotes the largest share of its S&T budget to international actions and specific scientific institutions. All other functional budget allocations are increasingly under the control of the regional authorities. Figure 4.4 illustrates the largest shares held by the Flemish Region in these other functional directions. Globally speaking, the main functional direction of the total public budget allocations to S&T activities is towards the higher education sector (34%). Next are international projects (17%), especially the space-related programmes (12%).

Thirdly, in addition to the emergence of regional authorities, there is a marked contrast between the two main regions with respect to public institutions engaged in science and technology activities, and private business firms known to be active in R&D activities. The first half of Table 4.8 gives the number of higher education institutions, research and technology organisations, and bridging institutions. The second half shows the number of firms carrying out R&D activities in each industry in the Flemish Region, the Walloon Region, and the Brussels-Capital Region. The Flemish Region has by far the largest number of private firms (1010) performing research activities. Next comes the Walloon Region with 817 private firms and then the Brussels-Capital Region with 533 firms.

This contrast between Flanders and Wallonia is also present for all the services and manufacturing industries, although to a lesser extent in the high-tech industries. In the latter, the number of firms carrying out R&D activities is still higher in Flanders than in Wallonia, but to a lesser extent. Maps 4.1 and 4.2 show a similar contrast at the district level in the number of private firms engaged in R&D activities, of libraries and documentation centres and of research centres. At least part of the observed difference between the regions is due to the relatively tighter budgetary situation in the Brussels Region and in the southern part of the country.

---

[2] As explained in the previous chapter, the Flemish Community and the Flemish Region actually merged into one entity. Except when comparing with the French Community, we will call it the Flemish Region for convenience sake.

Figure 4.4:   Functional destination of public budget allocations to S&T activities, by institution (1989 and 1996)

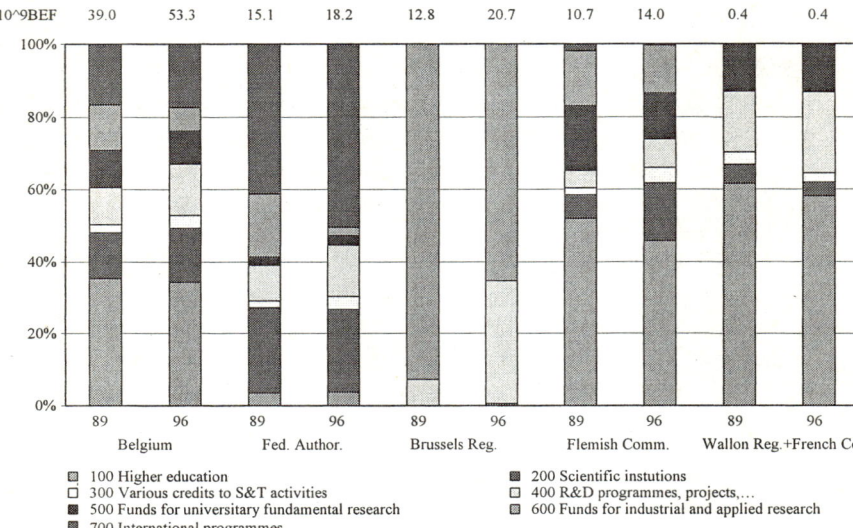

Sources: Commission Coopération Fédérale, Groupe de concertation CFS/STAT, October 1996 (FEBEDET).

Figure 4.5:   Institutional distribution of public budget allocations to S&T activities, by function (1996)

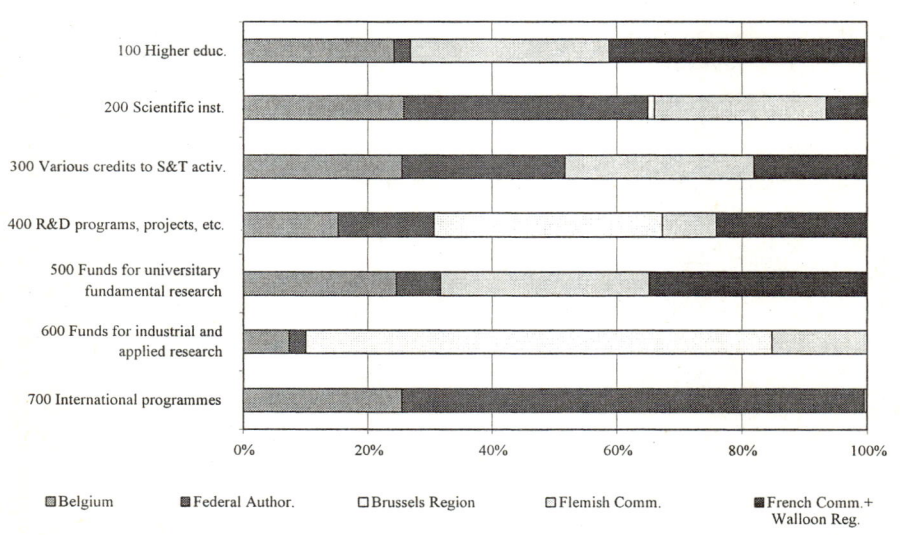

Sources: Commission Coopération Fédérale, Groupe de concertation CFS/STAT, October 1996 (FEBEDET).

Table 4.8:   **Number of HEIs, RTOs, bridging institutions and enterprises engaged in R&D activities**

	Belgium	Brussels	Flanders	Wallonia
HEIs	**95**	**28**	**39**	**28**
Universities	19	6	6	7
Autonomous university research centres	24	6	12	6
Other HEIs	52	16	21	15
RTOs	**172**	**78**	**68**	**26**
Federal central services				
Central services	16	8	8	0
Scientific institutions	38	29	8	1
Other public institutions	6	4	1	1
Flemish community central services				
Central services	4	2	2	0
Scientific institutions	5	2	3	0
Other public institutions	6	4	2	0
Walloon Region/French Community central services				
Central services	3	1	0	2
Scientific institutions	3	0	0	3
Other public institutions	7	2	0	5
Brussels-Capital Region central services				
Central services	1	1	0	0
Other public institutions	1	1	0	0
Subordinated institutions	13	1	8	4
Semi-public institutions	8	4	4	0
Non-profit making private institutions	13	7	6	0
Sectoral centres of collective research	43	10	23	10
International organisations established in Belgium	5	2	3	0
Bridging institutions[a]	**112**	**37**	**51**	**24**
University/HEIs Interfaces	9	4	6	3
Science parks	9	4	7	3
Number of firms housed		79		
Number of firms carrying out R&D activities				
Agriculture	**12**	**0**	**10**	**2**
Mining	**17**	**1**	**1**	**15**
High-tech industries	**186**	**55**	**74**	**57**
Drugs	43	20	9	14
Electronic equipment (excl. components)	31	9	15	7
Electronic components	24	4	16	4
Aerospace	7	1	2	4
Instruments and office machines	81	21	32	28
Medium high-tech industries	**428**	**75**	**205**	**148**
Chemicals (excl. drugs)	124	28	52	44
Non-electrical machines	191	30	100	61
Electrical machines	82	15	30	37
Motor vehicles	31	2	23	6
Medium low-tech industries	**164**	**13**	**76**	**75**
Refineries	6	0	5	1
Rubber and plastic products	62	6	31	25
Stone, clay and glass	69	6	25	38
Other transport	8	1	5	2
Shipbuilding	6	0	4	2
Other manufacturing	13	0	6	7

Table 4.8 (continued)

	Belgium	Brussels	Flanders	Wallonia
Low-tech industries	**516**	**58**	**261**	**197**
Food and beverage	117	13	69	35
Tobacco	2	0	2	0
Textile	71	4	48	19
Clothing	9	4	5	0
Leather and shoes	6	0	4	2
Wood and wood products	24	2	13	9
Paper	20	2	8	10
Printing	30	13	9	8
Iron and steel and non ferrous-metal	50	2	19	29
Metal products	166	14	74	78
Furniture	21	4	10	7
Total manufacturing industries	**1107**	**183**	**532**	**392**
Utilities	15	2	8	5
Construction	149	41	34	74
Wholesale and retail trade	230	82	90	58
Hotels and restaurants	2	1	1	0
Transportation and storage	18	3	10	5
Telecommunications	8	1	5	2
Financial intermediates	28	15	9	4
Software production	102	27	48	27
Computing services	59	15	30	14
Research and development	12	2	7	3
Other services to firms	219	91	60	68
Other services	195	51	81	63
Total services	**873**	**288**	**341**	**244**
Total	**2360**	**533**	**1010**	**817**

Notes: a) not exhaustive; b) based on the official R&D survey repertory of firms
Sources: OSTC, 1997.

Map 4.1:   The distribution of R&D firms across Belgian districts

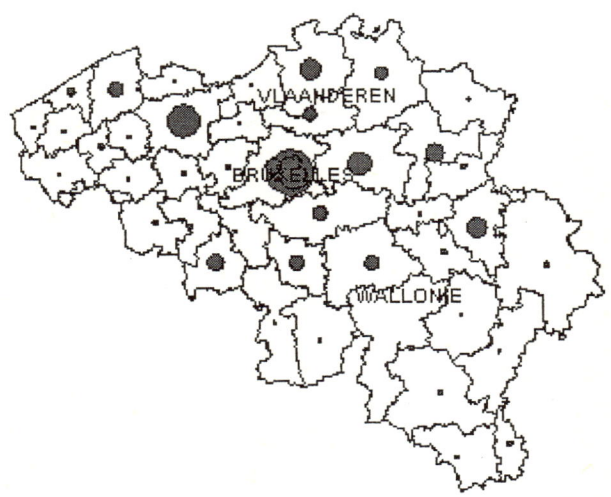

Map 4.2:   **The distribution of research centres across Belgian districts (public institutions, university centres, and research centres)**

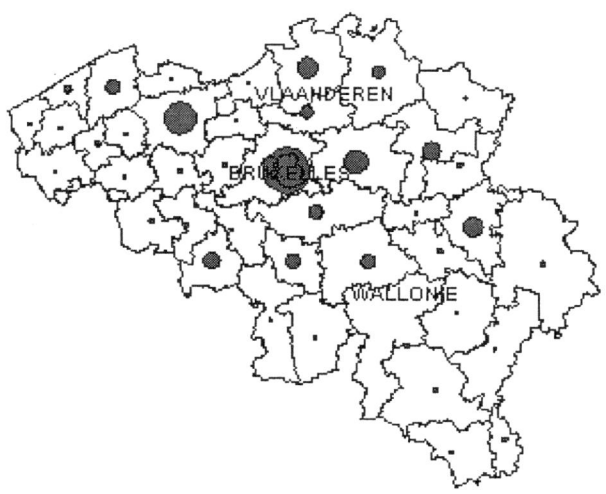

4.8. The performance of higher education

The educational sub-system, as part of the innovation system, has very intense interactions with other components, so it plays a central role in the process of knowledge transmission. More specifically, the number of graduates in science and engineering – the essential components of the research workforce – is a crucial parameter in this context.

Some indicators are presented below that give a global view of the role of higher education in the innovation system. As far as possible, the Belgian data are compared with those of similar countries. Given the scarcity of data, only some, albeit important, aspects are reviewed: higher education as a measure of the increase of the human capital stock and human-capital mobility, which in this context we limit to students and researchers. The latter phenomenon constitutes an important channel in the knowledge-acquisition process and in the participation in European framework programmes.

It is often said that some European countries have a deficit in graduating engineers and scientists. Table 4.9 shows that this is particularly true in Belgium. Despite the favourable evolution of the total number of university graduates, Belgium is under both the European and the Triad averages in this respect. Not only is the number of graduates in natural and applied sciences dramatically low compared to the main industrialised countries but, what is more disturbing, the gap is growing over time.

As pointed out by the OECD (1992), there is a growing concern among industrialised countries about serious shortages of scientists and engineers. In the case of Belgium, the main reason is not to be attributed to demographic factors but to decreasing interest in science among the student population. The study of EGOR (1990) reveals that there is a shortfall of 4000 scientists and engineers in Belgium. This deficit is, in relative terms, the highest of the European countries (see Table 4.10). Thus, an important mismatch of the Belgian educational system is identified. The low value of the index for the inflow of graduates in the theoretical and applied sciences does not allow one to expect an improvement of the situation in the near future.

Table 4.9:   Higher education graduates in Belgium (university degree)

	EUR15		TRIAD	
	1983	1991	1983	1991
Total share (%)	2.20	2.53	0.82	1.03
Natural and applied sciences share (%)	1.75	1.55	0.69	0.67
Total index	81	93	63	79
Natural and applied sciences index	65	57	53	52

Note: The indexes are the variables weighted by population divided by the similar
             value calculated for Europe and the Triad respectively.
Source: First European Report on S&T Indicators, own calculations.

Table 4.10:   Shortfalls of qualified engineers in some European countries (1990)

	BE	DE	UK	NL	SP	IT	DA	SW	FR	P
Shortfall (in thousands)	-4	0	-8	2.2	-5.3	-14.5	0.8	-0.3	-11	-1.5
Per thousand inhabitants	-.40	0	-.14	.15	-.14	-.26	.01	-.04	-.19	-.15

Source: EGOR (1990).

The increase of the degree of human capital mobility is another major way to speed up the transfer of tacit knowledge. Unfortunately, only some fragments of information are available in the Belgian case, and they are limited to the higher education sector. The role of Belgium in international human capital mobility can be partially appreciated through its position as a destination country for foreign students as well as an origin country of students moving to other countries. Table 4.11 gives a view of the Belgian position in both of these cases.

With regard to the Belgian position as a destination country, Belgium seems, at the European level, to benefit from a high power of attraction for foreign students, especially for students from Italy, Luxembourg, the Netherlands, and Spain. Nevertheless, around 53% of the foreign students come from developing countries because of Belgian's colonial past. Another reason is the large size of the foreign population residing in the country, about 9%. These two elements are certainly important sources of bias.

Table 4.11: Patterns of student mobility from and to Belgium

		Country of Destination			Country of Origin		
		EUR15	EUR, JAP, USA	Total	EUR15	EUR, JAP, USA	Total
Share	EUR15	11.7	9.9	7.5	3.0	2.5	0.9
	TRIAD	8.7	6.4	3.7	2.6	1.8	0.5
Index	EUR15	432	365	276	111	193	-
	TRIAD	670	493	285	96	139	-

Note: The indexes are the variables weighted by population divided by the similar value calculated
            for Europe and the Triad respectively.
Source: European Commission, 1994, and own calculations.

Turning to the Belgian students in foreign universities, we observe that Belgium is 11% above the European average for within-Europe exchanges and 4% below the European average when Japan and the USA are included as countries of destination. Around 53% of the Belgian students in other countries are concentrated in the neighbouring countries. The main countries of destination are France, the USA, the UK, Germany, and the Netherlands. The mobility of Belgian students is to a large extent comparable to that which is observed in other European countries.

Specifically regarding research mobility, we refer to the European Union programmes, which have specific measures in this field. Table 4.12 summarises the Belgian participation in this respect. The scores obtained are globally satisfactory in both categories of indicators, i.e. from the perspective of the partner as well as of the host country. Consequently, we can consider that the Belgian research teams are relatively well integrated into the European research network.

Table 4.12: Belgian participation in European actions (%)

Actions	Fellowships	Host Institutions
SCIENCE (1988-1992)	6	5
SPES (Economic science) (1989-1991)	2	28
Human Capital & Mobility (1992-1994)	4	6

Source: European Commission, 1994, and own calculations.

4.9.   The education and training challenge

The quality of human resources is a prime factor in economic growth and competitiveness. Past and present investment in human capital explains to a large extent the present and the future of the skills and capabilities of countries. More basically, education plays a prominent role in the effectiveness of the NIS. The acquisition of basic and high-level skills is a long-term process that requires major public investment in the educational and training infrastructure. No economic or social development can be achieved without the availability of an educated and properly qualified working force. Stimulating innovation and technology transfer capacity as well as technology diffusion will be only effective if there is sufficient absorption capacity. An in-depth analysis of the components of the absorptive capacity is a *conditio sine qua non* for the design of an efficient policy to ensure the transition to the learning economy.

Although this is not the place for a sustained analysis of the Belgian educational and training system, it is useful to highlight some characteristics that are directly linked to the innovation system: effectiveness of the early school system in the teaching of science-linked fields, the percentage of students in higher education in the 18- to 24-year-old population, and the level of qualification of the labour force. As some significant differences can be observed between the regions, regional differences also deserve examination.

Table 4.13:   Effectiveness of the education system (EUR15 = 100)

	French Community	Flemish Community	Belgium
Mathematics	101	108	105
Science	88	103	97
Higher education[1]	118	113	115

Note: ([1]) Foreign students are excluded from the data.
Source: TIMSS, 1997a,1997b.

The IEA Third International Mathematics and Science Study (TIMSS, 1997a, 1997b) gives a measure of the achievement in mathematics and science for a large number of countries. The achievement measure is based on comparable tests. Table 4.13 shows that, compared to other European countries, Belgium scores well for mathematics but scores lower in science. At the regional level, the data show that the students in the Flemish Community obtain better indicators than those in the French Community so there is a real mismatch in the teaching of science in the French Community. The indicator suggests that the French Community might in future be faced with an imbalance between supply and demand of scientific and technological skills, as well as with the weakening capacity of the population to take full advantage of the knowledge-based economy.

When, on the other hand, we look at the number of students in the higher education system, Table 4.14 shows that Belgium is well positioned among the European countries. Furthermore, we observe that the French Community here obtains a better index than its Flemish counterpart. Nevertheless, a closer look at the data given in Table 4.14 shows that, compared to the other community, more Flemish students choose technical training while more French-speaking students prefer teachers training. As shown in Chapter 3, the number of university students is, in fact, considerably higher in French-speaking universities than in Dutch-speaking universities, in absolute as well as in relative terms.

Why is there such an apparent lag of the Flemish Community in the number of university graduates? First, around 6% of students enrolled in French-speaking universities live in the Flemish Region (mainly French-speaking people in the Brussels suburban areas). Second, given the concentration of international institutions in Brussels (European Commission, NATO, etc.), the number of students of foreign nationality is high, and most of these students choose French-speaking instead of Dutch-speaking universities for language reasons. Around 20% of the university students in the French Community are, indeed, of foreign nationality. Globally, of the 15% foreign students enrolled in Belgian universities, about 80% are enrolled in French-speaking universities.

Table 4.14: Distribution of higher education students in 1997

Higher education (% of 18-24 year old population)		French Community	Flemish Community	Belgium
Total		31.1	29.9	30.4
Of which:	technical training	14.8	15.9	15.5
	teaching training	4.0	1.3	2.1
	university[1]	12.3	11.6	11.7

Note: ([1]) Foreign students not included.
Source: National Statistical Office.

If we turn to the evaluation of skills of the economically-active population as measured by the distribution of the working force according to the ISCED levels,[3] Table 4.15 shows that the Belgian distribution of the active population differs significantly from the European average. The high value of the indexes for the low and high qualification levels demonstrates that Belgium has a 'dual' labour force. Although this observation applies to the three regions, it is in the Brussels-Capital Region that the duality of the working force is most apparent. The general trend in upgrading the skill of the workforce in both manufacturing and services therefore calls for additional efforts to implement an effective training policy in Belgium in order to upgrade the average skill level of the active population. It is certainly a

---

[3] The ISCED (International Standard Classification of Educational Diplomas) is used to compare the levels of education and qualification. ISCED 1, 2, and 3 refer to the primary-school level, ISCED 4 to secondary-school level, and ISCED 5 and above to the post-secondary-school level.

critical challenge that Belgium has to take up if it wants to be successful with its economic restructuring and ensure its transition to the knowledge-based economy.

Within Europe, Belgium has one of the lowest employment rates: the level of employment as a percentage of the total population in 1996 was equal to 36% against 40% in Europe. If we take the active population instead of the employed population, the ratios were respectively equal to 41% and 45%. These data show that the country is faced with a double problem: first, with an unemployment rate of 9.6% in 1996, the labour-market performance must be improved, and, second, the low share of the working force in population suggests that the low activity rate could endanger the growth process and that there is a real problem with the effectiveness of the allocation of human resources. One should add that this last observation is mainly due to the increase in the age of obligatory school attendance (to the age of eighteen) and to the choice of the Belgian government to resort to a early-retirement system as a way of addressing the unemployment problem.

Table 4.15: Qualification level of the economically active population, 1997 (EUR15 = 100)

Qualification index	Wallonia	Flanders	Brussels	Belgium
Low	98	95	93	95
Medium	83	88	68	85
High	135	130	175	135

Notes: 'Low' = ISCED level 3 and below, 'Medium' = ISCED level 4, 'High' = ISCED level 5 and above.

Source :   Eurostat.

Table 4.16: Qualification level of the unemployed in 1991

Qualification level of unemployed (%)	Wallonia	Flanders	Brussels	Belgium
Low & undetermined	66	63	66	65
Medium	27	28	21	27
High	7	9	13	8

Source: 1991 Census and National Statistical Office.

Table 4.16 shows that the low-skilled working force accounts for two thirds of the unemployed in Belgium. Although the implementation of efficient training programmes is certainly one of the ways to tackle the unemployment problem, it should also be said that an important part of the unemployed have no specific or general skills and so in general do not have sufficient educational background to follow programmes aimed at improving their ability to use technology-intensive equipment. Even though the promotion of the development of low-skilled activities can be expected to resolve the unemployment problem in the short run, it might still lead the country to follow a growth trajectory that departs from the trend towards the knowledge-based economy.

4.10. R&D collaboration between Belgian firms and other actors of the NIS

In this section, we look at technological collaboration between Belgian firms and the principal actors of the NIS involved in R&D activities and located in Belgium or abroad. Among these actors, we distinguish customers, suppliers, other firms (including companies of the same group), universities, non-commercial research centres, collective research centres, and other partners. Collaboration is defined as a formal agreement concluded with other firms or research institutions for the re-alisation of R&D objectives. Collaboration can involve the exchange of informa-tion, the co-ordination of R&D activities, or joint development of new products or processes within a new physical structure or otherwise. The distinction is made between forms of collaboration with the same partner if it concerns different proj-ects.

Figure 4.6:   R&D collaboration between firms and other actors of the NIS

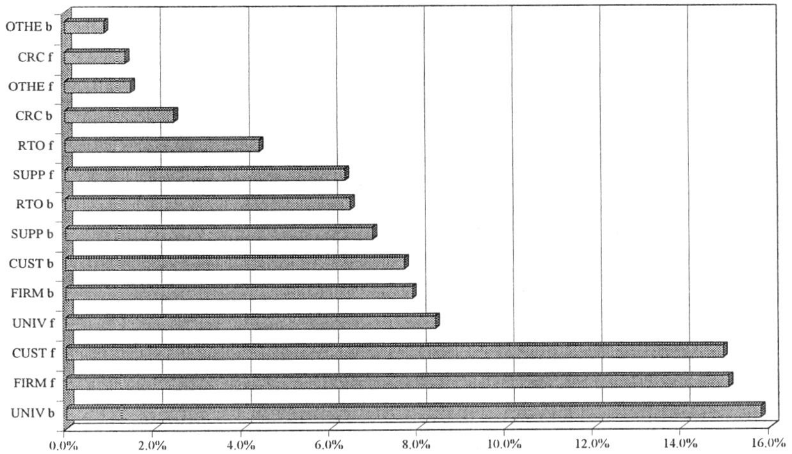

Notes: OTHE = other partners; CRC = collective research centres; RTO = research and technology organisation; SUPP = suppliers; CUST = customers; FIRM= firms; UNIV = universities; b = Belgium and f = Foreign.
Source: OSTC, 1997.

Among the main benefits of R&D collaboration suggested in the literature are the lower costs of developing new technologies by the reduction of duplication of research efforts, the sharing the risks of undertaking R&D, obtaining immediate access to new technologies and economical production sources, and the enhancing of the feasibility of large and complex research projects (Kumar and Magun, 1995). Figure 4.6 shows that the principal R&D collaboration partners of Belgian firms are the Belgian universities, foreign companies, and foreign customers. Indeed, these three types of partners indeed account for 45.7% of all collaborations. The fact that most of the R&D collaboration occurs between firms and universities is due to the desire of firms to share the ever-increasing higher costs and risks associated with undertaking basic or pre-competitive R&D activities. The high degree of R&D collaboration between Belgian and foreign firms and customers may be because of the high number of multinationals established in Belgium and the willingness of Belgian firms to develop international linkages with foreign customers in order to obtain access to new markets. The other important R&D collaborators are foreign universities (8.4%), other Belgian firms (7.9%), and customers located in Belgium (7.7%).

Figure 4.7: **R&D collaboration between firms and other actors of the NIS by industry sector**

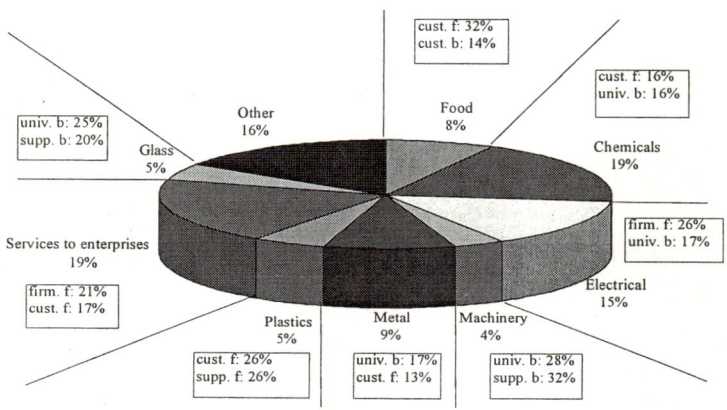

Notes: The percentages of collaboration of the two main partners are given for each industrial
           sector; supp=suppliers, cust=customers, firm=firms, univ=universities; b=Belgium and
           f=foreign.
Source: OSTC, 1997.

Since the beginning of the 1980s, there has been a rapid evolution in the development of collaborative agreements in strategic technologies. They have roughly quadrupled from 1980 to 1996 and are mainly located in core technologies: information technology, biotechnology, and new materials (European Commission, 1997a; National Science Foundation, 1998). Debresson *et al.* (1997) show that innovative Belgian firms have a relatively high tendency to engage in international networking with a high level of both inward and outward flows of information.

Figure 4.7 suggests that R&D collaboration in Belgium occurs mostly in the services-to-enterprises sector and the chemical and electrical industries (20%,

19%, and 15% of all collaboration, respectively). For the last two sectors, the collaboration mainly concerns Belgian firms, foreign firms and customers, and Belgian universities. Nevertheless, the two main actors that collaborate with Belgian firms operating in the services-to-enterprises sector (mainly engineering and specialised software firms) are firms and customers established abroad. The innovation-network profile of innovative Belgian firms does not differ significantly from that which is observed in Germany and other small European countries (Debresson *et al.*, 1997).

Figure 4.8:   R&D collaboration between firms and other actors of the NIS in the Brussels-Capital, Flemish, and Walloon regions

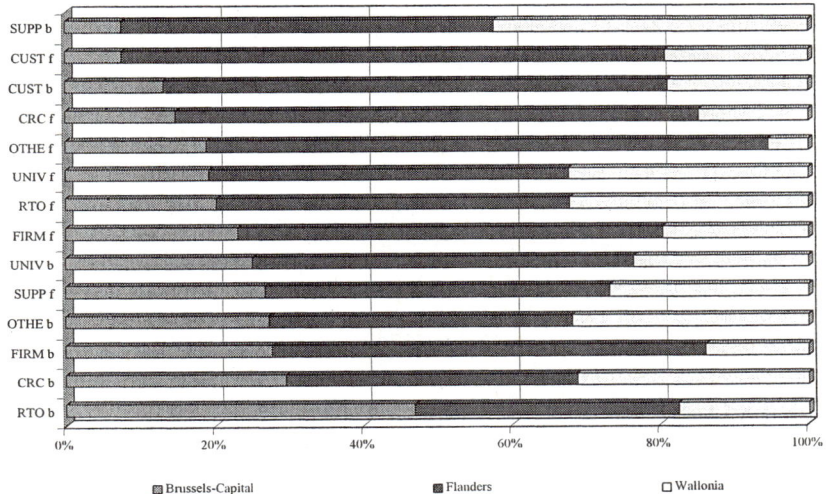

Notes: OTHE = other partners; CRC = collective research centres; RTO = research and technology organisation; SUPP = suppliers; CUST = customers; FIRM= firms; UNIV = universities; b = Belgium and f = Foreign.
Source: OSTC, 1997.

It follows from Figure 4.8 that the strategies developed by Belgian firms as regards R&D collaborations differ from one region to the other. Indeed, firms established in Wallonia appear to be oriented more towards domestic suppliers and collective research centres as well as foreign universities and public research and technology organisations. Flemish firms are more oriented toward their customers and other firms. Hence, the technological partnerships developed by firms in Wallonia tend to be vertically integrated and directed toward research institutions located upstream in the innovative process, while Flemish firms seem to have linkages mainly with actors located downstream in this process. This may suggest that firms in Flanders undertake more 'near market' or applied research with more rapid commercial results. This regionally differentiated behaviour of firms raises the question of the coherence and the integration of the Belgian NIS.

4.11. Conclusion

In the Belgian innovation system, the business sector is the most important source of, and destination for, R&D funding. Even though the country is a high-income economy, the main S&T indicators classify it in the medium R&D intensity range, with numerous characteristics similar to those of the average of the main industrialised countries.

The findings that emerge from this chapter may be summarised as follows:

- The relative R&D efforts in Belgium are greater than in Italy or Canada, but still less than those of the USA, Japan, and the large European countries. The share of government R&D in the total R&D outlay is relatively weak. The business sector is by far the largest financial source and the largest R&D-active sector in the Belgian economy.

- High-tech and medium high-tech industries account for only 8% of the total value added created by the business sector as a whole (including services) but at the same time account for 71% of total business R&D activities. The reverse is true for the services industry. The qualification level of total R&D personnel is much higher in the service industry than in the manufacturing industry. However, the manufacturing industry relies ten times more on R&D personnel than does the services industry.

- The service industry relies much more than does the manufacturing industry on outside funding of intramural expenditures and, more precisely, on funds from abroad and from the government. The service industry has also a higher propensity to finance extramural R&D.

- There is a trend towards the regionalisation of S&T policies and a reduction of the role of the federal authorities. Furthermore, the functional distribution of public-budget allocations varies substantially among the regional authorities, which indicates different regional stances regarding the organisation of their respective innovation systems.

- Despite a favourable positioning in the total number of graduates, Belgium is suffering from an insufficiency in the number of graduates in both theoretical and applied sciences. This deficit can be attributed to a mismatch of the higher education system. The role played by Belgian citizens in international human-capital mobility reflects the high degree of openness of Belgium in comparison with that of other European countries.

- Among the main actors involved in R&D collaboration with Belgian firms, Belgian universities and foreign firms and customers account for more than 45% of the collaboration. This collaboration predominates in the chemical and electrical industries and in the technology services supplied to firms. The R&D collaborative pattern differs across the Belgian regions: Flemish firms are directed more toward firms and suppliers while Walloon firms co-operate more with institutions that are located upstream in the innovation process, i.e. universities and public RTOs.

Chapter 5.   R&D Activities at the Firm Level

Klaus Vandewalle

5.1. Introduction

It is often said that the relatively weak performance of the Belgian economy in terms of innovativeness is due in part to the comparatively small average size of its firms and the scarcity of home-based multinational corporations. The question whether firm size is related to R&D intensity is, therefore, of particular importance for a country like Belgium. This section describes some aspects of the orientation of R&D activities of Belgian firms beginning with the distribution of the R&D activities of firms in several components: research versus development, process versus product innovation, and capital- versus labour-intensive R&D (Section 5.2). The Schumpeterian hypothesis concerning firm size and innovativeness is examined in Section 5.3. This section also includes a first analysis of the relationship between firm size and innovativity, as measured by the percentage of 'new products' in total sales. We conclude in Section 5.4.

5.2. The R&D orientation of Belgian firms

The R&D orientation of Belgian firms will be discussed only briefly. Vandewalle (1998) explains the design and the preparation of the analysis and also gives a full description and interpretation of the compounded tables.[1] The figures are for the year 1995, unless stated otherwise.

---

[1] Each of the firms in the sample used was examined individually. Dubious or clearly erroneous figures were corrected where possible, making use of the database of the Central Bank and of 'Trends Top 5000'; if anomalies were found and no correction was possible, the firms were excluded from the sample. At the end of this procedure, we retained 505 firms. Because the analysis was carried out starting from the survey database prior to the operations of inter- and extrapolation of the original data in function of the ANBERD calculations (see Capron, Meeusen *et al.*, 1999), the implied totals of R&D expenditures do not entirely match the statistics reported in Chapter 4.

5.2.1.   Research versus development

In the 1995 OSTC sample of firms active in R&D that was used, 424 out of a total of 505 gave details on the distinction between research and development activities. We found that three-quarters of the total intramural R&D budgets of these firms is used for the 'development' of new products and processes and one quarter was spent on 'research'.[2] Veugelers *et al.* (1995), taking into account the total R&D expenditure in 1993 of only the Flemish firms, reported a comparable research share of 28%. The same relative quantities are found for other European countries (see for instance Pavitt, 1984).

Nelson's opinion (1959, p. 299) in this context is of particular relevance: 'Research, and especially basic research, is an uncertain activity, yielding inventions and discoveries in unexpected areas. The firm with interest in a diversity of fields will generally be able to produce and market a higher proportion of these unexpected inventions than a firm whose product line is narrow.' This means that, in general, larger firms, mainly because of economies of scale, are expected to contribute a relatively larger share of their R&D budgets to research activities proper.[3]

The share of intramural research accounted for by the five largest firms of our sample is – and this is consistent with Nelson's statement – indeed well above their share of intramural development, and larger firms (500 employees and more) are found in general to be relatively more research-oriented. However, at the other end of the scale, the smallest firms (fewer than 25 employees) are also found to be relatively more research-oriented.

Calculation of the relative amount of intramural R&D expenditure in this sample, allocated to research and development, for the manufacturing sector as a whole and some sub-sectors revealed large interindustry differences. The chemical industry in Belgium, for instance, allocates on average more than a third of the total intramural R&D budget to research, while the electrical equipment and components industry allocates only about 10%. Taking the overall manufacturing shares as a reference, we can say that both the chemicals and the iron-and-steel and ferrous metals industry are, relatively speaking, much more research-oriented than the textile, electrical equipment and components, and non-electrical machines industries, which are preponderantly development-oriented.

Rather surprisingly, we found that, taken as a whole, the high-tech industries spent the smallest percentage of their total intramural R&D budget on research.[4] However, again, both the smallest firms and the firms employing from 500 to

---

[2] The OSTC is the Federal Government agency responsible for R&D policy. It centralises the results of biannual R&D surveys carried out on the regional level.

[3] This is because it is expected that larger firms will generally have a larger number of product lines and so are expected to have interests in a diversity of fields.

[4] We use the classification in high-tech, medium-tech (comprising medium-high-tech and medium-low-tech), and low-tech industries as defined by the OECD (1995) on the basis of average R&D intensities observed in the member countries.

1000 people in the high-tech industries contribute nearly 45% of their total intramural R&D budget to research activities. For firms employing between 25 and 50 people the share drops to 23%, and for the 50-100 size class it drops down to only 8%.

A similar research orientation is found for medium high-tech firms active in R&D. Again the smallest firms are the most research-oriented, with a share of about 42%. The next size class devotes only 26% to research, and the 50-100 size class less than 12%. The medium low-tech and low-tech industries show a different picture, with the medium-large firms (250 to 500 employees) and the largest firms (more than 1000 employees) being the most research oriented.

5.2.2. Product versus process innovation

In discussing the breakdown of the innovative effort into product and process innovation as measured by R&D outlays, it should be noted first that a relatively large share of the total intramural R&D of our sample (more than 15%) could not be allocated to either product or process innovation. In particular, very small firms seem to have some difficulty in assigning their intramural R&D expenditures to one of the two categories.[5] Taking this into account, we can, albeit with caution, say that about three quarters of the allocable intramural R&D expenditure is used for the innovation of products rather than processes. The larger the firm, however, the greater the importance of process innovations, except for the firms with more than 5000 employees, where again product innovation rises above the average of the sample. Pavitt *et al.* (1987) also found medium-sized firms to be mostly process oriented.

For the manufacturing sub-sectors, we found that one industry is an exception in the sense of being extremely process-oriented: the iron-and-steel and non-ferrous metals industry. This industry devotes no less than 70% of the total intramural R&D expenditure to the development of new processes. In contrast, innovation in the chemical, and even more in the electrical equipment and components industry, is more product oriented.

The share of intramural R&D expenditures allocated to either product or process innovation, according to the technological level, reveals that the Belgian high-tech sector is strikingly product-oriented, while the medium high- and medium low-tech sectors, although they too allocate more than 50% of their intramural R&D expenditure to the development of new products, also contribute to a considerable extent to the development of new processes. No clear conclusion could be made about the low-tech sector, as nearly 50% of the total intramural R&D

---

[5] More than 60% of the total intramural R&D expenditure of the smallest firms (fewer than 25 employees) cannot be assigned to either product or process innovation. This percentage falls sharply for large firms (500 employees and more), and even disappears for firms with more than 5000 employees.

expenditure of this group could not be assigned to either product or process innovation.

5.2.3.   Capital- versus labour-intensive R&D

To conclude this section on the R&D orientation of Belgian firms, we will take a
brief look at the capital- versus labour-orientation of the R&D active firms. The
degree of capital intensity is measured by the share of the R&D budget devoted to
investments (as reported in the 1995 OSTC survey). The labour intensity is similarly measured as the share of the R&D personnel expenditure in the total intramural R&D budget.

In addition to these two categories, the 1995 OSTC survey reports data on operational costs due to R&D activities. This category is shown to represent more
than one third of the total intramural R&D budget. Overall we can say that the
R&D activity of the Belgian firms is characterised by a high labour intensity, as
high as in Germany and higher than in most other European countries and in Japan. More than half of the total intramural R&D budget is used to cover R&D
personnel expenditure, while only a small 8% of the budget is used for capital
investment.

In function of the size classes, we can state that the small and medium-size
firms (up to 500 employees) are somewhat less labour oriented (in comparison to
the average values), but for the SMEs this is due to relatively high operational
expenditures. This implies that the SMEs cannot be labelled as being relatively
more capital intensive than is the average firm. Firms employing 250 to 500 persons, on the contrary, are relatively more capital intensive, with an investment
share of 14%. Firms in the size class of 500-1000 employees also report a relatively high investment share, and consequently are more capital intensive, again in
comparison to the average values.

Taking account of the manufacturing sector only, a similar breakdown between
size-classes is found. We encountered relatively strong inter-industry differences,
but these again boil down essentially to differences in the share of operational
costs. We should stress that the spread between the most and the least labour- or
capital-intensive sectors, after correction for these differences in operational costs,
was only 4.3 percentage points. This puts statements about higher or lower labour-
or capital-intensity in an ambiguous perspective.

We found that the operational expenditures represent a relatively large share of
the R&D budget for both high-tech and medium low-tech industries, depending on
the technological level. Omitting these costs, the medium low-tech industries are
found to be the most labour-intensive (with a labour share of 93.7%), while the
medium high-tech industries are the most capital-intensive, the spread between the
relative shares being 8.9 percentage points.

5.3. Firm size and R&D intensity

When studying the determinants of technological progress and the structure of the NIS, attention is often focused on the 'firm size - innovativeness', respectively 'firm size - R&D intensity' relation as being one of the more specific aspects of the Schumpeterian paradigm. As in the previous section, we will report the results in brief and refer the interested reader to the reports of Rayp *et al.* (1998) and Vandewalle (1998) for a more detailed discussion of the data for Belgium.

Our analysis of the relationship of firm size to R&D intensity consists of two parts. In the first part, the nature of the relationship is treated empirically. Making use of the OSTC database for 1995, we discuss a number of tables including the share of total and intramural R&D expenditure, the share of sales, and some proxy measures for R&D intensity. These tables relate to the sample as a whole as well as to sub-samples (specific industries, subdivisions by technological level, etc.), and provide an initial understanding of the nature of the size – R&D intensity relationship.

The second part contains regression results based panel data. Making use of the OSTC surveys for the years 1985 through 1989, we were able to build a quasi-panel of sufficient size covering these years. The qualifier 'quasi' is used because, rather than considering a true panel relating to a limited number of companies that were continuously present in the 1985 through 1989 samples, we collected data on average values within the period for the relevant inflation-corrected variables[6] for those companies for which we have data in at least two successive surveys. In order to discern the nature of the relationship, we estimated a simple loglinear regression with the dependent variable being R&D expenditures and size as the main explanatory variable.

5.3.1. Descriptive approach

The empirical analysis is based on OSTC data for 1995 in function only of the firms that reported R&D activity. Table 5.1 presents the 505 surveyed companies in a cumulative way according to their size, expressed in terms of the number of employees. Two R&D intensity measures are also reported, the first defined as total R&D expenditure related to sales, the second as total R&D expenditure related to total employment (Table 5.2).[7]

The statistics for the manufacturing sector as a whole reveal a relatively large degree of importance of small firms. Very small firms (fewer than 25 employees), in particular, are found to contribute more than a proportional share of R&D.

---

[6] Lacking an alternative, we used the GDP deflator.

[7] Following Scherer (1965b), we opted for firm sales as a meaningful size variable. The thresholds were chosen somewhat arbitrarily but as meaningfully as possible for the Belgian economy, which is defined as an SME economy.

While accounting for only 1.0% of the sales, their share of total R&D expenditure amounts to 2.2% and their share of R&D employees is an even larger 2.8%.

This result remains valid even if we extend our definition of small firms to firms with fewer than 250 employees. These firms account for 18% of the total R&D expenditure and 20.5% of R&D personnel but less than 11% of the total sales (Table 5.1). Small firms (in the narrower as well as the broader sense) in this sample of R&D-active companies clearly make a more-than-proportional contribution to the development of new products and processes.

Table 5.1:   Cumulative sales, share of total R&D expenditure and share of R&D employment for the 1995 sample, Belgium

Size (number of employees (n))	Sales (in %)	Share of R&D expenditures (in %)	Share of R&D employment (in %)
n < 25	1.0	2.2	2.8
n < 50	2.5	5.0	6.3
n < 100	4.2	9.1	10.8
n < 250	10.5	18.0	20.5
n < 500	33.1	26.3	29.6
n < 1000	48.5	37.6	39.1
n < 5000	78.9	79.0	80.8
Total	100.0	100.0	100.0

Source: OSTC database.

Table 5.2:   R&D intensity per size class in the manufacturing sector in Belgium (1995)

Size (number of Employees (n))	Total R&D-expenditures/ turnover (in %)	Total R&D-expenditures / number of employees (millions of BEF)
< 25	7.9	0.9
25 ≤ n < 50	6.7	0.6
50 ≤ n < 100	8.9	0.6
100 ≤ n < 250	5.1	0.4
250 ≤ n < 500	1.3	0.3
500 ≤ n < 1000	2.7	0.3
1000 ≤ n < 5000	4.9	0.4
5000 and more	3.6	0.2

Source: OSTC database.

Kleinknecht *et al.* (1991), studying the Dutch economy, also found that smaller firms, although having but little probability of engaging in R&D, are – when they do – certainly no less innovative than larger firms.

Medium-large firms contribute proportionally the least. But we also see that the contribution share of the largest firms (up to 5000 employees), when the total R&D expenditure and the R&D employment are considered, is high relative to their share in sales. These findings obviously also show up when R&D intensity (computed as the firm's R&D expenditure over sales) is considered (Table 5.2).[8] Firms with up to 250 employees report very high intensities. Once above 250 employees, the measure drops sharply to rise again for firms with more than 1000 employees.

Taking the R&D intensity measure as a proxy for innovativeness, our results seem to give some support to the hypothesis of a U-shaped relationship between firm size and innovativeness, with the importance of small firms being relatively larger. This concurs with a similar conclusion put forward by the European Commission in the 1994 issue of the *European Report on Science and Technology Indicators*. Veugelers *et al.* (1995), studying a group of Flemish firms, also found evidence in support of the U-shaped relationship. Firms with 200 to 1000 employees are found to contribute relatively the least, while SMEs (here defined as firms with fewer than 200 employees) and firms with more than 1000 employees are found to have an R&D intensity above the average. A word of warning though: the relatively concentrated R&D input in innovative activity among small and very large firms does not necessarily mean that innovativeness as such relates to firm size in a U-shaped way. We also stress once again that this result applies only to a sample of R&D-active firms, so it tells us little about SMEs in general.

Table 5.3 again shows the share of the sales, the share of total R&D expenditure, and the share of R&D employment according to firm size, but this time examined from a different angle, the firms of the sample being ranked by sales in descending order. The share of the R&D accounted for by the largest firms is well below their share of sales. Even if we look at the 250 largest firms in the sample, their contribution to the development of new products and processes is less than proportionate. These findings contrast with those of Soete (1979), Acs and Audretsch (1991) and others who – for other countries – found that the share of R&D accounted for by the largest firms slightly exceeded their share of sales.

As we noted above, a variety of possible relationships may underlie these results. Mansfield (1964) and Freeman (1974), for instance, have stressed that the nature of the relationship depends on the industry. In addition to analysing the manufacturing sector as a whole, therefore, we find it worthwhile to take a closer look at some specific manufacturing sectors. As claimed by Cohen *et al.* (1987, p. 545): 'Interindustry differences in technological opportunities and in the appropri-

---

[8] As stated by Acs and Audretsch (1987), ratios are more meaningful because absolute R&D expenditure is not standardised by an equivalent measure of firm size.

ability of returns from R&D investment may ... influence the degree to which size
confers advantages or disadvantages.' They go on to state that: 'a spurious statistical connection between R&D and size may arise as a consequence of failure to
take adequate account of interindustry differences.'

**Table 5.3:   Cumulative share of sales, total R&D expenditure and R&D employment
in the manufacturing sector, according to firm size (Belgium, 1995)**

Number of firms Ranked by sales	Share of sales (in %)	Share of total R&D expenditure (in %)	Share of R&D employment (in %)
First 5[*]	32.1	4.8	4.7
10	44.7	28.9	29.3
15	52.9	45.7	43.4
20	58.8	53.4	52.3
25	63.2	58.9	57.2
50	76.5	70.9	70.0
100	88.7	80.6	78.5
250	98.3	93.2	91.0
Total	100.0	100.0	100.0

Note: (*) This is not very robust: when we take the first six the share of R&D expenditures and
employment almost triples.
Source: OSTC database.

Table 5.4 reports similar findings for the main sub-sectors as for the whole of
manufacturing, with an exception for the chemical industry. Only in this industry
do we find that the share of the total R&D budget compared to sales is higher for
large firms than for small firms. For all the other sectors, we can again conclude
that the proportional R&D share for small businesses is most of the time substantially higher than the relative contribution of large firms. Consequently, we can
argue that small firms active in R&D contribute a more-than-proportional share of
R&D and are not, as stated by the Schumpeterian hypothesis, of less importance
for the development of new products and processes. However, we must stress that,
in general, the importance of small firms is found to be rather limited in industries
characterised by high capital and/or R&D requirements and high entry costs (e.g.,
aerospace, *motor vehicles*, and *pharmaceuticals*).

Although the nature of the relationship between size and R&D intensity seems
to be similar in most sub-sectors, there are considerable intersectoral differences in
the R&D intensities. The, in comparison, very high values for the electrical
equipment and components industry and, to a lesser extent, for the non-electrical
machines industry were also found by Acs and Audretsch (1991).[9] Scherer (1967)
argues that these kinds of interindustry differences are mainly due to the 'vigorous
scientific climate' typical of these industries.

---

[9] Acs and Audretsch (1991) also found relatively high R&D expenditures for the computer
and office-equipment industry.

Table 5.4: **R&D intensity, defined as total R&D expenditures over sales; in percent (Belgium, 1995)**

Size (number of employees (n))	Textile	Chemicals	Iron & steel and non-ferrous metals	Electrical machines	Electrical equipment & components	Non-electrical machines
< 250	1.1	2.5	1.4	4.3	14.2	5.0
250 ≤ n < 1000	0.6	3.6	0.3	3.4	11.8	3.7
1000 and more	0.5	6.4	1.2	3.0	11.4	5.1

Source: OSTC database.

Klevorick *et al.* (1995) explain the interindustry differences by differences in technological opportunities. *Electrical equipment and components* and *chemicals* (mainly drugs) are both labelled as 'high opportunity sectors'. They also note that R&D intensity in an industry is strongly correlated with the strength of the connections of that industry with several of the fields in science, and with the contributions made by university research and government laboratories. The authors further state that the interindustry differences in the amount of resources devoted to R&D, whether measured in absolute terms or in relation to sales, can be explained by two key variables: technological opportunity and ability to appropriate the returns from new developments.

Scherer noted in his 1965 articles that, in order to obtain a clear view on the nature of the relationship 'size-innovativeness', it can be worthwhile to divide the firms into different classes according to their relative level of innovativeness and then to estimate separate regressions for these subgroups. In Tables 5.5 and 5.6, therefore, we make a distinction in function of the technological level. We will distinguish high-tech, medium high-tech, medium low-tech, and low-tech industries, following the classification used by the OECD.

The relative contribution of large firms is found to be the highest in the high-tech industry. We also note that the lower the technological level, the higher the relative importance of small firms.

A particular problem when analysing total R&D expenditures arises because most firms report both intramural and extramural R&D expenditures. The extramural R&D contribution of one firm may be part of the intramural R&D expenditure of another. In order to avoid double counting, therefore, it is appropriate to have a closer look at the relationship between firm size and intramural R&D expenditure, all the more because the link between in-house R&D and innovativeness seems to be stronger than between total R&D and innovativeness (Griliches 1986).

Table 5.5:   Share of sales and total R&D expenditures for different technological levels (cumulative data), in percent (Belgium, 1995)

Size (number of employees)	High-tech		Medium high-tech		Medium low-tech		Low-tech	
	Share of sales	Share of R&D exp.	Share of sales	Share of R&D exp.	Share of sales	Share of R&D exp.	Share of sales	Share of R&D exp.
< 25	0.6	0.4	0.2	0.4	0.1	0.8	0.2	1.3
< 50	1.4	1.2	1.6	0.9	3.1	3.4	1.6	5.2
< 100	2.3	1.6	4.2	2.8	4.8	5.2	2.5	7.0
< 250	6.3	4.2	10.7	9.6	14.7	14.0	10.5	13.6
< 500	13.5	6.5	22.0	22.2	25.8	24.8	26.1	20.0
< 1000	23.9	14.7	28.1	27.2	69.4	66.3	48.5	38.7
Total	100.0	100.0	100.0	100.0	100.0	100.0	100.0	100.0

Source: OSTC database.

Table 5.6:   R&D intensity for different technological levels, in percent (Belgium, 1995)*

Size (number of employees (n))	High-tech R&D intensity	Medium-high-tech R&D intensity	Medium-low-tech R&D intensity	Low-tech R&D intensity
n < 25	8.9	6.3	18.8**	5.5
25 ≤ n < 50	11.4	1.2	1.5	2.8
50 ≤ n < 100	5.4	2.4	2.0	1.8
100 ≤ n < 250	8.1	3.4	1.6	0.8
250 ≤ n < 500	4.0	3.6	1.7	0.4
500 ≤ n < 1000	9.8	2.6	1.7	0.8
1000 and more	13.9	3.3	2.0	1.1

Notes: (*)   R&D intensity is defined as the total R&D expenditure over sales.
           (**)   Not very robust.
Source: OSTC database.

Starting from the original sample of 505 firms, we eliminated 11 firms that reported dubious figures on the division of intramural and extramural R&D expenditure. More than half of the remaining firms (51%) reported that they did not contract out any R&D and so only reported intramural R&D expenditures.

A in the mean time familiar pattern can be recognised in Table 5.7: small firms account for a relatively large share of the total R&D expenditure, although the observed differences are less pronounced than reported above (cf. Table 5.2).

We cannot stress it enough that the overall finding that small firms seem to contribute in a more-than-proportional way to R&D has to be interpreted with caution. First, because we took account of only of firms that conducted R&D on the basis of an OSTC sample. This implies that the previous findings are biased because of a serious sample-selection problem.

Table 5.7:   **Share of sales and of intramural R&D expenditures and R&D intensity for the reduced sample of 494 firms, cumulative and according to size class, in percent (Belgium, 1995)**

Size (number of employees)	Share of sales	Share of intramural R&D expenditure	Size (number of employees)	R&D intensity[*]
< 25	1.0	1.6	< 25	4.3
< 50	2.5	4.6	25 ≤ n < 50	5.2
< 100	4.2	8.8	50 ≤ n < 100	6.7
< 250	10.5	17.1	100 ≤ n < 250	3.5
< 500	33.1	26.4	250 ≤ n < 500	1.1
< 1000	48.5	38.7	500 ≤ n < 1000	2.1
< 5000	78.9	75.2	1000 ≤ n < 5000	3.2
Total	100.0	100.0	5000 and more	3.1

Note: ([*]) Defined as intramural R&D expenditure over sales.
Source: OSTC database.

Second, we know that many small firms often have no formal R&D activity (see for instance Kleinknecht, 1987). Reported 'technological innovation' is, in these cases, said to be the result of a (typically) poorly measured fraction of time worked by the engineers and managers of the firm. Thus, the individually reported R&D efforts of small firms may be over-estimated if reporting is not done properly in full-time equivalents. Third, as argued by Kleinknecht *et al.* (1991), there are indications that innovative firms might have a higher propensity to respond (and to do so more completely) to an innovation questionnaire than non-innovative firms. In other words, it could be that the large low-profile innovators (having better figures on their activities) respond more than do the small low-profile innovators, and consequently the relative efforts of small firms are over-estimated.

However, previous research also suggests that, generally speaking, as a result of non-response or bad reporting, the R&D contributions of small firms is systematically underestimated (see for instance Kleinknecht, 1987, and Mansfield, 1964). This would then suggest that our findings of a less-than-proportional relationship imply an even stronger rejection of the Schumpeterian hypothesis than might appear at first sight. Furthermore, studies for the UK and the US point out that the R&D *efficiency* of SMEs – particularly in some specific industries – is higher than that of large firms (Dodgson and Rothwell, 1994). This would imply that a higher proportion of innovative activities of SMEs occurs outside of what is formally defined as R&D, and that the contribution of SMEs to the development of new products and processes – by using R&D expenditures as a proxy for R&D efforts and innovativeness – is even underestimated.

In brief, the foregoing findings of the empirical approach have to be treated with caution, all the more so because, apart from taking account of R&D-performing firms only, we also only took firm size into account. In order to develop a provisional overview, we ignored several other factors that might influence innovative activity, such as subsidisation, openness to foreign competition, and foreign ownership.

5.3.2.   Regression results

Many of the earlier, mainly American, firm-level analyses are based on the 500 or 1000 largest firms in the manufacturing sector, and firms that reported no R&D were generally excluded. Apart from obvious measurement problems, this kind of design introduces the difficulty of sample-selection bias. By dealing with R&D-performing firms only, our analysis will also be subject to the same problem of sample-selection bias and thus similarly subject to criticism.

On the basis of the OSTC surveys we tried to construct a panel of Belgian R&D-performing firms.[10] However, because – when constructing a panel covering the years 1985 through 1989 – we were confronted with serious problems in terms of sample-size reduction, and an additional sample-selection bias due to the changing sample of firms that was selected in the consecutive surveys, we opted for a third-best solution that consists of defining a *sample of average values* for the firms with at least two observations over the period. Using a quasi-panel technique we were still able to focus solely on the independent variable that is most relevant to our present purpose, firm size, and to take account of individual effects and intra-industry effects via the incorporation of 2- and 3-digit industry dummies.[11]

The most neutral indicator of firm size is often considered to be 'sales' (Scherer, 1965b).[12] On the other hand, analyses using R&D employment, or patents or innovation counts, rather than R&D outlays, as a proxy measure for innovativeness seem to overestimate the R&D contribution of small firms (Soete, 1979; Acs and Audretsch, 1991). In view of these findings, so as not to introduce a bias for or against the Schumpeter hypothesis, we define our proxy measure for 'innovativeness' as the average R&D expenditure of the firm (*RD*). The size vari-

---

[10] The advantage of panel data is that, using the technique of the fixed-effects-model estimation, we are able, first, to concentrate on the main estimator (in this case, the size variable) by accounting for industry differences through the incorporation of industry dummies, and, second, to take account of omitted variables influencing the R&D activity through the incorporation of unobserved individual firm effects.

[11] For practical reasons, we assigned each sample firm to a primary industry using the two-digit NACE classification despite the warning of Cohen *et al.* (1987, p. 545) against such a practice. They argue that interindustry differences are not adequately accounted for by doing so, and there may be a risk of a spurious statistical connection between size and R&D.

[12] Scherer (1967) argues that the sales variable is most likely to be responsive to short-term changes in demand while it is neutral with respect to factor proportions. Sales have also been proven to be the principal scale variable considered in company R&D budget decisions.

able is defined as one period lagged (average) sales (S).[13] All the data are in fixed prices of 1985.[14]

For reasons of simplicity and transparency, we specified a simple linear regression between the firm's R&D intramural expenditure and sales. We finally opted for a logarithmic specification, as it has been shown to be the least sensitive to outliers and presents the best goodness-of-fit (see Rayp *et al.*, 1998):[15]

$$\log(RD_i) = \alpha + \beta \log(S_i) + \gamma D_i + \varepsilon_i \ , \qquad [1]$$

with D_i being a vector of the relevant 2- and 3-digit industry dummies.

Increasing returns would be reflected by the scale parameter β being greater than unity. When trying to estimate the sample as a whole (375 observations), we could not but strongly reject the normality hypothesis, apparently because of the overall heterogeneity of the dataset. In order to solve this problem, we divided the sample − on an *ad hoc* basis of prior homogeneity expectations − into eight sector-defined sub-samples, each having at least 20 observations. The sector dummies in that case are accordingly redefined as subsector dummies. The estimation results are given in Table 5.8. We report the coefficient of the scale parameter β, its 95% confidence interval, the sample size, the adjusted R^2, and the statistical problems encountered − at the 95% confidence level, unless otherwise specified − of each specification. The coefficients of the sub-sector dummy variables in each equation are not reported.

For all industries but two, we found a less-than-proportional relationship between R&D efforts and firm size. Only for textiles and the metal industry could the null hypothesis − a proportional relationship between R&D expenditure and firm size −not be rejected. These industries account for approximately 15% of the total R&D expenditure of the overall sample, a quarter of the sales, and represent some 30% of the number of firms in the sample.

Once again, these findings have to be handled with caution because, apart from concerning R&D-performing firms only, the logarithmic specification places a greater weight on small firms and so may lead to an over-estimation of the R&D contribution of these firms (Acs and Audretsch (1991)).

---

[13] The average sales are defined as the average of the one-period lagged sales in order to reflect the decision about the amount spent on R&D in period t generally being based on the sales (or cash flow) of the previous period.

[14] R&D expenditures were deflated using the general OECD Basic Science and Technology Statistics (BSTS) deflator, defined as Belgian R&D expenditures in current prices over the R&D expenditure in fixed 1985 prices. For the transformation of the current sales we applied NACE 2-digit deflators based on the added value of the specific industry.

[15] Rayp *et al.* (1998) use three specifications: a quadratic, a logarithmic, and an intensity specification. The best results are given by the logarithmic specification.

Table 5.8:   Estimation results for the eight sub-samples (equation 1)

Industry	β [95% conf. interval]	n	Adj. R^2	Estimation problems
Chemical	0.63* [0.47 ; 0.79]	64	0.60	Functional specification
Food	0.58* [0.26 ; 0.90]	24	0.73	
Textile	0.92 [0.64 ; 1.20]	22	0.69	Functional specification (CI-90%) Parameter stability (CI-90%)
Metal	0.95 [0.77 ; 1.13]	62	0.77	
Electrotechnical	0.75* [0.57 ; 0.93]	38	0.78	Functional specification
Wholesale	0.73* [0.53 ; 0.93]	20	0.74	
Ferrous & non-ferrous metals	0.57* [0.47 ; 0.67]	20	0.93	
Services for companies	0.63* [0.43 ; 0.83]	30	0.55	Parameter stability

Note: (*) Significantly different from unity at at least a 95% probability level.

However, similar results are obtained from analysis of the sample data by means of a more straightforward method. In order to test further the association between the two variables, size and innovativeness, we indeed now turn to an alternative measure for innovativeness that is closer to the output of innovative activities. We define innovativeness now as the percentage of new products in total sales.[16] However, the statistical reliability of this variable being low in our sample, we fell back on a crosstabs procedure applied to the categorised variable *NEWPROD*. We distinguished three categories for this variable: fewer than 10% of new products in total sales, between 10% and 30%, and more than 30%. The scale variable (*SIZE*), also categorised, discriminates between SMEs (firms with fewer than 250 employees) and large firms (250 employees and more).

According to the Schumpeterian hypothesis — large firms make a more than proportional contribution to the development of new products and processes — it is expected that the percentage of sales originating from new products is higher for large firms. That is, the observed number of large firms in the third category of *NEWPROD* is expected to exceed the number count on the basis of an equal distribution.

---

[16] By taking the percentage of new products in the total sales as a proxy measure for innovativeness, we are now dealing with an output measure (while the previously used R&D expenditure was an input-measure), and, strictly speaking, are taking account of product innovations only. However, the invention of new products is not rarely related to the implementation of new industrial or organisational processes.

The results — carried out on a OSTC sample of 518 Belgian companies — are given in Table 5.9.[17] It appears, first of all, that the observed number of SMEs (*SIZE* = 0) in the first category of our innovativeness variable (*NEWPROD* = 1; i.e. relatively low innovativeness) is less than the expected number and, second, that the number of SMEs that rely for their sales on a large percentage of new products (*NEWPROD* = 3) exceeds well the expected number. The opposite appears to be true for 'large' firms (*SIZE* = 1).

Table 5.9: **Results of the 'crosstabs' procedure: innovativeness versus size**

			NEWPROD			
			1	2	3	Total
SIZE	0	Observed	196	114	90	400
		Expected	205	114	80	400
		%	73.7%	77.0%	86.5%	77.2%
	1	Observed	70	34	14	118
		Expected	61	33.7	23.7	118
		%	26.3%	23.0%	13.5%	22.8%
		Total	266	148	104	518

Note:　*SIZE* category '0' consists of SMEs, '1' of large' enterprises; *NEWPROD* categories '1', '2', and '3' consist of low, medium, and high innovativeness, respectively, as measured by the percentage of new products in total sales.

Four measures of association were computed (Pearson chi-square, likelihood-ratio chi-square, phi, and Cramer's *V*), all indicating that there is a significant difference between the two size categories. Taking account of the direction of the difference we can only conclude that large R&D-active firms are not found to be more innovating than small ones.

5.4. Conclusion

We found little evidence for a Schumpeterian relationship between firm size and innovativeness as measured by expenditures on R&D. However, we did find some indications for the existence of a U-shaped relationship, witnessing to a relative larger R&D intensity for small and for very large firms. Medium-sized firms displayed the lowest intensity. This was found to be true for manufacturing taken as a whole, for most subsectors, and for nearly all the technological levels.

Similar U-shapes were also found when we focussed on the difference between research and development and between product and process innovation.

---

[17] The size of the sample examined in this exercise increased from 505 to 518 because some firms that reported inconsistent R&D-expenditure and employment data apparently supplied trustworthy data with respect to the *NEWPROD* variable.

To conclude this chapter, we need to stress two points. The relationship between technological change and innovativeness cannot be seen as a static one, with small and large firms operating in isolation from each other. Small and large firms do interact, mainly because of the existence of 'dynamic complementarities' that can be exploited (Dodgson, 1991). Some industries, like the ICT industry and the biotechnology industry, can be described as having a 'life cycle'-structure of *innovation*. In the early stages, mainly small firms are involved in innovation, because small firms (more than large firms) seem to be able to take advantage of basic research by universities and government labs and of venture capital. The fruits of the specific R&D efforts by small firms often 'flow' in a later stage to established (generally) larger firms. The advantages related to mutually complementary relationships between small and large firms become an increasingly important factor for further technological progress. Because of the limitation of SMEs in the act of innovation – mainly due to the lack of a 'critical mass' and accumulated knowledge stock – they, in particular, will benefit from networking.

The last point concerns the life-cycle structure of *firms*: successfully innovative SMEs often enter a growth stage so that they eventually end up in the class of medium-sized or even large enterprises. In trying to detect a relationship between innovativeness and size, therefore, we should, in a more thorough investigation, try to take full account of the dynamics of firm growth rather than relying only on cross-section data.

Chapter 6. The National Innovation System and its International Linkages

Henri Capron, Michele Cincera and
Bruno van Pottelsberghe de la Potterie

6.1. Introduction

Because of its size, its geographical location, and its openness, the Belgian innovation system interacts intensely with foreign countries. The influence of foreign innovation systems on Belgium technological and economic performance is shown both by the impressive number of R&D co-operation links between Belgian and foreign firms, and by the substantial share of foreign-based firms in the Belgian production capacity and knowledge base. Patel and Pavitt (1991), for instance, estimate that about 40% of the technological activity in Belgium comes from large non-Belgian firms. This ratio is one of the highest of the industrialised countries.

More generally, government policies have been challenged by the growth of international flows of goods, capital, and technology in recent years. The increased internationalisation process makes governments less and less able to reap the economic returns of domestic technology policies. Therefore, international collaborative ventures, foreign-investment decisions, technology transfers, offshore R&D centres, and the transnationalisation of firms are critical issues that have to be investigated.

This chapter presents some of the main indicators of potential and effective technology transfers both to and from Belgium. The second section briefly defines the various concepts and channels of international technological transfers. The sections that follow each focus on one particular channel, including imports and exports of high-tech products (Section 6.3), technology payments (Section 6.4), foreign direct investments (Section 6.5), and the collaboration in European R&D networks (Section 6.6). Section 6.7 concludes this chapter.

6.2. International technology transfers: concepts and channels

Given their inherent complexity, international technological spillovers are not measured in a widely accepted way. They relate to many forms of R&D externalities that emanate from one country and benefit other countries. Two concepts may be distinguished: rent and knowledge spillovers (Griliches, 1992). International *rent* spillovers relate to the fact that the prices of imported intermediate input and capital goods do not completely embody the product innovation or the quality improvement that results from innovation activities. Therefore, indirect benefits may emanate from the technological improvement of imported goods and services produced by trade partners. International *knowledge* spillovers, on the other hand, arise because of the imperfect appropriability of innovative output. They are generally characterised by the international transfer of technology, which may occur via different routes: foreign direct investments, foreign technology payments,[1] international R&D collaboration, reverse engineering of foreign technologies, publications in technical and scientific journals, and migration of scientists and skilled labour forces. Since these knowledge-spillover channels are often associated with one or another economic transaction, the extent to which they also reflect rent spillovers is not clear cut.

Some international technology transfer processes can be defined as 'active' because they imply a transaction between a home country (where the technology originates) and a host country (where the technology is used). Both countries share the benefits coming from such 'active' transfers. International knowledge spillovers can also be 'passive' in the sense that the home country, where the technology originates, is not involved in the international diffusion process of its own technology. In this case, R&D spillovers would be the outcome of imitation, reengineering of imported goods, or technology-sourcing practices. Here, the host country (or the imitator) captures all the benefits ensuing from the technology transfer, and the home country receives little or no compensation. The different channels are summarised in Table 6.1.

Table 6.1:   The role of the country of origin in the channels of international technology transfer

	Active	Passive
Direct	Inward foreign direct investments[*] Foreign technology payments[*] R&D joint-ventures Foreign R&D investments	Human capital mobility Technology sourcing[*] Imitation and re-engineering
Indirect	Trade[*]	Technical publications

Note: An asterisk indicates the channels that are analysed in this chapter.

Given this categorisation of the international diffusion of innovation, the issue that logically arises is the evaluation of the relative importance of these channels in the Belgian case. Concerning the relative importance of all these modes of

---

[1] Foreign technology payments include royalties, licensing fees, and patent sales.

technology transfer, it should in general be noted that most of them are interrelated and that they are closely associated with activities of multinational enterprises (MNEs). This is obvious for inward foreign direct investment (FDI), R&D joint ventures, foreign R&D investments, and technology sourcing. Foreign technology payments and international trade are also two channels of technology transfer that are mostly governed by multinational corporations.[2] Similarly, the increasing, though still relatively weak, internationalisation of R&D investment is essentially driven by MNEs. Since both indicators and international trade are for a large part dominated by MNEs, they should be closely related to FDI flows. This underlines the need to take international flows of capital into account in any attempt to measure international technological transfers.

Figure 6.1:   **R&D investments, technology payments and net FDI in Belgium, 1983-1995**

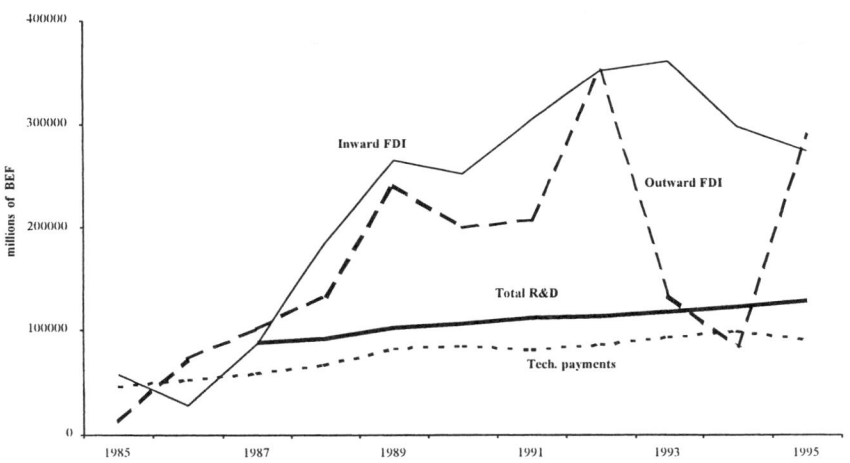

Note: All variables are in constant 1990 prices.
Sources: Banque Nationale de Belgique; OECD BSTS.

Figure 6.1 illustrates the relative importance of total R&D investments and the three channels of technology transfer from abroad in Belgium. Total R&D investments have, in constant 1990 prices, slightly increased through the 1980s from about 83 billion BEF in 1983 to more than 110 billion BEF in 1995. Technology payments to foreign countries have leapfrogged R&D investments over the same period, passing from 50 billion BEF in 1983 to 110 billion BEF in 1990. In the early 1990s, technology payments decreased slowly to about 100 billion BEF in

---

[2] Vickery (1986) provides evidence that the major part of foreign technology payments takes place between OECD countries and is dominated by MNEs.

1994. Net inward and outward investments underwent a drastic upsurge from the early 1980s to the early 1990s. Fluctuating under 100 billion BEF from 1983 to 1986, their real values passed far beyond investments in R&D in the late 1980s, to reach about 300 billion BEF in 1995.

These different aggregates are obviously not directly comparable but they do clearly indicate that foreign technology bases most probably yield benefits for Belgium in net terms. But this cuts both ways. Technology payments and the substantial presence of foreign firms within the national boundaries also show a significant technological dependence of Belgium on outside technology. Symmetrically, these indicators also show that the Belgian technology base benefits foreign countries. These channels are analysed below for Belgium in both the inward and outward directions. Our concern is to determine the main countries whose technology bases may benefit Belgium. Similarly, the geographical pattern of the technology that emanates from Belgium is analysed.

6.3.   Imports and exports of high-tech products

The analysis of export/import ratios for the different categories of industries sheds further light on the positioning of Belgium in the international technological competition. Despite the mismatches identified in the Belgian NIS, it remains that the educational, scientific, and technological base is acknowledged to be of high quality. One important thing is to know the extent to which Belgium succeeds in converting this advantage into high performance in terms of high-tech trade.

Table 6.2 gives data about the global Belgian pattern in world trade. These data cover the Belgo-Luxembourg Economic Union. Exchange coverage ratios in function of the technology intensity of products and the export market share for both the manufacturing and high-tech industries should allow us to obtain a clear idea about its international competitiveness.

Table 6.2:   Trade balance trends of Belgium-Luxembourg

	Coverage ratios in the manufacturing industry			Export market share	
	High-tech	Medium-tech	Low-tech	Manufacturing industry	High-tech industry
1975	0.81	1.0	1.16	-	2.45
1980	0.79	0.9	1.14	5.30	2.50
1985	0.80	1.0	1.21	4.65	2.00
1990	0.77	1.1	1.21	4.96	1.98
1995	0.98	1.2	1.27	5.16	2.18

Source: OECD.

Although Belgium appears highly specialised in international trade, its export market share in highly R&D-intensive products is only less than half that of the manufacturing industry as a whole and has sharply decreased in the 1980s. Nevertheless, the 1990s are marked by an improvement of the export share of high-tech industry. The analysis of coverage ratios tells a similar story. Indeed, we observe a favourable evolution of the coverage ratios in the different categories of industries. While specialisation in low-tech industries has increased, the increase of specialisation in medium-tech industries has been higher. Last but not least, the specialisation in high-tech industries has registered the most favourable evolution, with a coverage ratio now close to equilibrium.

These comparative advantages of the Belgian economy are mainly located in low- and medium-tech industrial sectors. However, it is important to keep in mind that Belgium is, in relative terms, highly specialised in international trade, so that the lower coverage ratio for the high-tech industry must be interpreted cautiously. Without being a technology leader, Belgium has developed competitive advantages in some high-tech as well as leading-edge industries such as pharmaceuticals and telecommunications (European Commission, 1997a). A sectoral analysis of high-tech export is discussed in the next chapter (Section 7.7).

6.4.   The balance of technology payments

Figure 6.2 shows the evolution of the balance of technology payments over the period 1983-1994. Both the payments of foreign technology and the receipts from Belgian technology have increased during the period from about 50 billion BEF to more than 100 billion BEF. Even though the deficit of the balance of technology payments worsened in the late 1980s, it became less important in the early 1990s, and was close to equalisation between payments and receipts in 1994 (minus one billion BEF).

Figure 6.3 illustrates the geographical destination of the technology payments made by Belgium during two sub-periods: 1983-1985 and 1993-1995. During these two periods, the USA was the main destination of technology payments by Belgium, accounting for more than 25% of all technology payments to foreign countries. Four European countries receive half of the payments: France, Germany, the UK, and the Netherlands. The main change in the distribution of payments from the early 1980s to the early 1990s is the increasing share of Italy, Spain, and the other European countries. The share accounted for by all European countries in total technology payments by Belgium increased from 54% in the early 1980s to 62% in the early 1990s.

That the Belgian technology balance of payments is largely in deficit with respect to the USA is due to American technological leadership. Other deficits, but of a lesser amplitude, also appear with France, the UK, and the Netherlands (cf. Table 6.3).

Figure 6.2:   The technology balance of payments and R&D investments in Belgium, 1983-1994

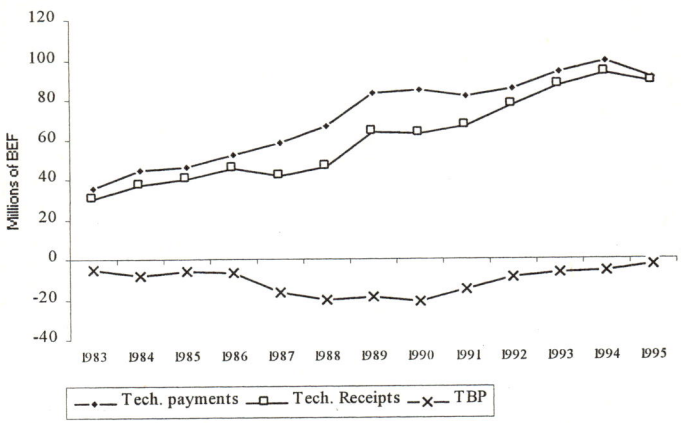

Sources: Banque Nationale de Belgique.

Figure 6.3:   Technology payments (top) and receipts (bottom) by country of origin, 1983-85 (left) and 1993-95 (right)

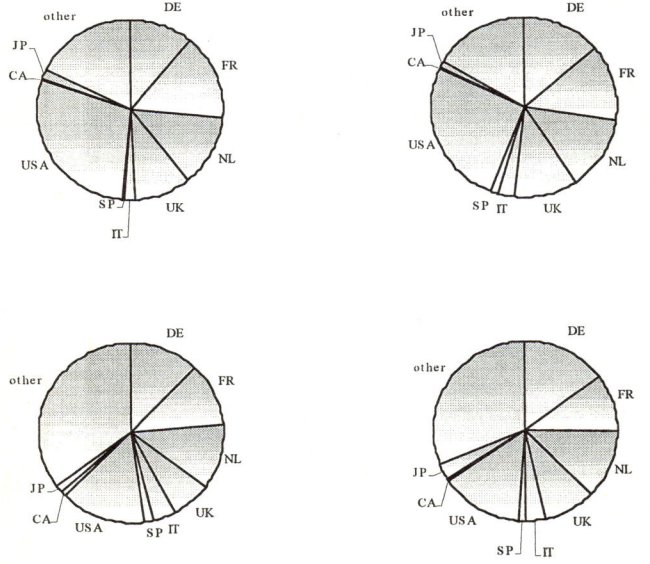

Sources: Banque Nationale de Belgique, own calculations.

The geographical distribution of the Belgian technology receipts is also mainly oriented towards the major European countries and the USA. More than half (53%) of the technological receipts came from European countries in the early 1980s, especially from Germany, France, and the Netherlands. In the early 1990s, this share increased to 58% thanks to an increase in technological receipts from the other countries of continental Europe and the UK.

The technological balance of payments is brought roughly into equilibrium by technical assistance in the framework of development co-operation. When licensing-out technology is compared to licensing-in, a sharp imbalance is observed. Thus, Belgium compensates for its low technology production by a high external technology-expertise capacity.

The share of the total receipts originating from the USA has been stable around 15%. This is the principal difference with the geographical distribution of technology payments, where the USA accounted for a share twice as large as its share in technological receipts. The reverse was true for the Eastern and African countries, the cumulated share of which in technological receipts was 20% in the early 1980s but dropped to 9% in the 1990s.

Table 6.3:   **The Belgian technology balance of payments**
by geographical area, in billions of BEF,
average for the early 1980s and the early 1990s

	1983-85	1993-95
Germany	-490	353
France	-2844	-3163
the Netherlands	-1364	-1167
UK	-1981	-2104
Italy	819	503
Spain	703	310
Northern Europe	905	65
USA	-8491	-11335
Canada	96	-90
Japan	-273	1385
Rest of Asia	365	271
Africa	3457	915
Latin America	-33	410
Central and Eastern European countries	309	471
Middle East	900	1175
Others	894	9429
Total	-7	-2

Source: Banque Nationale de Belgique.

6.5.   Inward and outward foreign direct investments

Important flows of foreign direct investments (FDI) are another indicator of the internationalisation of economic activity. Figure 6.4, which shows the share of net inward FDI in national gross fixed-capital formation, leads basically to three conclusions. First, there has been a general trend toward globalisation in most countries. From the early 1980s to the mid-1990s, net inward FDI have increased faster than domestic investments both within the European Union and within the OECD area. Second, OECD countries are characterised by a significant heterogeneity with regard to the presence of MNEs within their borders. The first group, which is composed of the Netherlands, Belgium, and the United Kingdom, is characterised by a ratio of net inward FDI on total investment well above the 10% since the early 1990s. The second group, with countries like the United States and France, is in an intermediate position. Japan and Germany belong to the third group, where inward FDI accounts for less than 2% of the total investments. Third, for at least two decades, the presence of MNEs in Belgium is the largest, in relative terms, within the OECD area.

Figure 6.4:   **The share of inward FDI in gross fixed-capital formation (GFCF), OECD, 3 sub-periods**

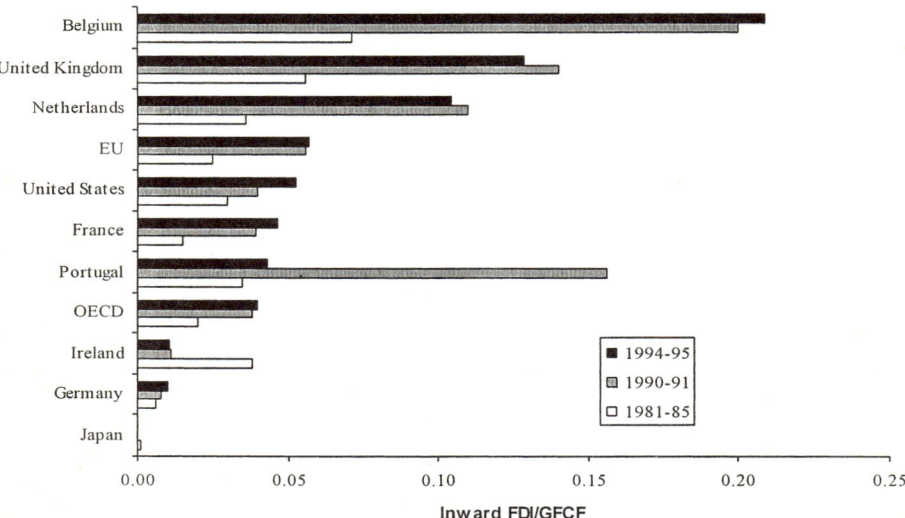

More than 20% of total investment in Belgium comes from abroad (this is a lower bound ratio since we use net inward FDI). In comparison with the UK (13% in the mid-1990's), the Netherlands (11%), and the average for OECD member countries (4%), Belgium is the most globalised country with respect to the breadth of foreign presence within its national borders. What are the potential consequences, if any, of such a high reliance on foreign capital?

The answer is far from clear cut.[3] Caves (1974) classifies the externalities arising from FDI into three categories: (i) the improvement of allocative efficiency (there will be fewer monopolistic distortions if a foreign company enters industries with high entry barriers); (ii) the inducement of higher technical efficiency (increased competitive pressure would spur local firms to more efficient use of existing resources); and (iii) increasing rates of technology transfer towards the host country. Therefore, it is conceivable that the presence of foreign firms within the national boundaries may foster international technology transfers from the home country.

An alternative way of looking at the likely effects of inward FDI would be through the determinants of these investments. The three traditional incentives are (i) offshore production (in order to benefit from one's own managerial or technological comparative advantages); (ii) market proximity (which allows for an adaptation to changing demand structures); and (iii) defence investment (in order to counter future protectionist measures, such as tariff and non-tariff barriers, higher transportation costs, or voluntary export-restraint measures). More recently, two new incentives emerged: (iv) control of international trade (through intra-company shipments between companies and their majority-owned subsidiaries), and (v) technology sourcing (in order to learn or to source knowledge-intensive assets from the host country).

The potential transfers of knowledge associated with inward FDI may have two directions. In the case of offshore production the host country may benefit from technological externalities emanating from the foreign companies. Yet, if foreign companies try to copy or to source the domestic knowledge, their home country may benefit from potential spillovers emanating from domestic firms. In Dunning's (1981) paradigm, a firm would decide to invest abroad if the three following conditions are fulfilled: ownership, localisation, and internalisation advantages. Otherwise, the firm would take advantage of the foreign market through exports or licensing. The 'internalisation' incentive suggests that FDI may be motivated by the desire to avoid the diffusion of firm-specific technological assets abroad. This idea is corroborated by Patel and Pavitt (1991) who provide evidence that the production of technology by large multinational corporations remains far from being globalised and is in the first place a domestic affair: foreign companies keep their knowledge activities in their home country. Therefore, caution is called

---

[3] See van Pottelsberghe de la Potterie (1997) for a more detailed analysis of potential effects and policy implications related to the globalisation of technology and economy.

for in the analysis of inward FDI with respect to any potential technology transfer generated by foreign companies.

The countries that are technological leaders have accumulated substantial scientific and technological capabilities. These technological assets are likely to be accessible to foreign companies that set up production and research facilities inside the technological leader's boundaries. The benefits for the host country are that the foreign research laboratories[4] or foreign production lines may contribute to improve domestic technological capacities. The mechanisms underlying the main determinants and impacts of FDI are illustrated in Figure 6.5.

Figure 6.5:   The ambiguous net effect of inward FDI

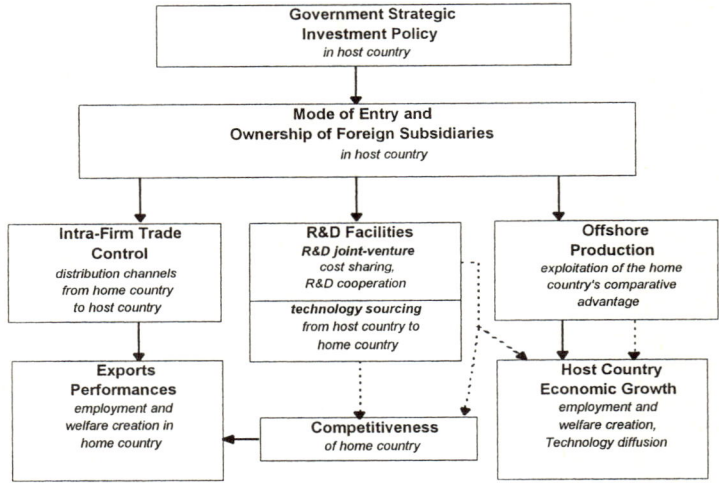

- - - - - - -► : *spillovers of technological and managerial know-how*

The degree to which foreign ownership is fully accessible to MNEs may be one of the motivations for undertaking the sourcing of foreign intangible assets. This may further allow one to control intra-company trade between the host and the home countries. In these two particular cases, inward FDI is more likely to benefit the home country than the host country. Nevertheless, in the cases of R&D co-operation and of the establishment of an offshore production line, inward FDI may be a source of value-added and employment creation as well as technology diffusion in the host country. In a nutshell, the net effect of inward FDI is unpredictable. As regards our present concern – the diffusion of technology – it would

---

[4] It is worth noting, however, that some foreign R&D investments do not contribute at all to technological improvement in the host country because their activities are only related to minor projects (cf. Chesnais, 1986).

also be precarious to expect an automatic transfer from the home country to the host country.

It is clear that the likely impact of inward FDI depends on its motivation for it. According to Dunning (1994), there is support both for the proposition that inward FDI may lessen domestic innovative capacity and for the proposition that it will increase it. However, he further argues that 'What does seem very plausible is that where foreign production adds to domestic production, the R&D base of the investing company is strengthened – whatever the nationality of the firm' (Dunning, 1994, p. 81). If the sourcing of the domestic technology base is the principal goal of inward FDI, the latter may become a Trojan horse and is unlikely to foster international R&D spillovers from the home country to the host country. Lichtenberg and van Pottelsberghe (1996) evaluated the extent to which inward FDI, outward FDI, and imports have been efficient channels of technology transfer between 13 industrialised countries from 1971 to 1990. Their empirical results suggest that outward FDI flows and import flows are two simultaneous channels through which technology is internationally diffused. Therefore, they support the hypothesis of technology sourcing. The technology embodied in inward FDI flows did not seem to contribute to the productivity growth of the host countries. In summary, the efficiency of FDI flows as a channel of international technology transfer is unpredictable. Inward FDI may either inflate or deflate the technology base of the host country and improve the technology base of the home country.

Figure 6.6:   **Inward foreign direct investments in Belgium, 1983-94 (receipts, payments and net FDI)**

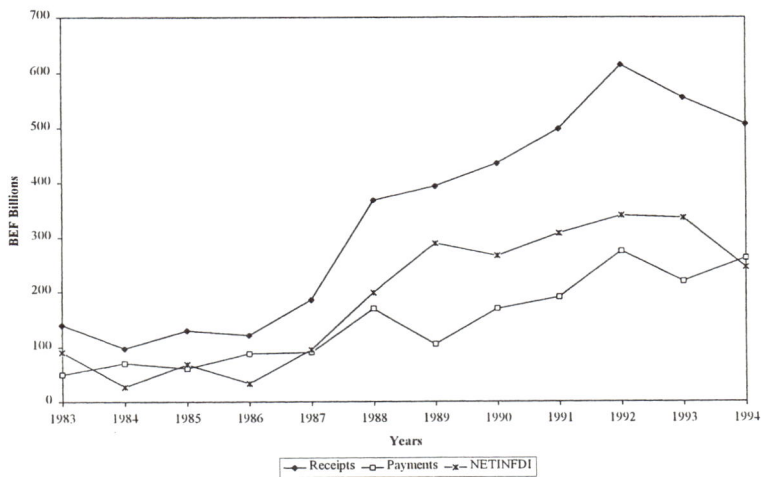

Source: Banque Nationale de Belgique.

Figure 6.6 presents the evolution of gross inward FDI (receipts) in Belgium, the payments made by foreign companies, and net inward FDI (the difference between receipts and payments). Net inward FDI has been positive all through the period 1983-94 and increased sharply from 1987 to 1992. The decrease in net inward FDI between 1993 and 1994 is due to the decrease in gross inward FDI and also to the increase in the payments of foreign companies established in Belgium.

Figure 6.7 shows that European countries accounted for about three fifths of total inward FDI in Belgium in the early 1980s. At that time, Germany, the Netherlands, the UK, the USA, and, to a lesser extent, France were the largest foreign investors in Belgium. The European share increased during the 1980s and came close to 75% in the early 1990s at the expense of the USA position, which declined from 22% in the 1980s to 12% in the 1990s.

Figure 6.7:   Inward (top) and outward (bottom) foreign direct investments, receipts by country of origin, 1983-1985 (left) and 1993-1995 (right)

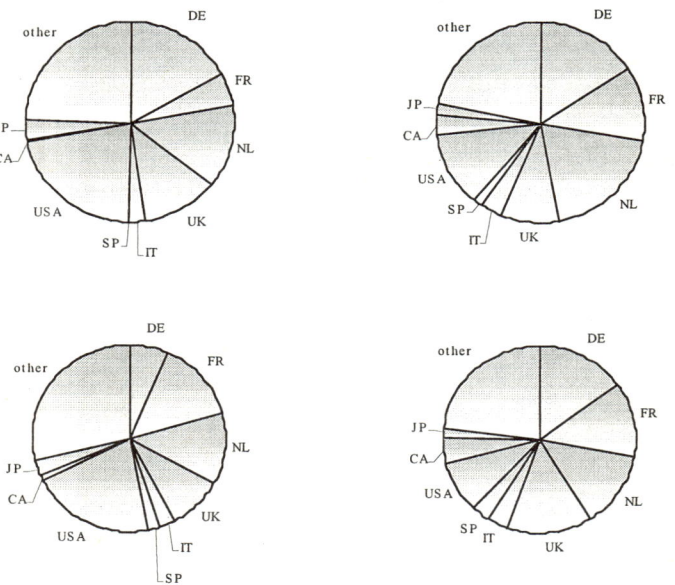

Sources: Banque Nationale de Belgique, own calculations.

Like the net inward FDI in Belgium, net outward FDI from Belgium also dramatically increased from about 17 billion BEF in 1985 to more than 300 billion BEF in 1992. Figure 6.8 shows that the sharp decrease from 1992 to 1994 is due to very high receipts from foreign subsidiaries. From the early 1980s to the early 1990s, the share of outward FDI directed to European countries jumped from 55% to 75%, Germany, the UK, the Netherlands, and France being the main beneficiaries.

Figure 6.8:   Outward foreign direct investments (receipts, payments, and net FDI)

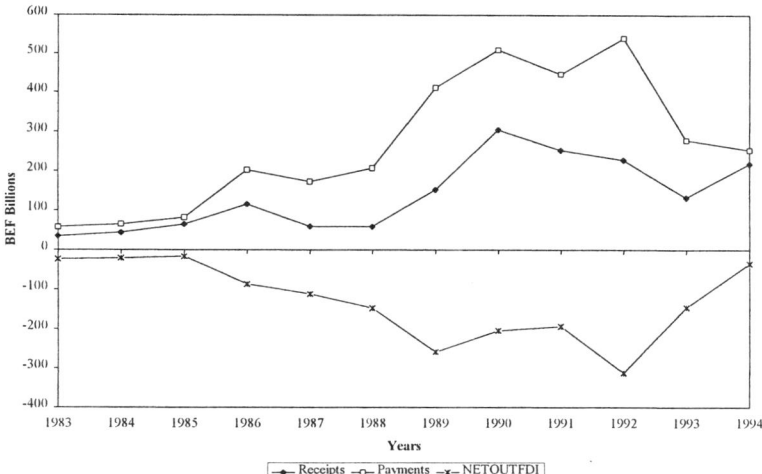

Source: Banque Nationale de Belgique.

The flow in the direction of the USA economy has diminished: it accounted for only 9% of the Belgian outward FDI in the 1990s, down from a share of 21% in the early 1980s. The figures show that the potential sourcing of foreign technology is more likely to come from European technological leaders than from the USA in the near future.

In short, assessing the net effect of FDI is a difficult task. Many direct and indirect effects, which are not easily measurable, have to be taken into account. Nevertheless, policies might be implemented to maximise the positive externalities of FDI and minimise the negative ones. Insofar as the focus is on technological externalities, government should strengthen the public infrastructure for training and research activities to improve the adaptive capabilities of local firms to inflows of technology. In a similar vein, R&D subsidies could be made conditional on collaboration with foreign high-tech firms. Outward FDI should also be stimulated, especially if technology sourcing is part of its strategy. In this respect, fostering educational exchanges between Belgium and the main scientific poles seems to be an essential policy element.

6.6.   Participation in European networks

The significant increase of cross-border collaboration over the last two decades is one of the most prominent components of the technological globalisation process. Technological complementarity and reduction of the innovation time-span are two main motives often put forward to account for the formation of international joint ventures in core technologies (Hagedoorn and Schakenraad, 1990; Hagedoorn, 1990, 1995). In order to appreciate to what extent Belgian organisations are engaged in world-wide research networking and transfer, three types of information are examined: (i) the pre-competitive collaboration, (ii) near-market co-operation, both supported by European and national public authorities, and (iii) strategic alliances formed on a private basis.

Although the European collaborative programmes may not have improved competitiveness in a direct way, it is recognised that they have stimulated the acquisition of new competencies and sharpened research skills. The Belgian participation to European R&D programmes is very high as can be seen in Table 6.4. Nevertheless, the per-capita participation index, which gives a measure of the degree of participation independently of the technological base, as well as the per-researcher participation index, which gives a measure of the degree of participation by including the technological base, show that other small countries perform better than Belgium. In fact, these indexes show that small countries are, in relative terms, the main beneficiaries of the research networks created under the impulse of the EU technology policy. In absolute terms, however, the five largest member states account for two thirds of the participation. Another important observation is that collaboration is largely influenced by geographic and/or cultural proximity (Capron and Cincera, 1999). In the case of Belgium, it appears that the weight of collaboration with the neighbouring countries is particularly important.

Further information on the evolution of Belgian participation in Framework Programmes is provided in Table 6.5. Three types of indexes are considered – the participation, distribution, and collaborative links indexes– and the focus is placed on the R&D projects in the Fourth Framework Programme (FWP). The Belgian indexes of partnership as well as collaborative links exhibit downward trends. This *a priori* negative observation is explained by the partnerships as well as the collaboration that become more diversified over time as a consequence of both the increasing participation of third countries and the enlargement of the EU.

All things otherwise being equal, the distribution index shows the extent to which the distribution of participation among the different categories of actors is similar to the one observed at the European level. With a value of 33% higher than the European average, the higher education sector appears to play a prominent role in the explanation of both the high indexes of participation and collaborative links. Inversely, the one obtained for large enterprises is 22% below the European average. In fact, the combination of the three indexes allows one to appreciate the real position of the different Belgian categories of actors within the European networks. Indeed, the participation index of Belgium as measured by the number of participations per capita relative to the European average shows that Belgian participation is 58% above the European average. Consequently, although the distribution index for the large enterprises is below the European average and weaker compared to other types of organisations, we cannot conclude that their degree of participation is below par. Indeed, the combination of both the participation and the distribution indexes produces the participation index of large enterprises in

European Programmes. In the 4th Framework Programme, their index of participation is 123, considerably above the European average. However, universities are
the most committed participants in networking with an index of 210 for the same
programme.

Table 6.4:   **Participation and collaborative links indexes of countries
participating in shared-cost research under the EU
Framework Programmes**[a]

Third Framework Programme			Fourth Framework Programme[b]					
Per capita participation index		Per researcher participation index		Per capita participation index		Per researcher participation index		Mutual collab. spatial special. index
DK	251	GR	450	FI	222	GR	444	LU	317
IR	234	IR	219	DK	208	IR	189	NL	123
NL	171	PO	200	IR	201	PO	171	FR	112
BE	**170**	DK	183	SW	195	LU	164	PO	105
GR	157	NL	172	NL	159	NL	160	DE	103
UK	110	**BE**	**166**	**BE**	**158**	**BE**	**154**	**BE**	**99**
PO	106	IT	109	GR	155	DK	151	SP	99
FR	104	SP	102	LU	151	FI	149	UK	95
SW	102	UK	96	UK	94	SW	131	FI	92
DE	99	FR	88	FR	94	AU	127	IR	91
LU	78	LU	85	DE	92	SP	123	IT	90
FI	75	DE	69	AU	91	IT	114	AU	87
IT	65	SW	68	PO	90	UK	82	GR	86
SP	55	FI	50	IT	68	FR	80	DK	80
AU	29	AU	40	SP	67	DE	64	SW	76

Notes: a) See the appendix for the definition of the indexes;
              b) Data about the 4th FP are limited to the period 1994-1996.
Sources: Second European Report on S&T Indicators; own calculations.

The SMEs are characterised by a high index value for their participation to the
FP (169). The category of actors least committed in the FPs seems to be the research organisations, the index value of which is 'only' 104. This can be due to
historical factors such as the decision of the Belgian government to sustain 'collective research centres'.

Table 6.5:   Belgian participation to European R&D programmes

	Financing			Participations		
Programmes	Second	Third	Fourth	Second	Third	Fourth
Collaborative links				-	174	149
Participation				193	170	158
Distribution						
- Large Enterprises	49	59	63	59	64	78
- SMEs	88	107	93	99	117	107
- Research Centres	137	86	75	84	76	66
- Higher Education	183	157	151	146	132	133
- Others	117	194	153	133	183	122

Note: See the appendix for formal definitions.
Sources: European Commission (1994, 1997a), own calculations.

At the regional level, the French-speaking universities appear to be more integrated into the European networks than their Flemish counterparts. The Flemish firms and research centres, however, have more propensity to collaborate at the European level than their Walloon counterparts (Capron, 1998, Capron and Cincera, 1999).

Table 6.6:   EUREKA projects up to 1996

	Projects		Participations		Organisations		Budget		Indexes		
	#	%	#	%	SME	RTOs & HEIs	total budget	% country	# of proj.	# of part.	budget
DE	452	14.4	921	16.1	264	288	14739	25.8	66	73	94
UK	307	9.8	619	10.8	195	148	8764	7.9	62	69	24
FR	431	13.7	981	17.2	350	248	17446	32.9	87	109	197
IT	211	6.7	405	7.1	78	131	14928	18.1	44	46	95
SP	287	9.1	448	7.8	179	106	8599	8.5	87	75	37
NL	349	11.1	524	9.2	228	91	13469	15.5	266	219	269
GR	39	1.2	54	0.9	13	24	541	5.0	44	34	5
BE	**166**	**5.3**	**233**	**4.1**	**87**	**61**	**12195**	**5.4**	**194**	**150**	**130**
PT	131	4.2	208	3.6	76	58	869	13.1	158	138	23
SE	230	7.3	288	5.0	110	61	9002	2.6	307	212	53
AT	164	5.2	237	4.1	86	67	8825	2.6	242	192	57
DK	159	5.1	198	3.5	73	45	5855	4.8	359	245	107
FI	147	4.7	254	4.4	85	47	10259	4.8	341	323	192
IE	34	1.1	333	5.8	13	9	4690	1.1	110	591	28
LU	11	0.4	14	0.2	4	0	800	1.6	308	215	62

Sources: EUREKA database (1998), own calculations.

In summary, despite a slight reduction of both the participation and collaborative links indexes from the 2nd FP to the 4th one, the integration of the different categories of organisations into the European R&D networks remains very high. The high value of both the collaborative links and participation indexes gives evidence of the active Belgian role in European networking. It appears that the Belgian S&T system is well integrated into the European S&T network. Its position could certainly be improved given that its score remains relatively inferior to those observed in some other highly industrialised countries. A question remains with respect to the extent that this phenomenon at the pre-competitive level is translated into an equally favourable position in near-market research and strategic alliances.

EUREKA's focus on near-market research aims at complementing the pre-competitive EU programmes. Although Belgium is involved in 12.6% of the total number of projects, the Belgian teams represent only 4.1% of the participating EU organisations, and its financial contribution is limited to 3.6% of the total EU funds. In order to appreciate the importance of the Belgian participation in comparison with that of other European countries, some indexes are reported in Table 6.6. All the Belgian indexes are above the European average.

Nevertheless, two other small countries are more active in European networks but with a financial participation generally less than that of Belgium: the Netherlands and Finland. Among the large countries, France and, at the second level, Germany are the two large countries most active in the European networks. Both countries participate in more than 50% of the funds. The UK appears to be the country that is the least engaged in European networks. When we look at the Belgian participation in EUREKA projects, both Flemish universities and enterprises are more involved in collaboration than the French-speaking ones: around 70% versus 30% (Capron, 1998, Capron and Cincera, 1999). These observations seem to indicate that the Walloon research system is less business-oriented than the Flemish system. Despite the high level of its university research, the Walloon Region has many difficulties in valorising its R&D potential, for example, by promoting near-market research. Consequently, we can conclude that there is an important spatial mismatch in the Belgian NIS.

The globalisation of markets and the acceleration of technological change are both elements that account for the present trend towards the formation of strategic partnerships. Besides the Framework Programmes and the EUREKA projects, enterprises decide to enter into alliances on a private basis in order to expand their market, to reduce risk, and to share technological competencies.

If we consider the data published in the *Second European Report on S&T Indicators* (European Commission, 1997a) on technological co-operation between enterprises in the world, the very high degree of internationalisation of the Belgian R&D system as exemplified by its participation to European R&D programmes needs to be substantially qualified. Of a total of about 5000 international technology alliances between EU members and the USA and Japan, only 57 involve Belgian enterprises. If we consider only strategic alliances with at least one EU partner, as shown in Table 6.7, the participation indexes are 106 for the per-capita index and 103 for the per-researcher index. The scores obtained by other small countries like the Netherlands, Sweden, and Ireland suggest that Belgium could improve its performance.[5] Nevertheless, the high degree of multinationalisation of

---

[5] The Belgian positioning in the European average is largely dependent on the very low scores obtained by technological laggards. When the indexes are calculated excluding the four countries drawing the lower scores, the new indexes obtained for Belgium are 90 for the per-capita index and 97 for the per-researcher one.

the country could explain this very mediocre position. Indeed, in a country whose economic structure is largely dominated by foreign companies, participation in international strategic alliances could be hampered by the worldwide strategies of these companies.

Table 6.7:   **International technology alliances of**
             EU countries (1984-1995)[a]

Distribution (%)		Per capita partici-pation index[b]		Per researcher participation index[b]	
UK	28.2	SW	193	NL	192
DE	23.2	NL	191	UK	148
FR	17.7	UK	169	SW	129
NL	8.4	DE	134	IR	117
IT	7.5	IR	125	**BE**	**103**
SW	4.9	FR	107	DE	93
BE	**3.0**	**BE**	**106**	FR	91
ES	2.2	FI	103	IT	77
FI	1.5	DK	86	FI	69
IR	1.3	IT	46	DK	62
DK	1.3	ES	20	ES	37
PO	0.4	PO	15	PO	29
GR	0.3	GR	9	GR	26
LU	-	LU	0	LU	0

Notes: a) The alliances taken into account refer to the major trading
           blocs: the EU, the USA, and Japan;
           b) cf. the appendix for definitions.
Sources: European Commission (1997a), own calculations.

These results show that its position as a partner in strategic alliances is still relatively weak even though Belgium has developed its European collaboration considerably thanks to the EU programmes and the EUREKA initiative. In the present era of globalisation of markets, the Belgian public authorities should do more to promote more strategic partnerships of Belgian firms at the world level. Thus far, its good performance in pre-competitive research as well as in near-market research does not seem to have stimulated its participation in strategic alliances very much. In the framework of a benchmarking approach, Belgium should almost double the number of its participations in order to be, in relative terms, at the top of the ranking.

Because of the importance of the phenomenon of R&D co-operation in the technological globalisation process and the position of Belgium in this respect, the next chapter is completely devoted to this subject.

6.7. Conclusion

International trade, inward and outward FDI flows, R&D collaboration, and technology payments are four important channels that may foster the international diffusion of technology. Trade flows and FDI are however not *automatically* associated with international R&D spillovers. Therefore, the analysis of their evolution constitutes only an indicator of the *potential* technology transfers that may occur between countries.

The most salient observations of the present chapter can be summarised as follows:

- The analysis of all four indicators has shown that Belgium relies substantially on research activities from abroad and, other things being equal given its size, contributes substantially to foreign technology bases. However, the balance seems to tilt towards greater dependence from abroad than towards contribution to foreign technology bases.
- Technology payments, or the extent to which Belgium takes advantage of foreign technology, have increased during the 1980s and have remained at that level. During the entire period, the main destination of technology payments was the USA. Next in order of importance come four neighbouring countries: the UK, the Netherlands, Germany, and France, which received about half of the technology payments to foreign countries.
- Technology receipts and inward and outward foreign direct investment have also substantially risen in the late 1980s, and their geographical distribution is comparable to that of the technology payments. From the early 1980s to the early 1990s, the most noticeable change in their geographical distribution was the strong reduction of the USA share to the advantage of neighbouring countries.
- The geographical distribution of the various channels of technology diffusion shows that technology transfers are facilitated by geographical proximity, technological endowments, and the size of the countries from which the technology originates.
- The analysis of its trade-specialisation pattern shows that Belgium is specialised in declining commodity classes. In a dynamic sense, however, companies are generally moving into classes with increasing technology intensity. With regard specifically to high-level technology commodities, the position of Belgian firms is growing stronger. The country, however, remains specialised largely in medium- and low-tech industries.
- The position of Belgium with respect to the European average regarding technology-based strategic alliances shows that its very good performance in terms of collaboration in pre-competitive and near-market research (as shown by its participation in European programmes and EUREKA projects) does not guarantee that Belgium has enough advantages to enable it to integrate efficiently into the globalisation process.

Appendix: Definition of indexes

Per capita participation (or project or budget) index:	$100*(P_i/pop_i)/(P_E/pop_E)$
Per researcher participation index:	$100*(P_i/res_i)/(P_E/res_E)$
Distribution index:	$100*(P_{ij}/P_i)/(P_{Ej}/P_{Ei})$
Per capita collaborative-link indexes:	$100*(L_i/pop_i)/(L_E/pop_E)$
Mutual collaboration spatial specialisation index:	$100*(L_{il}/L_i)/(L_{1l}/L_E)$,

where: P_i = number of participations of country i *(alternatively projects or budget)*;

Pop_i = population of country i;

Res_i = number of researchers of country i;

P_{ij} = number of participations of the category of actors j in the country i

L_i = number of collaborative links of country i;

L_{il} = number of collaborative links between the country i and the country l;

E = subscript for Europe.

Chapter 7.   The Network of Joint Research Projects and Alliances

Michel Dumont and Wim Meeusen

7.1.   Introduction

In this chapter, we will present results of a graph-theoretical analysis of the Belgian network of research co-operation and research agreements as it is operationalised in the projects falling under the general heading of the R&D Framework programmes of the EU, the projects of the EUREKA initiative, and finally the private agreements and other forms of co-operation registered in the MERIT/CATI database.

There are two reasons to embark on a study of joint R&D projects as an approach to the national innovation system. The first is of a purely practical nature. Data on joint R&D projects and agreements are readily available and can be quantified in a straightforward way in a network context. The second reason is a fundamental one. Joint research projects often give access to funds, equipment, and new markets, and, most of all, nearly always to new information. They can be seen as one of the most powerful ways of disseminating knowledge and know-how within a NIS. But network analysis applied to technological systems is still, despite the burgeoning literature, poorly developed. Therefore, a word of caution is appropriate at this stage, for the ambition of the present analysis is modest. We will determine 'who co-operates with whom' and look at a number of features of this co-operation, but we will not deal with the results of joint R&D projects.

In Section 7.2, we characterise the graph in general terms and describe in some detail the data that are being used. We also present a summary of a number of results obtained so far. In Section 7.3, we address the clustering issue. In Section 7.4, we propose a new approach to compute intra- and intersectoral knowledge flows. In Section 7.5, we present some regional aspects of R&D collaboration. In Section 7.6, we analyse the participation of Belgian organisations in international R&D co-operation. In Section 7.7, we try to establish the extent to which specialisation in R&D collaboration matches the specialisation pattern in high-tech trade. We conclude in Section 7.8. A more detailed analysis of Belgian participation in international R&D co-operation can be found in Meeusen and Dumont (1997a,b) and an analysis of co-operation from a regional viewpoint with incorporation of data on Flemish R&D projects is given in Meeusen and Dumont (1998) and Dumont and Meeusen (1999a).

7.2. The mapping of the network of joint R&D projects between firms, research institutions and universities

7.2.1. The model and the data

The observations are defined on the level of microeconomic agents: companies, research institutions, and universities, i.e., the *nodal* points of the graph. The network criterion is whether two actors are partners in the same research project or alliance, thereby creating a *line* in the graph, or not. The obtained graph can be specified as being valued (individual lines may be weighted) and being a *multigraph* (two entities can be linked by several lines with different weights). The graph consisting of nodes and lines together with their corresponding information is defined as a *network*. We distinguish between three different types of projects and agreements:

a) R&D projects in one of a selected list of EU RTD Framework programmes (source: the CORDIS database of the European Commission (EC));[1]

b) EUREKA projects (source: the EUREKA on-line database);

c) Private technological co-operative agreements (source: the Belgian part of MERIT-CATI database on strategic agreements).

So as not to overburden the graph and avoid crossing computational thresholds, we discarded the project lines between the foreign partners in the project or agreement. The actors in the point set of the graph are identified by an 8-character acronym. The first character of the acronym is a country code. The lines of the graph (in the line set) are identified by the 'head-tail' sequence of the corresponding acronyms. In addition to the basic point and line data, the values of a number of variables are attached to the points and lines. A more detailed description of the model and the data that are used is given in Meeusen and Dumont (1997a,b).

7.2.2. Description of the complete graph

7.2.2.1. General features

The complete graph contains 3753 nodes and 14918 lines.[2] Of these lines, 3078 are directed (i.e., connect a main contractor with a partner). These figures actually give an inflated picture of the density[3] of the graph, since a relatively large num-

---

[1] The selected projects must have at least one Belgian private firm as one of the partners.

[2] The software used is GRADAP v. 2.10, a social network analysis programme developed at the University of Groningen (Sprenger and Stokman, 1989).

[3] The density of a graph is defined as the actual number of lines in proportion to the maximum number possible ($n(n-1)/2$).

ber of nodes are connected through multiple lines. After having combined all the multiple lines between two points into one aggregated line, 10634 single lines remained, which means that the density of the combined graph is 0.0015. Of the 3753 actors, 776 are Belgian, 626 of which are private companies (private research institutes and consulting firms not included). There are 553 French and German actors and 451 British, 290 Italian, 229 Spanish, and 227 Dutch actors.

In Table 7.1, the Belgian companies are classified by size (number of employees and value added). It can be seen that a relatively large number of participating companies are SMEs (the share of SMEs in the total number of Belgian participants was above the EU15 average, both in the Third and the Fourth FWP (European Commission, 1997a, p.551; see also Chapter 6, Section 6.6). However, as will be shown later on, most of these SMEs only participate occasionally and large firms co-operate more frequently.

Table 7.1:   Classification of Belgian companies according to
size (number of employees and ranking by
value added)

	#	%
Number of employees (n)		
n > 5000	14	2
5000 > n > 1000	33	5
1000 > n > 500	26	4
500 > n > 250	35	6
250 > n > 100	50	8
100 > n > 50	43	7
50 > n	425	68
National ranking by value added		
TOP 100	34	5
TOP 500	74	12
TOP 1000	105	17
TOP 5000	178	28
TOP 10000	212	34
TOP 30000	271	43
Not ranked in TOP 30000	355	57

Source: Trends Top 30000.

In Table A.7.2, the Belgian co-operating companies are classified by NACE sector,[4] and in Table A.7.3 the share of NACE sectors in the graph is compared with the share of the corresponding sectors in the Belgian economy and in the repertory of 'all' Belgian R&D active firms.[5] High-tech and medium high-tech sectors generally have relatively higher shares of companies represented in the graph as compared to the economy as a whole, although some particular medium low- and low-tech sectors also have relatively high shares (i.e., the low-tech sector 27: *Metallurgy*). A different pattern emerges when the number of companies in a NACE sector present in the graph are compared to the share of that sector in the so-called 'repertory'. Medium-high and high-tech companies are more represented in the repertory than in the graph, while some medium low- and low-tech companies and two specific service sectors (NACE 72 and 73) are better represented in the graph than in the repertory. The latter result might indicate that R&D surveys underestimate the innovativeness or at least do not sufficiently account for the participation in co-operative R&D projects of low-tech and service sectors. It also supports the findings of Kleinknecht and Reijnen that R&D co-operation is not an exclusive phenomenon of 'R&D intensive' companies (Kleinknecht and Reijnen, 1992).

Table 7.2 shows the Relative Specialisation Index (RSI) of Belgian organisations for participation in EU and EUREKA projects and in technological agreements. For EU projects the RSI was computed using the number of prime contractors instead of overall participation, both in projects that are completed and in projects that are still in progress (1997).

For the projects that are still in progress, Belgian actors are apparently relatively specialised in telecommunications, medical technology, and IT. The RSI increased for these disciplines. When the indexes for completed and ongoing projects are compared, Belgian actors are shown to be relatively specialised in completed EU projects related to biotechnology, but the RSI fell below unity for the projects that are still in progress. Belgium seems relatively unspecialised in environmental technology, aerospace technology, and transports. Moreover, with the exception of the last technological discipline, the RSI further decreased. The distribution of the lines over the points is very skew: a small group of actors accounts for a large number of lines, and there is therefore a large group of actors with low involvement (cf. Steurs and Cortese, 1993; Cortese, Steurs and Kesteloot, 1990; Garcia-Fontes and Geuna, 1995). Gambardella and Garcia-Fontes (1994) interpret this as a result of the so-called 'Matthew effect' through which the probability of an organisation to receive subsidies depends largely on having benefited from subsidies in an earlier phase.

---

[4] The sector classification used is the so-called NACE-BEL one, which is the Belgian version of NACE Rev.1.

[5] This repertory is compiled by the federal Office for Scientific, Technical and Cultural Affairs (OSTC) based on a number of bi-annual R&D surveys, and is an attempt to map all Belgian companies that are active in the field of R&D.

Table 7.2:   **Relative Specialisation Index of Belgian participants in EU and EUREKA projects and in technological agreements (situation as of 1997)**

	RSI			
	PR(C)	PR(E)	EUREKA	CATI
Aerospace Technology	0.97	0.88	-	1.10
Information Technology	0.96	1.13	1.36	0.47
Telecommunications	0.93	1.26	0.64	1.64
Materials Technology	0.97	0.98	1.19	0.76
Biotechnology	1.28	0.78	0.94	1.31
Energy	0.90	1.01	0.54	-
Environmental Technology	0.95	0.88	0.88	-
Medical Technology	1.58	1.19	-	0.00
Transport	0.69	0.92	1.01	-
Robotics	-	-	0.82	0.27
Laser	-	-	1.82	-
Chemicals	-	-	-	3.28

Notes: RSI = $(NP_{i,Bel}/ NP_{Bel}) / (NP_i / NP)$ ($NP_{i,Bel}$ is the number of projects or agreements in the ith technological discipline with a Belgian organisation as prime contractor, NP_i and NP_{Bel} are partial totals, and NP is the overall total of projects (resp. agreements));
PR(C): Prime contractors in completed EU projects (1997);
PR(E): Prime contractors in ongoing EU projects (1997).

Sources: Own calculations based on EC (1997b), Eureka (1998), and Hagedoorn and Narula (1996).

7.2.2.2. Component analysis

We define a component C of a graph as a maximally connected subgraph, i.e., every node of C is connected to at least one other node of C and no node outside C is connected to any node of C. There are 45 components in the complete graph. The largest component contains 3626 actors and 10528 lines. At multiplicity '4' there are 10 components left with the largest component containing 200 actors and 470 combined lines. The large CORDIS subgraph (3247 actors) has 'only' 16 components and is denser (0.0018 versus 0.0006) than the smaller EUREKA subgraph, which has 42 components and 600 nodes. The CATI subgraph has 29 components and a density of 0.0194.

The choice of multiplicity '4' is a pragmatic one. It appears to be the lowest level at which components of reasonable size can be detected (at lower levels, there is one very large component with numerous very small ones). Furthermore, the analysis at sufficiently high multiplicity levels avoids the need to take into account occasional, 'once-only', links that do not involve any significant form of collaboration and are very often only a statistical by-product of collaboration between more central actors in larger projects.

7.2.2.3. Centrality indicators

Freeman (1979) distinguishes between three types of point-centrality indicators based on degree, closeness, and 'betweenness', respectively. Degree centrality is the most straightforward of the three. A node is considered to be more central than another if more nodes are adjacent to it. The actors with the highest unweighted degree centrality in the complete graph and the main subgraphs are given in Meeusen and Dumont (1997a,b).

An unweighted degree centrality does not take into account the multiplicity of the lines between nodes or the different weights each line may carry. We might consider assessing projects according to their financial value, give more weight to lines backed by a personal tie and to lines in programmes that are 'nearer to the market', discriminate between directed and undirected lines, or take the number of partners into account.

The formula for this weighted degree centrality measure takes the following form:

$$C_i^W = \sum_{\substack{j=1 \\ j \neq i}}^{n} \sum_k w_{ij}^k$$

where w_{ij}^k is the weight of the kth line running between i and j .

In Table 7.3, we recompute the degree centrality in the set of the 200 most central actors and report the results for the 35 most central ones in the new definition: we actually account for multiple lines while combining the last two higher mentioned criteria, giving the undirected lines in a project the weight $1/NP$, where NP is the number of partners in the project, and the directed lines a double weight of $2/NP$. In this way we want to stress – in a way that is unavoidably somewhat arbitrary – that projects with a large number of partners suggest less 'intimacy' between them. The acronyms of the actors in Table 7.3 are given in Table A.7.1.

Table 7.3:   The 35 actors with the highest weighted degree-centrality

BIMEC	51.52	GSIEMENS	11.44	BSCK	8.03	BSOLVAY	5.07	BKARMAN	3.92
BALCATEL	28.16	FTHOMSON	10.57	FCNRS	7.41	BEURDEV	4.82	UBT	3.92
BKUL	19.41	BWTCM	10.37	BLMSINT	7.11	FRANTEL	4.52	BEEIG	3.69
BUG	17.48	FALCATEL	9.69	BVITO	6.11	BBARCO	4.47	BSOCBIO	3.60
BMIETEC	14.56	BUNIVL	9.45	GFRAUN	5.81	BPGS	4.35	GALCATEL	3.51
NPHILIPS	13.03	BVUB	8.98	FMATRA	5.71	BWTCB	4.09	VTT	3.50
BUCL	11.65	BBELGACO	8.11	FCEA	5.24	BULB	4.05	ICSELT	3.40

7.2.2.4.   The relation between the position in the R&D-network and firm characteristics

In this section we report on some relations between the participation in R&D co-operation projects and alliances and the position in the R&D network as measured by the unweighted centrality of each firm and a number of firm characteristics (share of new products in turnover, number of employees, and return on equity (ROE).

a) Innovativeness
We linked the data on R&D co-operation to the results of the 1996 Belgian R&D survey. In this survey, firms were asked to report the share of their 1995 turnover that was realised from products or services that had not been on the market for more than 2 years. Possible answers were 'less than 10%', 'between 10% and 30%', and 'more than 30%'. The χ^2 test on a simple cross-tabulation revealed that responding firms that participate in international R&D projects or agreements were not significantly more innovative than those that did not participate in any such project or agreement. On the other hand, firms participating in projects financed by the Flemish Region were more innovative than respondents that did not (see Meeusen and Dumont, 1998). Comparable results for the other two regions are not available.

b) Size
The plot of the centrality of firms against their size (number of employees) reveals a very scattered pattern with no clear-cut linear or increasing functional relationship. The same holds true on the sectoral level (2-digit NACE). In Table 7.4, we present the average centrality for six size-classes.

The higher the number of employees, the higher the average centrality. The size classes are not normally distributed, and the variances differ considerably. Thus, the necessary conditions for a variance analysis are not met. We performed the non-parametrical Kruskal-Wallis test to compare the 6 classes, the mean ranks of which are given in Table 7.4. The Kruskal-Wallis statistic reveals that the 6 size-classes differ significantly (0.001) from one another with regard to centrality. However, the Kruskal-Wallis test is not a very powerful one, and the significance obtained might as well relate to significant differences in distribution as to differences in population location.

In Table 7.5, we present the average centrality of the 15 main 2-digit NACE sectors in the graph. Once again, the Kruskal-Wallis test is significant (0.002). Not surprisingly, the main sectors are those that are related to the main technological disciplines in the EU Framework programmes and EUREKA, especially *IT* and *telecommunications*.

c) Return on equity
Finally, there is no clear relationship between centrality and ROE for all firms combined, or on the sectoral level.

Table 7.4:   Average degree-centrality in size classes (number of employees in 1995; standard deviations between parentheses)

Number of employees (n)	Centrality	Mean rank (Kruskal-Wallis)
n > 5000	61.46 (72.52)	292.73
1000 < n ≤ 5000	18.18 (30.92)	208.88
500 < n ≤ 1000	14.59 (23.14)	197.04
250 < n ≤ 500	10.26 (9.92)	173.84
50 < n ≤ 250	9.99 (11.21)	169.65
n ≤ 50	9.99 (11.05)	171.37

Table 7.5:   Average centrality in the 15 main NACE sectors (standard deviations between parentheses)

NACE rev. 1		Centrality	Mean rank (Kruskal-Wallis)
32	Electrical equipment	53.43 (71.13)	200.07
64	Telecommunications	42.40 (66.55)	189.20
73	R&D	22.20 (23.29)	159.90
72	Informatics	15.65 (14.85)	156.96
27	Metallurgy	14.88 (20.38)	148.84
24	Chemicals	11.93 (27.83)	106.22
15	Food and beverage	11.82 (10.86)	143.55
28	Metal products	10.93 (9.07)	138.73
74	Other services	10.71 (9.97)	132.86
17	Textiles	9.48 (6.79)	130.37
29	Non-electrical machines	8.18 (9.44)	100.35
31	Electrical machines	7.08 (6.64)	101.50
25	Rubber and plastics	6.00 (5.37)	93.06
33	Instrum. and office mach.	5.80 (3.03)	101.10
26	Stone, clay and glass	5.00 (4.06)	83.95

7.2.2.5. Coincidence of different types of lines

In the complete graph, 13151 of the 14918 project lines are related to RTD Framework programmes financed by the EU. These projects are labelled pre-competitive as they are often closer to basic research than to the development, production, or marketing of new products or to the introduction of new processes. This is reflected in the large degree of participation of research institutes and institutions of higher education in the EU Framework programmes (61.3% in the 3rd Framework, 54.4% in the 4th Framework (European Commission, 1997a, p. 520)). With respect to innovation, the 'near-market' EUREKA projects and the technological agreements contained in the MERIT-CATI database provide in this respect information that is more relevant to our present purpose, albeit that they only account for 1156 and 104, respectively, of the 14918 project lines.

With regard to the pre-competitive RTD lines, it is interesting to analyse the extent to which they coincide in the global graph with EUREKA and CATI lines and how often they precede these lines in time, particularly because of the relatively recent nature of the phenomenon of joint European R&D projects.[6] The linear causal model of innovation would lead us to expect that near-market co-operation between firms would follow an earlier phase where this co-operation follows the looser and more informal channels of pre-competitive research, and not the other way round. However, from the evaluation of EUREKA cited in European Commission (1994), we learn that 'The original policy conception of a "pipeline model", whereby pre-competitive EC projects are followed by nearer-market EUREKA projects has not materialised to date. Rather there has emerged a complex picture in which involvement in EC programmes could either precede or follow a EUREKA project.' Peterson comes to similar conclusions about the nature of the relation between EUREKA and the EU's RTD programmes on the basis of two behavioural surveys of EUREKA participants (Peterson, 1993). In Dumont and Meeusen (1999b), the regression results for the number of links generated by the EU RTD projects, EUREKA projects, and private alliances in telecommunications also seem to suggest that a systemic approach to the effect of subsidised pre-competitive R&D on near-market R&D and private alliances is more appropriate than an approach following the traditional model of a linear causal process starting with basic research and finally resulting in the development of new products.

In our graph, only 36 Belgian firms (out of a total of 626) appear in both at least one RTD project and at least one EUREKA project, and there is a coincidence of 256 EUREKA and CORDIS lines. The RTD projects in information technology and telecommunications (ESPRIT, ACTS, RACE, TELEMATICS) coincide by far the most with EUREKA in these disciplines with 234 lines, the other technological disciplines accounting for only 22 coinciding lines. This is not all too surprising, given the importance of information technology and telecommunications both in the EU Framework programmes and EUREKA. Nevertheless, there seems to be a disproportional coincidence between RTD and EUREKA lines in these disciplines. Of the 256 CORDIS lines 149 (58.2%) precede EUREKA lines.[7] Moreover, involvement in some specific RTD programmes seems even

---

[6] A sequence analysis loses meaning when the period in which joint projects have been set up grows longer. The reason is a 'demographic' one: R&D initiatives in a mature stage, set up between two partners, will in that case more often co-exist with new initiatives between the same partners as time proceeds.

[7] The observed difference between 149 lines where RTD Framework projects precede EUREKA projects and 107 where the opposite is true or RTD and EUREKA projects started in the same year, is statistically significant (compared to a 50-50 proportion) at a level of 99%.

more often to precede involvement in EUREKA projects (e.g. 74 of 88 ESPRIT lines precede EUREKA lines). Thus, in our graph the 'pipeline model' seems to be materialised to a certain extent, especially for the projects in *IT* and *telecommunications*.

Meeusen and Dumont (1997a,b) also analysed the coincidence of project lines with personal lines. Most of the actors in the 'strong line' set[8] are actors who are involved in a good number of joint projects. The results of the 'strong line' analysis do not support the idea that personal influence becomes more important as R&D co-operation moves closer to direct market applicability. On the other hand, we find it difficult to believe that personal influence would be more often instrumental in obtaining 'easy' government subsidies for more or less noncommittal research than in making strategic choices with respect to the development of new products and the entry on new markets. A possible explanation for the low number of strong lines in near-market contexts might be that non-equity agreements seem to become more important than equity agreements, especially in high-technology industries (Duysters, 1996; Hagedoorn and Narula, 1996), and that these kinds of agreements are less likely to result in 'interlocking directorates' than in equity agreements (see also Meeusen and Cuyvers, 1985).

7.3.   Clusters in the National Innovation System

7.3.1.   Concepts and methodologies of cluster approaches

In studies dealing with innovation clusters and cluster-based policies, a wide variety of cluster definitions and concepts is used. A clear distinction must be made between cluster approaches using traditional cluster analysis techniques to detect objects that are similar or proximate with respect to some relevant characteristic(s) (i.e., cluster analysis in the traditional, statistical, sense) and those approaches that focus on relationships between actors or groups of actors (firms, sectors, branches) in networks. Another distinction concerns the level of aggregation used in the analysis.[9] Meeusen and Dumont (1997a) give a more detailed analysis and theoretical underpinning of the graph-theoretical cluster approach used to detect clusters in the 'Belgian R&D' network.

---

[8] A 'strong line' is defined as a project line that coincides with a 'personal' line created by an interlocking directorate.

[9] The cluster concept is also sometimes used in an a-prioristic, non-analytical, context. An example is the concept used by the Flemish regional government, which considers (and in a number of cases, finances) clusters as formal organisations of firms in a particular industrial sector or active in the same field, formed on a voluntary basis, that perform co-ordination and advisory tasks with respect to product and process innovation on behalf of its members (see Debackere and Vermeulen, 1997, who place this cluster concept in a more general perspective).

7.3.2.   Cliques and micro-clusters of R&D co-operation

In what follows we specialise the rather loosely defined concept of 'cluster' to the graph-theoretical concept of 'clique'. n-cliques can be defined as subgraphs of which all points are linked with one another through a path with maximum length equal to *n* in such a way that no point outside the subgraph has the same quality.

The detection of n-cliques poses some problems for the complete graph due to the size of the graph and the programme because of limitations of central memory. In order to reduce computational complexity, the multiplicity of the lines was taken into account. For the complete graph 1-cliques could be detected from a multiplicity level of 8 onwards. The subgraph at multiplicity level 8 (containing all actors inter-linked by at least 8 lines) has four components. The largest contains 56 actors and 108 multiple lines. At the multiplicity level of 12, two components remain. The largest contains 35 actors and 53 multiple lines. At the multiplicity level 8 there are 20 1-cliques. 3 of which contain 4 actors and 17 contain 3 actors. Although the result of a straightforward detection procedure for the complete graph, i.e., without having introduced any bias or correction in the methodology as to specific technological disciplines, the 20 cliques without exception are generated by RTD projects related to *IT* or *Telecommunications* and are themselves linked to one another to a high degree.

The dominance of links related to *IT* and *Telecommunications* clearly reflects the dominance of these disciplines in the EU Framework programmes, and to a lesser extent in EUREKA and MERIT-CATI, and the relative specialisation of Belgian actors.

With regard to the distinction between R&D and innovation, it is worthwhile to note that the dominance of *IT* is less pronounced in near-market projects (EUREKA) and in technological alliances (CATI) than in pre-competitive EU projects, and that the number of strategic IT alliances in which Belgian partners are involved is low, both absolutely and relatively, compared to other countries (see also Hagedoorn and Narula (1996)).

The European Commission calls the poor link between scientific, technological, and economic performance the 'European paradox'. Belgium is cited as one of the countries in which this paradox appears to be the most significant (European Commission, 1997a, p. 180). A possible explanation for this may be the high dependence on subsidiaries of foreign multinationals in Belgium (see also Chapter 8). These subsidiaries often actively participate in pre-competitive collaboration (e.g. Alcatel Bell and Alcatel Microelectronics), but the low participation in private alliances of Belgian subsidiaries may indicate a poor valorisation of research efforts within Belgium (Switzerland is a clear counter-example; see OECD (1999)).

In Figure 7.1, which can be seen as the core of the 'Belgian' international R&D network, the interlinkage of the cliques is shown. All actors (except foreign education establishments) appearing in at least one clique (at multiplicity level 8) are shown with their links in the cliques. The thick lines are 'strong lines' (project lines backed up by a personal link between the actors). The central triangle of IMEC, Alcatel Bell, and Alcatel Microelectronics (formerly Mietec) consists of these strong lines. The multiple line (46 projects) between IMEC and Philips (NL) and the multiple line (42 projects) between IMEC and Siemens (DE) are also backed up by a personal link. The density of the network is underestimated as existing links between foreign actors are not considered.

It was found that the density of the networks related to *IT* and *Telecommunications* in EU projects increased over time (see Meeusen and Dumont (1997a)). An analysis on the level of some specific technological areas is provided by the same authors (1997a,b).

Figure 7.1:   Interlinkage of the cliques in the complete graph (multiplicity ≥ 8)

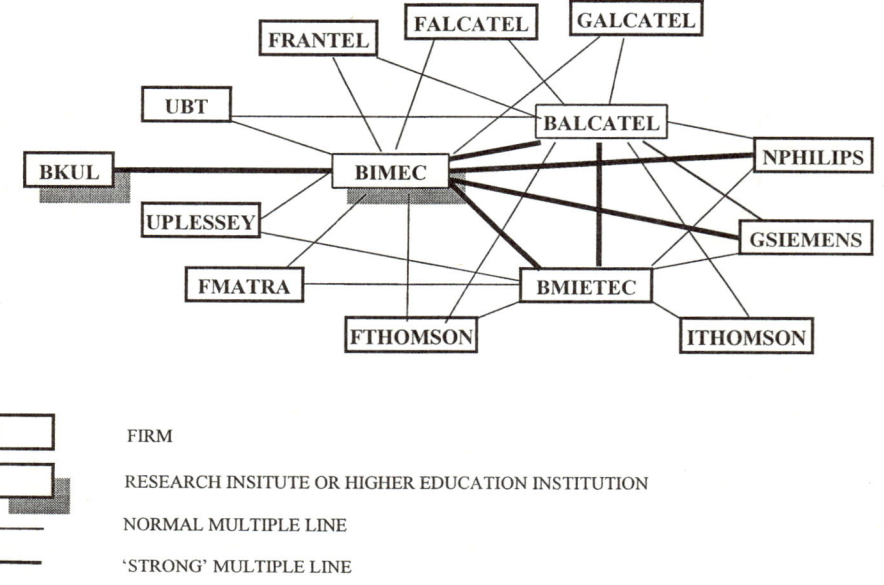

FIRM

RESEARCH INSITUTE OR HIGHER EDUCATION INSTITUTION

—— NORMAL MULTIPLE LINE

—— 'STRONG' MULTIPLE LINE

7.4.   Knowledge spillovers through R&D co-operation

Since the emergence of the endogenous growth theory, the interest in knowledge spillovers as a source of economic growth has increased considerably. Further progress in this area is, in Griliches' view, essentially to be expected from a more accurate definition of 'the changing multi-dimensional space of technological opportunities' (Griliches, 1992, p. S44). Griliches distinguishes between two notions of R&D spillovers. He considers spillovers to be 'embodied' if they relate to the purchase of goods and services. 'Disembodied spillovers' are seen by Griliches as 'ideas borrowed by research teams of industry *i* from the research results of industry *j*. It is not clear that this kind of borrowing is particularly related to input purchase flows' (*ibid.*, p. S36). They are considered by Griliches to be more significant. Unfortunately, computing 'embodied' spillovers is easier and more straightforward than computing 'disembodied' spillovers, since methods borrowed from more or less traditional input-output analysis can be used for the former. The study of the intra- and intersectoral aspects of R&D co-operation may be a useful alternative.

In what follows, we will propose a method for calculating intra- and intersectoral knowledge flows based on the data on R&D co-operation between Belgian firms in EU RTD and EUREKA projects and in technological agreements (MERIT-CATI). This method measures 'disembodied' knowledge flows between firms co-operating in R&D projects. The basic hypothesis is that the number of joint co-operation links between firms is a proxy measure for the underlying knowledge flows.

We constructed an asymmetric matrix of intra- and intersectoral knowledge flows. The asymmetry was obtained by hypothesising that on balance more knowledge flows from the main contractor – often the technologically more advanced partner – to other contractors in R&D projects than the other way round, whereas knowledge flows between 'normal' partners are assumed to be balanced. Furthermore, we assume knowledge flows to be inversely related to the total number of participants in each project or agreement. In this way, we take account of the importance of 'intimacy'. The hypothesis that as a rule in joint R&D projects more knowledge flows from the main contractor to another partner than the other way round, is open to discussion. The results that follow, therefore, should be interpreted with some reserve.

We performed our analysis at the NACE 2-digit level due to insufficient data for an analysis at a more disaggregated level. Thus, for example, if a Belgian firm belonging to NACE sector 32 is the main contractor in a project or agreement that involves 5 partners of which one is another Belgian firm belonging to NACE 72, we assume a knowledge flow of 0.4 (2/5) 'units' from NACE 32 to NACE 72 and a knowledge flow of 0.2 (1/5) 'units' from NACE 72 to NACE 32. However, if none of the firms is the main contractor both knowledge flows equal 0.2. The resulting matrix is given in Table 7.6.

The column sums give the amount of knowledge flowing into a given sector and the row sums give the amount of knowledge flowing out of the given sector. The overall intersectoral spillover measures per sector are calculated as the amount of knowledge flowing from a given sector to the other sectors (*Spill-out*), and from the other sectors to the given sector (*Spill-in*). Apparently, the overall intersectoral spillovers are high for all sectors, with the exception of NACE 17 (*Textiles*) and NACE 26 (*Manufacture of Non-metallic Mineral Products*), which reveals that co-operation occurs more between sectors than within sectors, even at a rather high level of aggregation. It also reveals that co-operation between 'national' competitors in international R&D projects and technological agreements,

Table 7.6: Matrix of intra- and intersectoral knowledge flows in R&D co-operation

NACE-Bel	15	17	24	25	26	27	28	29	31	32	33	34	36	45	64	70	72	73	74	Total	Spill-out	DIFF	INT
15	0	0	0	0	0	0	0	0	0	0	0	0	0	0	0	0	0	1.33	0	1.33	1.00	0.2	0.14
17	0	3.27	0.07	0	0	0	0	0.05	0	0.07	0	0	0.05	0	0	0	0	0	0.05	3.56	0.08	0	0.18
24	0	0.07	0	0	0	0	0	0	0	0.07	0	0	0	0	0	0	0.04	0.11	0	0.29	1.00	-0.14	0.05
25	0	0	0	0	0	0	0.12	0	0.5	0	0	0	0	0	0	0	0.2	0	0.06	0.88	1.00	0.03	0.22
26	0	0	0	0	0.55	0	0	0	0	0	0	0	0	0	0	0	0	0	0	0.55	0.00	0	0.07
27	0	0	0	0	0	1.23	0.27	0.07	0	0.6	0.03	0	0	0	0	0	0	0	0.46	2.66	1.00	-0.06	0.15
28	0	0	0	0.12	0	0.27	0.92	0.27	0	0.2	0	0	0.05	0	0	0	0	0	0.65	2.23	0.59	-0.05	0.48
29	0	0.05	0	0	0	0.07	0.27	0	0.25	0.4	0	0	0.05	0	0	0.33	0	0	0.19	1.40	1.00	-0.03	0.29
31	0	0	0	0.25	0	0	0	0.25	0	0.24	0	0.06	0	0	0.14	0	0	0	0	0.94	1.00	-0.18	0.12
32	0	0.07	0.07	0	0	0.6	0	0.4	0.49	1.64	0.5	0	0.17	0.18	0.86	0	0.67	0	0.18	5.83	0.72	0.11	0.06
33	0	0	0	0	0	0.03	0	0	0	0.25	0	0	0	0	0	0	0	0	0	0.28	1.00	-0.28	0.11
34	0	0	0	0	0	0	0	0	0.06	0	0	0	0	0	0	0	0	0	0	0.06	1.00	0	0.04
36	0	0.05	0	0	0	0	0	0.05	0	0.17	0	0	0	0	0	0	0	0	0.05	0.32	1.00	0	0.08
45	0	0	0	0	0	0	0	0	0	0.18	0	0	0	0	0	0	0	0	0.05	0.24	1.00	0	0.33
64	0	0	0.04	0	0	0	0	0.16	0	0.45	0	0	0	0	0.13	0	0	0	0.13	0.85	0.85	-0.17	0.07
70	0	0	0	0	0	0	0	0	0	0	0	0	0	0	0	0	0.2	0	0	0.36	1.00	-0.17	1
72	0	0	0	0.4	0	0	0	0	0	0.47	0	0	0	0	0	0.2	1.32	0	0.17	2.59	0.49	-0.03	0.07
73	0.83	0	0.22	0	0	0	0	0	0	0	0	0	0	0	0	0	0	0	0	1.05	1.00	-0.14	0.17
74	0	0.05	0	0.06	0	0.86	0.92	0.25	0	0.18	0	0	0	0.06	0.13	0	0.33	0	0.34	3.22	0.89	0.14	0.14
Total	0.83	3.56	0.4	0.83	0.55	3.05	2.49	1.49	1.44	4.53	0.53	0.06	0.32	0.24	1.25	0.53	2.76	1.44	2.33				
Spill-in	1	0.08	1	1	0	0.6	0.6	1	1	0.64	1	1	1	1	0.9	1	0.52	1	0.94				

which can be followed on the main diagonal of the matrix, is rather limited, although, as pointed out by Griliches (1992), data for this kind of analysis should ideally be collected at the business-unit level rather than on the firm level. In our analysis, major R&D-active firms that are competitors for some of their activities span several sectors, even at the 2-digit level used.

As co-operation seems to occur more between than within industries and as firms within sectors can be expected to be more technologically related than firms from different 2-digit sectors, the relationship between spillovers and proximity is probably not a clear-cut, monotonically increasing one. Mowery, Oxley, and Silverman (1996) find mixed evidence for the effect of alliances on the technological distance between partners. In a substantial part of the alliances, collaboration seems, according to them, to have increased specialisation (i.e., divergent development of capabilities of the collaborating partners). However, technological proximity can be essential for the absorption of transferred knowledge.

The advantage of the matrix is that it does not depend on any distance measure but calculates knowledge flows in a rather straightforward manner. The intra- and intersectoral elements may be used as weights for the computation of within- and between-industry disembodied R&D spillovers.

In the matrix obtained, diffusion can be measured for each sector as the logarithm of the row sum related to the column sum (see Den Hertog *et al.*, 1995). In the line of Pavitt (1984), science-based sectors can be expected to be characterised by 'positive' diffusion and supplier-dominated sectors by 'negative' diffusion. NACE 15 (*Food and Beverages*), NACE 74 (*Other Services to Firms*), NACE 32 (*Electronic Equipment*), and NACE 25 (*Rubber and Plastic Products*) have a positive diffusion index. When account is taken of the number and magnitude of intersectoral flows, NACE 32 in particular, diffuses a great deal of knowledge to other sectors. NACE 33 (*Instruments and Office Machines*), NACE 31 (*Electrical Machines*), and NACE 64 (*Telecommunications*) have, in our definition, the highest negative diffusion index.

For each sector, the last column in Table 7.6 gives the share of national links for each sector. With the exception of NACE 28 (*Metal Products*) and NACE 29 (*Machinery*), this share is fairly low. With data on the sector classification of foreign firms, a denser and more revealing matrix could in principle be computed that would allow the study of intra- and intersectoral knowledge flows on an international level. International 'disembodied' spillovers could then be computed.

7.5. The regional dimension of Belgian R&D collaboration

The last section of the foregoing chapter mentioned a few differences between the three Belgian regions in participation in the Framework programmes of the EU and in EUREKA.

In the R&D network that was considered in this chapter, the most central Belgian actor is IMEC, an institute created by the Flemish government in 1982 in order to conduct research in microelectronics and to support the valorisation of research results (see Chapter 3). The institute has been active in EU projects from the outset and is the co-ordinator for a considerable number of projects. Indeed, a large part of the apparent relative Belgian specialisation in IT can be attributed to IMEC.

Another Flemish research institute, VITO, which conducts research in materials, environmental, and energy technology, is in the 18th position of central Belgian actors. The Walloon Region has no such research institutes of its own in specific technological domains.

In the top 35, there are 2 sectoral centres of collective research, WTCM and WTCB. These centres, which are funded by the federal government as well as by the three regions, have laboratories in all three of them and can therefore be seen as carrying out research that benefits these regions.

There are three Flemish as well as three Walloon universities in the top 35, and no regional differences in academic participation could be detected. The most important difference between the regions, therefore, is once again related to business orientation.

There are seven Flemish firms in the top 35 but only one from the Walloon Region and one from Brussels. Especially in ICT, there are very few Walloon industrial participants. This might be an indication of the importance of regional research institutes in increasing the participation of firms in R&D collaboration and, from a more long-term perspective, in strengthening the economic fabric in specific technological domains.

In a similar way as in Table 7.6, a matrix of intra- and interregional knowledge flows within Belgium can be computed (see Meeusen and Dumont, 1998). This matrix reveals that scale effects are also significant on the regional level as the largest Belgian region, Flanders, is more 'self-reliant' (in this particular context of R&D co-operation) than Brussels and Wallonia. Somewhat surprisingly, Flanders has a negative diffusion index while Wallonia and Brussels have positive indexes, which would mean that more knowledge flows from the smaller regions to the largest region than the other way round. Again, of course, this result depends on the definition of the direction of the knowledge spillovers (main contractor to partner). Furthermore, the three indexes do not seem to indicate statistically significant differences.

7.6. The Belgian R&D network in an international context

That national and international R&D co-operation has become an increasingly important feature of economic development certainly holds true foremost for small countries. Table 7.7 shows the total number of collaborative links within each country as a percentage of the total number of links for the 4th EU Framework programme. Large countries clearly have a larger share of links *within* their borders: the Spearman rank correlation between country size and share of collaborative links is significant at the 5% level. For private technological alliances the correlation between the percentage of intra-national links and population is also significant at the 5% level.

Table 7.7:   Share of collaborative links within a country as a
             percentage of its total number of links (4th Framework
             Programme and technological alliances, 1992-95)

Country	% (FWP)	% (alliances)	Population (1997)
Germany	11	11	82190
France	11	12	58543
United Kingdom	10	11	58201
Italy	9	5	57236
Spain	9	7	39718
the Netherlands	7	4	15661
Greece	7	0	10522
Belgium	4	4	10188
Portugal	7	0	9803
Sweden	6	8	8844
Austria	5	n.a.	8161
Switzerland	3	n.a.	7277
Denmark	5	0	5248
Finland	5	7	5142
Norway	6	n.a.	4364
Ireland	3	8	3559
Luxembourg	4	n.a.	417

Source: Own calculations based on European Commission (1997a), p.560 and p.613.

With regard to the analysis of participation of EU countries in RTD projects, we applied the method used by Lichtenberg (1996) to evaluate the participation in the ESPRIT program. Lichtenberg computed cross-country regressions of the logarithm of the number of participating organisations on the logarithm of population and the logarithm of GDP (in purchasing power parities) separately, and with both independent variables combined. He found that the number of organisations is more closely related to population than to GDP. The residuals of the model with both independent variables show those countries with a relatively high (positive residual) or a relatively low (negative residual) number of participating organisations.

Instead of using the total number of organisations of each country, we used its total number of prime contractors, thus also measuring the ability of the actors of a country to act as project leaders. In RTD programmes, the role of project leader is mostly assumed by large firms, and SMEs participate mostly as associate partners (European Commission, 1997a, pp. 529-30). We used the 1992 GDP measured in current international prices (Penn World data). Unlike Lichtenberg, however, we included an intercept in the regression equation. Its apparent significance in 5 of the 8 equations suggests that there is a structural effect not accounted for by population or GDP. For all the RTD programmes present in the CORDIS database, the number of prime contractors is related to GDP, albeit only at the 90% level of significance, and not to population, controlling for GDP.

For ESPRIT, contrary to the findings of Lichtenberg on the total number of participating organisations, the number of prime contractors is significantly related to GDP and not to population, again controlling for GDP. The coefficients for all the RTD programmes (CORDIS) and for the major RTD programmes are shown in Table A.7.4. The residuals are ranked in decreasing order. Positive residuals indicate a high number of prime contractors, given the size of the country, whereas a negative residual indicates that a country has a comparatively low number of prime contractors relative to its size.

We also computed cross-country regressions for participation in EUREKA with the total number of projects as the dependent variable. Again, we find that the number of EUREKA projects is significantly related to the GDP of a country but not to its population. This does not come as a surprise. EUREKA projects are more 'near market' than RTD Framework projects and do not imply a European subsidy. The EUREKA partnerships are therefore probably more determined by straightforward economic rationality of its members, and less by opportunistic reasons related to the maximisation of the prospect to obtain European funding.

The UK is the only country with positive residuals for all the RTD programmes that were considered. Belgium has negative residuals for BRITE/EURAM, JOULE/THERMIE, and EUREKA, and positive residuals for all the other RTD programmes and for overall RTD participation. The high number of Belgian prime contractors relative to its size might be partly because the European Commission has its seat in Belgium. Indeed, Lichtenberg suggested that the intensity of involvement of countries in ESPRIT projects might significantly depend on their distance from Brussels.

For the complete CORDIS database, the four countries with the highest positive residuals are Belgium and three of its neighbouring countries. For specific RTD programmes and for EUREKA, this appears to be less pronounced. Germany has only negative residuals except for one RTD programme (RACE). Although these results at first glance seem to yield a relatively positive picture about Belgian participation, Steurs and Cortese (1993) and European Commission (1994) show that this high participation is mainly due to universities and research institutes, and that Belgian firms have a low relative rate of participation compared with the EU average (see also Chapter 6).

We performed a hierarchical cluster analysis with data on prime contractors for 10 major RTD subject index codes for a group of 11 countries and found three important clusters. A first cluster consists of the UK, France, the Netherlands, and Belgium with Belgium and the UK having a similar distribution over the subject codes. The countries of the first cluster, relative to other countries, participate highly in agriculture, biotechnology, and medicine. A second cluster is composed of Germany, Italy, and Spain with relative strength in materials technology, aerospace technology, and electronics. The third cluster is composed of Greece, Denmark, Portugal, and Ireland with relative strength in environmental protection and renewable sources of energy. The first two clusters to a large extent coincide with the two scientific clusters detected by Archibugi and Pianta (1992, p. 99).

In European Commission (1997a, p. 558), it is shown that France, Germany, Great Britain, and Italy were, in decreasing order of importance, the most significant partners for Belgian organisations in both the Third and the Fourth FWP.

In Table 7.8, we show the number of lines between Belgian companies and foreign organisations. Germany, France, Great Britain, Italy, and the Netherlands are the main countries in terms of the number of collaborative links in the complete graph, as well as for all RTD programmes combined (CORDIS). The ranking for EUREKA and MERIT-CATI is somewhat different (e.g. Spain as the third country for EUREKA and Great Britain as the main country for MERIT-CATI).

Table 7.8:   **Collaborative links between Belgian companies and foreign partners and Revealed Comparative Preference (RCP)**

	Total	CORDIS	RCP	EUREKA	RCP	CATI	RCP
Germany	1309	1173	1.01	132	0.92	4	0.52
France	1230	1059	0.97	165	1.22	6	0.84
Great Britain	964	864	1.01	87	0.82	13	2.31
Italy	684	593	0.98	88	1.17	3	0.75
the Netherlands	585	490	0.95	84	1.30	11	3.22
Spain	524	428	0.92	96	1.66	0	0.00
Greece	266	260	1.11	6	0.20	0	0.00
Denmark	247	231	1.06	16	0.59	0	0.00
Portugal	203	198	1.10	5	0.22	0	0.00
Sweden	184	167	1.03	17	0.84	0	0.00
Ireland	140	138	1.12	2	0.13	0	0.00
TOTAL	6336	5601		698		37	

Notes: $RCP_{ij} = (NL_{ij}/NL_i)/(NL_j/NL)$;

NL: Number of Collaborative Links between Belgian companies and foreign organisations;

i : country, j : programme/technological area.

Sources: Own calculations based on European Commission (1997b), EUREKA (1998), and MERIT-CATI (1998).

In order to obtain a more precise view of technological collaborative patterns in the joint R&D projects, we computed the relationship of collaborative links of a foreign country with Belgian companies in a technological area or programme to the overall number of collaborative links with Belgian companies in that specific area or programme. We call this measure the 'Revealed Comparative Preference' (RCP) since, to some extent, it reveals the preference of Belgian companies for co-operating with organisations of a given country in a given technological area or programme compared to the overall distribution of collaborative links.

In Table 7.8, the RCP is computed for all the collaborative links in CORDIS, EUREKA, and MERIT-CATI. In Table A.7.5, the RCP is computed for all the main links proceeding from the directed graph, i.e., the graph consisting only of the directed lines going from main contractors to the partners. The RCP measure apparently varies less between countries for the 'pre-competitive' RTD projects (RCP close to unity) than for the 'near-market' EUREKA projects or technological agreements contained in CATI. Apparently, the nearer to the market the more pronounced the preference of Belgian companies for partners from certain countries. In Table A.7.6, we computed the RCP for all the links of Belgian companies with foreign partners for major RTD programmes. These programmes were classified by technological area. The RCP of links in these areas are reported in Table A.7.7.

Finally, we performed a hierarchical cluster analysis with the data given in Table A.7.6 along with RCP data on co-operation in EUREKA. We found three major clusters of countries with similar RCP patterns of co-operation with Belgian actors. Germany and the Netherlands have the most similar RCP pattern and form the first cluster. They have high RCPs for CRAFT and Materials (EUREKA) and low RCPs for ECLAIR and COST. The second cluster is composed of Italy, Denmark, and Spain with high RCPs for COST and RACE and low RCPs for DRIVE and JOULE/THERMIE. The third cluster consists of France, the UK, and Greece with high RCPs for JOULE/THERMIE and low RCPs for COST, CRAFT, and RACE. Portugal, Switzerland, Ireland, and Sweden are somewhat isolated at the outside of the central group of these three clusters.

7.7. The Belgian specialisation pattern in high-tech trade

There are sufficient indications that Belgium, due to its early industrial development, ensconced itself in traditional industrial activities at the expense of later growth in emerging high-tech domains, in spite of the scientific and technological potential of the country. Acknowledgement of this has led regional governments, since the federalisation of the country in 1990, to stimulate innovation in domains like ICT, biotechnology, and new materials (i.e., domains that are also favoured by the EU in its FWPs). However, it remains to be seen if this has resulted in a redirection of trade flows.

In this section, we will analyse the Belgian specialisation pattern in high-tech trade, and we will try to establish the degree to which the trade pattern matches specialisation in R&D collaboration.

With regard to R&D intensive products, Edquist and Lundvall, making use of data compiled by Dalum, obtained a low overall 'Revealed Comparative Advantage' (RCA) index for Belgium for the period 1961-1987 (Edquist and Lundvall, 1993, p. 286; Dalum, 1989). Van Essen and Verspagen (1997) also reported a low Belgian RCA in high-tech trade. And, as has already been shown in Table 6.2 in the previous chapter, Belgium has a low export market share in high-tech products compared to its overall market share in the manufacturing industry. Grupp, on the contrary, using bilateral correlation analysis, concluded that Belgium in 1988 had good high technology competitiveness in the EU context (Grupp, 1992)[10].

If we turn from market shares to the trade balance, the picture becomes even less clear. Indeed, the Belgian trade balance in high-tech products in the beginning of the 90s is reported to be roughly in equilibrium (European Commission, 1994 and European Commission, 1997a; see also Daniels, 1993). It becomes however positive in 1995, both for leading-edge commodities and for high-level technology commodities (see Chapter 6).[11,12] Belgium is clearly in a borderline situation, and trade balance figures can change sign in function of the period considered or the definition of the commodity classes.

Some unambiguous features however do emerge. Belgium shows strength in pharmaceuticals and some other chemical commodities and also in leading-edge and high-level telecommunications-related goods. Weak trade performance can be found in electronics and most areas of machinery with the exception of advanced electrical machinery. The data show also that a country can very well have a positive trade balance for a broadly defined class of R&D-intensive goods without being a 'specialist' on the world-trade scene for these goods. However, we do find a high and increasing RCA in advanced organic chemicals and advanced industrial abrasives despite trade deficits in both of these classes. This might indicate significant flows of intra-industry trade.

Another way of analysing the trade-specialisation pattern of a country is with a 'constant-market-share' analysis (CMS). Overall changes in commodity export shares can be decomposed into three effects. The share effect measures the part of the overall change of the share due to changing shares in each sector measured at a constant share composition at the global level. In other words, it is a pure competitiveness effect. The 'composition effect' measures the part of the overall change caused by the changing composition of shares at the global level measured at constant shares in each sector. The third effect, the 'market adaptation effect' or 'interaction effect', is the residual that corresponds to the product of the changes in the sectoral shares in the country studied and the commodity-share changes at

---

[10] Grupp further distinguishes between so-called high-level technology and leading-edge commodities, the latter being defined as the upper segment subset of high-tech commodities. For high-level technology commodities, i.e., not including the leading-edge ones, he finds a positive relationship between the number of patents per GDP (1984-1986) and RCA (1988). The relationship for leading-edge commodities is more complicated, and no clear pattern emerges, which probably reflects the relatively lesser importance of formalised property rights in the leading-edge technology sector, due to the nature itself of the activities in this sector and to their being subject to strong government intervention and protection.

[11] Calculations based on United Nations (1996).

[12] The high-level technology commodity class is defined as being the class of R&D-intensive goods, not including the so-called leading-edge commodities.

the global level. When positive, it indicates that companies on balance increase their market share in worldwide expanding commodity classes and/or are moving out of declining ones (see Fagerberg and Sollie, 1987). As such, the 'decomposition effect' is a measure of a possible mismatch between the evolution in a country and the evolution worldwide. We performed a CMS analysis for both leading-edge and high-level technology commodity classes for which data were available. The results for the RCA and the trade balance for leading-edge and high-level technology commodities as well as the results of the CMS analysis are presented in the appendix (Tables A.7.8 and A.7.9).

Belgian companies showed an overall trade surplus in leading-edge classes and increased their overall share by 5.28% between 1991 and 1995. However, the overall share of Belgian companies in high-level technology classes decreased by 5.58% between 1991 and 1995. The decomposition of the overall effect shows that, with regard to leading-edge commodities, the overall improvement between 1991 and 1995 was caused essentially by Belgian companies gaining shares. The negative composition effect shows that Belgium is specialised in declining commodity classes. Finally, the positive adaptation effect shows that Belgian companies are generally moving out of declining leading-edge classes or into classes with growing importance. With regard to high-level technology commodities, the declining position of Belgian firms is due to the loss of shares, the 'wrong' specialisation pattern, and the 'wrong' adaptation pattern – all three effects being negative. Another CMS analysis for the high-level technology commodities, this time for the period 1991-1994, reveals that Belgium, just behind Germany, has the sharpest decline in high-tech market shares in a group of 12 European countries and is one of the few countries with all three CMS effects being negative (Van Essen and Verspagen, 1997).[13]

If we look at the results for specific commodities, we see that Belgium has a large trade surplus, an RCA well above 1, and a positive overall CMS effect for leading-edge commodities like agricultural chemicals and pharmaceutical products. This illustrates the well-known strength of Belgium in chemicals and pharmaceuticals. This strength can be found in scientific performance, R&D collaboration, and strategic alliances as well as in trade. Biotechnology is also a discipline that is supported strongly by the regional authorities in Belgium (e.g. the creation of VIB in Flanders and BCR in Wallonia).

For other domains, the match between scientific, technological, and economic performance is less pronounced or even non-existent, which illustrates the 'European paradox', already mentioned above in Section 7.3.2.

---

[13] The CMS analysis can also be performed on R&D expenditure shares, as did Laursen and Christensen (1996), who found a negative structural effect for small countries like Denmark and Finland indicating a 'wrong' specialisation pattern. They however add that, due to the path-dependent nature of technological change, countries cannot dramatically alter their specialisation pattern.

As already mentioned above, Belgium is well-represented in IT-related pre-competitive R&D collaboration but not in private R&D alliances. Trade performance in IT commodities is in general very poor. For automatic data-processing machines, Belgium has a large trade deficit and a low RCA. For office machines, there is a small trade surplus but also a low RCA. However, for both commodities the RCA increased, and the overall CMS effect is positive in the 1991-95 period.

With regard to electronics, the results are mixed. For advanced electrical machinery, Belgium has a large trade surplus and an RCA above 1. However, the RCA decreased and the overall CMS is negative for the 1991-95 period. For medical electronics, there is a trade deficit, a low and decreasing RCA, and a negative CMS effect. For semi-conductor devices, Belgium has a large trade deficit and a very low and stable RCA. The overall CMS, however, is positive for 1991-95. For electrical distributing equipment there is a trade surplus, a low and decreasing RCA, and a negative CMS effect, and finally, for traditional electronics, a trade deficit, a low but increasing RCA, and a small but positive CMS effect.

These results do not indicate in a straightforward way that government support and the specialisation in pre-competitive collaboration have so far resulted in an improvement of the position of Belgian firms in IT and electronics, although for some leading-edge and high-level IT commodities, the performance has clearly ameliorated. The improvement is more pronounced if we look at intermediate innovative output (i.e., patents). Belgium is second in the world for average annual growth of EPO shares for computers and office machinery with an average annual growth of 89.3% in the period 1986-95 and eighth for electronics, with a 12.1% growth in the same period (European Commission, 1997a, p. 161). See also Chapter 8.

For telecommunications, for which Belgium has an RSI above unity in ongoing EU projects as well as for private alliances, the data again do not allow for unambiguous conclusions. For four high-tech telecom-related commodities, Belgium has a trade surplus, but in 1995 all the RCA were below unity. For telecommunications equipment and TV and video equipment, the RCA decreased. For telecommunications equipment overall, the CMS was positive because of a positive composition effect while the share and adaptation effect were both negative. For TV and video equipment, the overall CMS was negative. Radio-broadcast and sound and video recorders showed an increase in the RCA and a positive CMS, which was largely due to a positive share effect.

By far the worst trade performance is found in aircraft and spacecraft. For this commodity class, Belgium has a trade deficit, a small and decreasing RCA, and a large negative CMS. This matches the low Belgian RSI for EU projects. However, it conflicts with Belgium's high contribution to, and participation in, ESA programmes.

It should perhaps be stressed that the terms 'right' and 'wrong' with respect to specialisation are not unambiguous. Dalum, Laursen, and Verspagen (1996), for instance, point to the risks of a policy aimed at stimulating growth by steering specialisation in the 'right' direction. Because of the relative stickiness of specialisation patterns, the outcome of an active policy remains very uncertain. Giving up strong positions in declining sectors may, for the same kind of reasons, also be questionable.

7.8.   Conclusion

In this phase of the research on the network of R&D co-operation, at least one thing became abundantly clear, and it comes – in the light of previously published research – as no surprise for those studying national innovation systems. The international network aspects of Belgian R&D activities are very pronounced and 'markets and hierarchies' are obviously transcended.

We cannot, of course, but realise that the shape of the networks we find gives a somewhat biased view of national innovation systems. Because the EC in the last decade selected a number of S&T fields that they considered of growing importance in terms of international competitiveness and future growth potential, heavy emphasis was placed in the EU Framework programmes on such fields as ICT, new materials, bio-engineering, and new forms of energy. The result, of course, is an R&D co-operation network in which the highest connectivity can be found in precisely these fields. However, there is no way of denying the overall importance of the EU Framework programmes.

The following conclusions clearly emerged:

- The network of R&D collaboration involving Belgian actors (firms, research labs, and institutions of higher education) showed to be highly connected. Two subsets of domestic actors with the highest, weighted degree centrality could be distinguished: first, firms active in *IT* and, second, universities and interuniversity research laboratories also active in *IT*. Another important subset consisted of foreign multinationals active in *IT* and telecommunication. This feature of the network was confirmed by the analysis of clique configurations.
- Belgium is clearly more active in pre-competitive R&D collaboration than in near-market co-operation or in private technology alliances, which indicates a certain lack of valorisation of research efforts within Belgium that can be explained in part by the high dependence on foreign multinationals.
- Simple cross-tabulations revealed that the R&D active firms that participate in international R&D projects or agreements were not significantly more innovative than those that did not participate in any such project or agreement.
- The study of the coincidence of project lines indicated that partnerships between firms in the pre-competitive sphere continued in more near-market projects only to a limited extent.
- The matrix of intra- and interregional and international knowledge flows implicit in R&D partnerships reveals that scale effects are as relevant on the re-

gional level as on the international level: the largest Belgian region, Flanders, is more 'self-reliant' in this particular context than Brussels or Wallonia.

- A hierarchical cluster analysis with data on prime contractors for 10 major RTD subject index codes for a group of 11 countries yields three important clusters. The first cluster consists of the UK, France, the Netherlands, and Belgium with Belgium and the UK having a very similar distribution over the subject codes. The countries of the first cluster, relative to other countries, highly participate in agriculture, biotechnology, and medicine. The second cluster is composed of Germany, Italy, and Spain with relative strength in materials technology, aerospace technology, and electronics. The third cluster is composed of Greece, Denmark, Portugal, and Ireland with relative strength in environmental protection and renewable sources of energy.

- The closer to the market the more pronounced is the preference of Belgian companies for partners from certain countries.

- The comparison of the pattern of high-tech trade of Belgium with the pattern of R&D collaboration reveals a number of mismatches or at least significant delays in the transmission of the results of co-operation.

Appendices

Table A.7.1: List of actors

LABEL	NAME	YPE	NAT
BALCATEL	Alcatel Bell	IND	BE
BBARCO	Barco	IND	BE
BEEIG	European Renewable Energy Centers Agency	NCL	BE
BBELGACO	Belgacom	IND	BE
BEURDEV	Frontier Design (former European Development Centre)	IND	BE
BIMEC	Interuniversity Micro-Electronics Centre (IMEC)	ROR	BE
BKARMAN	Von Karman Institute For Fluid Dynamics	ROR	BE
BKUL	Katholieke Universiteit Leuven	EDU	BE
BLMSINT	LMS International	IND	BE
BMIETEC	Alcatel Microelectronics (formerly Mietec)	IND	BE
BPGS	Plant Genetic Systems	IND	BE
BSCK	Study Centre for Nuclear Energy	ROR	BE
BSOCBIO	Sociéte de Biotechnologie	IND	BE
BSOLVAY	Solvay	IND	BE
BUCL	Université Catholique de Louvain	EDU	BE
BUG	Universiteit Gent	EDU	BE
BULB	Université Libre de Bruxelles	EDU	BE
BUNIVL	Université de Liège	EDU	BE
BVITO	Flemish Institute for Technological Research (VITO)	ROR	BE
BVUB	Vrije Universiteit Brussel	EDU	BE
BWTCB	Scientific Technological Centre of the Building Industry	ROR	BE
BWTCM	Scientific Technological Centre of the Metal Industry (WTCM)	ROR	BE
FALCATEL	Alcatel-Alsthom	IND	FR
FCEA	Commissariat à l'Energie Atomique (CEA)	ROR	FR
FCNRS	Centre National pour la Recherche Scientifique	ROR	FR
FMATRA	Matra Cap Systemes	IND	FR
FRANTEL	France Telecom	IND	FR
FTHOMSON	SGS-Thomson (France)	IND	FR
GALCATEL	Alcatel Sel AG	IND	DE
GFRAUN	Fraunhofer Gesellschaft	IND	DE
GSIEMENS	Siemens	IND	DE
ICSELT	Centro Studi e Laboratori Telecomunicazione	ROR	IT
ITHOMSON	SGS Thomson (Italy)	IND	IT
NPHILIPS	Philips	IND	NL
UBT	British Telecommunications	IND	GB
UPLESSEY	Gec Plessey	IND	GB
VTT	Technical Research Centre of Finland (VTT)	ROR	FI

Table A.7.2: Classification according to the percentage of project lines in which Belgian R&D co-operating firms of a given NACE sector are involved (1984-1997)

SECTOR NACE (rev. 1)		% lines	# firms	%
Audio-, video- and telecommunication equipment	32	11.26	14	3.32
Informatics	72	6.71	50	11.85
Other business services	74	4.05	66	15.64
Post and telecommunications	64	3.20	4	0.95
Textile industry	17	1.96	27	6.40
Research and development	73	1.75	6	1.42
Metallurgy	27	1.71	17	4.03
Food and beverages	15	1.69	20	4.74
Manufacture of metal products	28	1.50	28	6.64
Chemical industry	24	1.37	37	8.77
Machinery and tools	29	1.25	37	8.77
Electrical machines	31	0.90	16	3.79
Manufacture of other means of transport	35	0.80	7	1.66
Medical and optical instruments, fine mechanics	33	0.73	10	2.37
Rubber and synthetic materials	25	0.47	14	3.32
Agriculture	1	0.40	7	1.66
Furniture industry	36	0.38	5	1.18
Building industry	45	0.34	10	2.37
Manufacture of non-metallic mineral products	26	0.33	11	2.61
Manufacture of motor vehicles	34	0.29	4	0.95
Wholesale trade machinery	51	0.21	28	6.64
Rent and sale of real estate	70	0.10	4	0.95
Total			**422**	**100.00**
Other or unknown			204	
Overall total			**626**	

Table A.7.3: Comparison per NACE sector of the total number of companies and the number of companies represented in the OSTC repertory and in the graph

NACE	TOTNUM	NUMGR	%	TOT-SHARE	GRSHARE	G/T	REP	% REP	REP/GRSHARE
High-tech	*827*	*24*	*2.90*	*2.08*	*8.99*	*4.32*	*112*	*14.91*	*1.66*
244	99	5	5.05	0.25	1.87	7.52	26	3.46	1.85
32	177	12	6.78	0.45	4.49	10.09	41	5.46	1.21
353	38	3	7.89	0.10	1.12	11.75	5	0.67	0.59
33	513	4	0.78	1.29	1.50	1.16	40	5.33	3.56
Medium high-	*2546*	*56*	*2.20*	*6.41*	*20.97*	*3.27*	*223*	*29.69*	*1.46*
24	618	21	3.40	1.56	7.87	5.06	78	10.39	1.32
29	1152	17	1.48	2.90	6.37	2.20	84	11.19	1.76
31	480	15	3.13	1.21	5.62	4.65	46	6.13	1.09
34	296	3	1.01	0.74	1.12	1.51	15	2.00	1.78
Medium low-	*3924*	*27*	*0.69*	*9.88*	*10.11*	*1.02*	*124*	*16.51*	*1.63*
23	30	1	3.33	0.08	0.37	4.96	7	0.93	2.49
25	633	9	1.42	1.59	3.37	2.12	41	5.46	1.62
26	1204	7	0.58	3.03	2.62	0.87	41	5.46	2.08
35, excl. 351,352	198	5	2.53	0.50	1.87	3.76	6	0.80	0.43
351	109	2	1.83	0.27	0.75	2.73	6	0.80	1.07
36, excl. 361	1750	3	0.17	4.40	1.12	0.26	23	3.06	2.73
Low	*8007*	*70*	*0.87*	*20.15*	*26.22*	*1.30*	*189*	*25.17*	*0.96*
15	3307	14	0.42	8.32	5.24	0.63	58	7.72	1.47
16	31	1	3.23	0.08	0.37	4.80	2	0.72	0.71
17	1276	24	1.88	3.21	8.99	2.80	46	6.13	0.68
27	255	13	5.10	0.64	4.87	7.59	24	3.20	0.66
28	3138	18	0.57	7.90	6.74	0.85	59	7.86	1.17
Construction	*19945*	*6*	*0.03*	*50.19*	*2.25*	*0.04*	*27*	*3.60*	*1.60*
Services	*4257*	*79*	*1.86*	*10.71*	*29.59*	*2.76*	*76*	*10.12*	*0.34*
72	4167	76	1.82	10.49	28.46	2.71	63	8.39	0.29
73	90	3	3.33	0.23	1.12	4.96	13	1.73	1.54
TOTAL	39736	267	0.67	100.00	100.00	1.00	751	100.00	1.00

Notes: The totals in the TOTNUM and REP columns are related to the database that was used in the present analysis; they do not coincide with those mentioned in Chapter 4 since other and stricter selection criteria were used;
TOTNUM: total number of companies belonging to this sector; NUMGR: number of companies in each sector represented in the graph;
% = NUMGR/TOTNUM*100 ;
TOTSHARE = TOTNUM/TOTAL TOTNUM*100 ;
GRSHARE = NUMGR/ TOTAL NUMGR*100 ;
G/T = GRSHARE/TOTSHARE ;
REP = total number of this sector's companies in the OSTC R&D repertory ;
% REP = REP/TOTREP*100.

Sources: OSTC (1997).

Table A.7.4: EU RTD projects and country size

MODEL: log(number of prime contractors) = C + α log(Population 1992) + β log(GDP 1992) + ε							
(t-statistics between brackets; * = 10% level of sign.; ** = 5% level of sign.)							
	CORDIS	ESPRIT	BRITE	RACE	JOULE	CRAFT	BCR 4
C	-11.38	-21.62**	-17.59**	-19.57	-24.39**	-1.87	-48.78**
	(-1.69)	(-3.09)	(-3.04)	(-1.47)	(-3.65)	(-.28)	(-3.20)
α	-.96	-1.35	-1.18	-1.45	-2.25*	.95	-4.22**
	(-1.27)	(-1.73)	(-1.81)	(-.97)	(-3.00)	(1.26)	(-2.48)
β	1.46*	2.03**	1.72**	1.87	2.60**	-.19	4.76**
	(2.03)	(2.73)	(2.79)	(1.31)	(3.64)	(-.27)	(2.94)
	Ranking of residuals						
	UK (+)	UK (+)	UK (+)	UK (+)	UK (+)	**BE (+)**	UK (+)
	FR (+)	**BE (+)**	IE (+)	IE (+)	NL (+)	ES (+)	NL (+)
	IE (+)	FR (+)	FR (+)	FR (+)	DK (-)	NL (+)	**BE (+)**
	BE (+)	IE (+)	**BE (-)**	DE (+)	DE (-)	FR (+)	ES (+)
	NL (+)	NL (-)	DE (-)	**BE (+)**	IE (-)	UK (+)	FR (+)
	DE (-)	DE (-)	DK (-)	NL (-)	ES (-)	DE (-)	DK (-)
	IT (-)	IT (-)	IT (-)	DK (-)	FR (-)	IE (-)	IE (-)
	DK (-)	ES (-)	NL (-)	IT (-)	**BE (-)**	DK (-)	DE (-)
	ES (-)	DK (-)	ES (-)	ES (-)	IT (-)	IT (-)	IT (-)

Table A.7.4 (continued): EUREKA participation and country size

MODEL:	log(number of projects) = C + α log(Population 1992) + β log(GDP 1992) + ε
	(t-statistics between brackets; * = 10% level of sign.; ** = 5% level of sign.)
	EUREKA
C	-19.60*
	(-2.37)
α	-1.63
	(-1.76)
β	2.09*
	(2.37)
Ranking of residuals	
	NL (+)
	ES (+)
	DK (+)
	FR (+)
	UK (-)
	BE (-)
	DE (-)
	IE (-)
	IT (-)

Sources: own calculations from European Commission (1997b) and EUREKA (1998).

Table A.7.5: Main collaborative links between Belgian companies and foreign partners and Revealed Comparative Preference (RCP)

	TOTAL	CORDIS	RCP	EUREKA	RCP	CATI	RCP
Germany	233	223	1.06	10	0.47	0	0.00
France	311	264	0.94	47	1.66	0	0.00
UK	216	202	1.04	10	0.51	4	3.04
Italy	129	123	1.06	5	0.42	1	1.27
the Netherlands	146	107	0.81	36	2.70	3	3.38
Spain	97	89	1.02	8	0.90	0	0.00
Greece	43	43	1.11	0	0.00	0	0.00
Denmark	53	53	1.11	0	0.00	0	0.00
Portugal	40	38	1.05	2	0.55	0	0.00
Sweden	17	15	0.98	2	1.29	0	0.00
Ireland	30	30	1.11	0	0.00	0	0.00
TOTAL	1315	1187		120		8	

Sources: own calculations from European Commission (1997b), EUREKA (1998), and MERIT-CATI (1998).

Table A.7.6: Revealed Comparative Preference of Belgian companies in the major RTD programmes

	ESPRIT	RCP	BRITE	RCP	CRAFT	RCP	JOULE	RCP	BCR 4	RCP	RACE	RCP	ACTS	RCP	TELEMAT	RCP
Germany	302	1.05	208	1.21	105	1.65	30	0.94	125	1.03	146	0.93	51	0.86	18	0.63
France	251	0.97	190	1.23	54	0.94	33	1.15	119	1.09	89	0.63	36	0.68	21	0.81
UK	253	1.21	110	0.88	6	0.13	41	1.77	107	1.21	103	0.91	38	0.88	24	1.15
Italy	150	1.02	84	0.95	14	0.43	10	0.62	51	0.82	119	1.49	32	1.06	17	1.16
the Netherlands	98	0.85	54	0.78	54	2.11	7	0.55	55	1.13	67	1.07	24	1.01	8	0.69
Spain	112	1.09	48	0.78	14	0.62	5	0.44	30	0.69	72	1.29	24	1.13	16	1.56
Greece	52	0.78	38	0.95	8	0.54	12	1.63	17	0.61	35	0.97	20	1.46	9	1.35
Denmark	31	0.56	31	0.93	15	1.21	6	0.97	40	1.70	44	1.45	7	0.61	8	1.43
Portugal	37	0.76	12	0.41	39	3.63	1	0.19	17	0.83	30	1.14	16	1.60	5	1.03
Sweden	33	0.80	39	1.58	0	0.00	4	0.88	10	0.58	14	0.63	5	0.59	7	1.70
Switzerland	32	0.96	8	0.40	1	0.14	3	0.81	12	0.85	31	1.71	27	3.91	3	0.90
Ireland	50	1.45	17	0.82	0	0.00	3	0.79	7	0.48	11	0.59	9	1.27	4	1.16
Total	1401		839		310		155		590		761		289		140	

Table A.7.6 (continued)

	AIR	RCP	DRIVE	RCP	NFS	RCP	ÉCLAIR	RCP	AERO	RCP	COST	RCP	BIOTECH	RCP
Germany	14	0.45	35	0.74	8	0.93	4	0.31	28	0.93	4	0.34	22	1.06
France	24	0.85	75	1.76	5	0.65	24	2.07	25	0.93	8	0.75	17	0.91
UK	20	0.87	18	0.52	7	1.12	9	0.96	23	1.05	2	0.23	22	1.46
Italy	24	1.50	3	0.12	5	1.14	5	0.76	11	0.72	14	2.30	7	0.66
the Netherlands	19	1.50	19	1.00	3	0.86	3	0.58	17	1.41	4	0.83	8	0.96
Spain	20	1.78	18	1.06	2	0.65	9	1.95	8	0.75	6	1.41	12	1.62
Greece	8	1.10	23	2.09	12	6.01	1	0.33	7	1.01	0	0.00	4	0.83
Denmark	5	0.82	3	0.33	0	0.00	4	1.59	7	1.20	4	1.73	5	1.24
Portugal	10	1.88	0	0.00	0	0.00	2	0.91	6	1.18	4	1.99	1	0.29
Sweden	2	0.44	29	4.27	0	0.00	0	0.00	6	1.40	7	4.11	0	0.00
Switzerland	2	0.55	6	1.09	0	0.00	0	0.00	1	0.29	3	2.17	1	0.41
Ireland	5	1.33	2	0.35	0	0.00	2	1.29	7	1.95	2	1.40	2	0.80
Total	153		231		42		63		146		58		101	

Notes: ESPRIT: Information Technology; BRITE: Industrial technologies and advanced materials; CRAFT: part of BRITE/EURAM oriented towards SMEs; JOULE: Non-nuclear energies/Rational use of energies; BCR 4: Measurement/Reference materials; RACE-ACTS-TELEMATICS: Telecommunications; AIR: Agro-Industrial research; DRIVE: Transport/Telecommunications; NFS: Nuclear Fission Safety; ECLAIR-BIOTECH: Agriculture/Biotechnology; AERO: Aeronautics; COST: Co-operation in Scientific and Technological Research.

Source: own calculations from European Commission (1997b).

Table A.7.7: Revealed Comparative Preference of Belgian companies for the main technological areas of the EU Framework programmes

	IT	RCP	TELECOM	RCP	MATERIAL	RCP	ENERGY	RCP	BIOTECH	RCP	TOTAL
Germany	356	0.96	215	0.88	341	1.28	38	0.93	40	0.61	990
France	359	1.09	146	0.67	269	1.14	38	1.06	65	1.12	877
UK	302	1.14	165	0.94	139	0.73	48	1.66	51	1.09	705
Italy	178	0.94	168	1.34	109	0.80	15	0.72	36	1.08	506
the Netherlands	127	0.87	99	1.02	125	1.18	10	0.62	30	1.16	391
Spain	133	0.98	112	1.24	70	0.71	7	0.47	41	1.71	363
Greece	88	0.97	64	1.07	53	0.81	24	2.42	13	0.81	242
Denmark	41	0.63	59	1.38	53	1.14	6	0.84	14	1.22	173
Portugal	46	0.73	51	1.22	57	1.26	1	0.14	13	1.17	168
Sweden	66	1.23	26	0.73	45	1.17	4	0.68	2	0.21	143
Switzerland	38	0.88	61	2.14	10	0.32	3	0.64	3	0.39	115
Ireland	65	1.39	24	0.77	24	0.71	3	0.58	9	1.09	125
Total	1799		1190		1295		197		317		4798

Sources: own calculations from European Commission (1997b).

Table A.7.8: Trade balance, RCA and constant-market-share effects of leading-edge commodities, Belgium-Luxembourg (1991-1995)

	EXP-IMP (1000 US $)	RCA 91	RCA 95	OVERALL	CMS Analysis		
					SHARE	COMPOSITION	ADAPTATION
Agricultural chemicals	606429	1.46	5.41	5.38	6.72	-0.34	-0.99
Pharmaceutical products	796682	2.98	3.33	5.78	4.76	0.87	0.15
Advanced organic chemicals	-131116	2.54	3.01	0.53	0.98	-0.36	-0.09
Advanced electrical machinery	375457	2.06	1.51	-1.79	-4.10	3.00	-0.70
Nuclear, water, wind power engines	-32118	0.32	0.98	0.30	0.47	-0.05	-0.11
Telecommunications equipment	258309	1.10	0.95	0.22	-1.36	1.74	-0.16
Radio-active materials	19506	0.39	0.76	0.03	0.49	-0.23	-0.23
Advanced measuring instruments	-209978	0.74	0.74	-0.80	0.32	-1.06	-0.05
Automatic data processing ma-chines	-838484	0.56	0.71	3.68	2.91	0.57	0.20
Turbines and reaction engines	13408	0.73	0.67	-1.26	-0.10	-1.19	0.03
Medical electronics	-126047	0.76	0.62	-0.45	-0.21	-0.27	0.04
Advanced optical instruments	-46548	0.31	0.34	0.07	0.04	0.03	0.00
Aircraft and spacecraft	-317167	0.63	0.31	-8.04	-5.34	-5.24	2.54
Semi-conductor devices	-363881	0.16	0.16	1.64	0.18	1.35	0.10
Total	4452			5.28	5.75	-1.19	0.73

Source: United Nations (1996), own calculations (data on SITC classes 575 and 891 not available for Belgium).

Table A.7.9: Trade balance, RCA and constant-market-share effects of high-level technology commodities, Belgium-Luxembourg (1991-1995)

	EXP-IMP (1000 US $)	RCA 91	RCA 95	CMS Analysis			
				OVERALL	SHARE	COMPOSITION	ADAPTATION
Advanced industrial abrasives	-26773	2.60	2.94	-0.06	0.02	-0.08	-0.00
Photo and cinema supplies	1155388	2.39	2.47	-0.48	-0.13	-0.35	0.00
Motor vehicles for persons	10438121	1.90	2.01	-4.20	-0.34	-3.89	0.02
Pigments, paints	512217	1.61	1.73	0.38	0.04	0.34	0.00
Miscellaneous chemicals	578248	1.54	1.47	-0.27	-0.60	0.37	-0.04
Mineral manufactures	165569	1.35	1.35	-0.04	-0.10	0.06	-0.00
Medical instruments	58507	0.62	1.18	0.94	0.88	0.03	0.02
Heterocyclic chemistry	-354662	2.21	1.13	-2.38	-2.41	0.06	-0.03
Rare Inorganic chemicals	-8712	1.23	1.07	-0.80	-0.45	-0.43	0.08
TV and video equipment	384687	0.91	0.69	-0.77	-0.68	-0.13	0.04
Synthetic fibres	-70190	0.40	0.69	0.20	0.14	0.03	0.02
Railway vehicles	71464	0.54	0.68	0.02	0.08	-0.05	-0.00
Advanced metalworking equipment	-7566	0.67	0.66	-0.11	-0.06	-0.05	0.00
Electrical distributing equipment	46141	0.88	0.65	-0.17	-0.63	0.66	-0.20
Printing and bookbinding	-761	0.30	0.64	0.41	0.50	-0.05	-0.05
Synthetic colouring matter	-33951	0.61	0.63	-0.11	-0.02	-0.09	0.00
Mechanical handling	-180310	0.47	0.62	0.42	0.43	-0.00	-0.00
Radio-broadcast	33859	0.27	0.61	0.82	0.72	0.05	0.05
Heating, cooling and equipment	68543	0.53	0.58	0.17	0.08	0.09	0.00
Other non-electrical machinery	-225128	0.28	0.56	0.52	0.62	-0.05	-0.05
Sound and video recorders	30487	0.28	0.43	0.26	0.31	-0.04	-0.02
Traditional electronics	-153158	0.34	0.40	0.59	0.23	0.32	0.04
Traditional measuring equipment	-36758	0.35	0.38	0.02	0.00	0.02	0.00
Office machines	1646	0.08	0.38	0.46	0.52	-0.01	-0.05

Table A.7.9 (continued)

	EXP-IMP (1000 US $)	RCA 91	RCA 95	CMS Analysis			
				OVERALL	SHARE	COMPOSITION	ADAPTATION
Phot. apparatus and machines	-40703	0.28	0.37	0.12	0.09	0.02	0.00
Essential oils, perfume	-24330	0.32	0.35	0.00	0.00	0.00	0.00
Advanced machine tools	-122673	0.39	0.34	-0.32	-0.46	0.16	-0.03
Ind. food-processing machinery	-61562	0.34	0.32	-0.07	-0.03	-0.04	0.00
Precious non-ferrous base metals	-27929	0.25	0.30	0.03	0.01	0.01	0.00
Paper and pulp machinery	-106510	0.17	0.17	-0.05	-0.01	-0.04	0.00
Advanced parts for computers	-312237	0.27	0.15	-0.81	-1.05	0.44	-0.20
Optical fibres, contact	-85141	0.13	0.13	-0.00	-0.00	-0.00	0.00
Total	**11570558**			**-5.58**	**-2.36**	**-2.86**	**-0.35**

Source: United Nations (1996), own calculations (data on SITC classes 542, 574, 731, 733, 735, 746 and 525 are not available for Belgium).

Part III

The Outputs of the National Innovation System
and Conclusion

Chapter 8.   Technological Performance

Henri Capron and Michele Cincera

8.1. Introduction

Research and development expenditure is the most commonly used indicator to gauge the technological position of countries. However, there are large differences between countries in their allocation of R&D expenditure. Some countries devote more effort to fundamental research while others are more oriented to applied research and experimental development. Moreover, R&D expenditure is an input measure. Thus, it is important to know how to measure the outcome of inventive activity. In other words, efforts in the field of R&D are only important as far as they yield results in terms of innovation. Indeed, this contention should be taken to its logical conclusion. Innovation is only important insofar as it leads to tangible results with respect to what is really economically and socially important: a high per capita income and its fair distribution and, therefore, good performance in terms of economic growth and, especially for a small, open economy like Belgium, international competitiveness. We will deal with the last element in the next chapter.

Patent and scientific-publication data are the output indicators most commonly used to measure technological and scientific activities. A double advantage of patent data is that they can be broken down by technological classes and provide internationally comparable information. They also constitute a main form of codified information. Their main disadvantages are well known: not all inventions are patented or patentable, and the propensity to patent differs greatly across technological classes.[1] With regard to bibliometrical indicators, only a subset of world publications is contained in the available databases, and there is a bias in favour of English-language publications. Nevertheless, these shortcomings are generally considered not to affect substantially the relevance of this type of data.

A far less common output indicator relates to trademark data, although in recent years a number of studies have started to use them (see e.g. Allegrezza and Guarda-Rauchs, 1998; Meeusen and Rayp, 1998a).

---

[1] For the relevance of patent statistics as an indicator of the output of science and technology activities, see, for instance, Bound *et al.* (1984), Basberg (1987), Glismann and Horn (1988) or Griliches (1990).

We will first go deeper into the matter of two first-level output indicators: patents (our main focus of attention) (in Sections 8.2. to 8.5) and scientific publications (in Section 8.6). We turn to trademarks as a second-level technological output indicator in Section 8.7. We conclude in section 8.8.

8.2.   Patents

Despite their limits, patents appear to be a relevant indicator for studying the impact of inventiveness on the economic environment and for tracing the interactions and technology flows across sectors and countries. Recent studies show that the productivity achieved by a firm depends on both its own research effort and knowledge from other firms. This aspect of the analysis of patents as a knowledge flow is not covered in this chapter. The data used here concern Belgian patenting statistics reported in the European and US patent offices from 1980 to 1996.

The Belgian patents are identified on the basis of applicants, not of inventors. This choice is not without consequences for the analysis because, for Belgium, the number of patents based on the applicant criterion is only three quarters of the number of patents based on the inventor criterion. This means that the Belgian NIS depends to a large extent on strategies developed by foreign multinationals.

8.2.1.   The Belgian position inside the European Union

The Belgian propensity to patent is less than the European average. The indexes of the number of Belgian patent applications per capita compared to the average for the European Union (EUR15 = 100) are equal to 61, 63, and 65 for 1980-1985, 1986-1990, and 1991-1996, respectively (the indexes are established on the basis of EPO data). While the index increases over time, we observe that Belgian firms seem to be less innovative than the average on the basis of this criterion. It is worth noting in this context that Belgium is one of the richest countries of the European Union, its GDP index being equal to 113. Thus, Belgium is more a technology user than a technology producer.

As the index of patents per capita is the product of the index of R&D expenditure per capita with the patent-index of R&D productivity, the lower Belgian propensity to patent can be explained in part by these factors. First, the index of Belgian R&D expenditure per capita compared to the European average is 89 (91 for business R&D expenditures). Second, the R&D productivity index as measured by the ratio of patent applications on R&D expenditures is 74. Consequently, a relatively large part of the observed gap cannot be explained by lower R&D expenditures. Actually, the low R&D productivity index apparently plays a larger role than the low R&D intensity. However, as the measure of the propensity to patent is based on the applicant criterion, a correction has to be made with respect to those patents that have to be attributed to Belgian inventors but whose registration is not claimed by the Belgian subsidiary of the multinational company. When such a correction is made, we obtain a Belgian propensity to patent roughly comparable to the European average.[2]

What can we conclude from this first glance at the Belgian technological performance? One clue is that the Belgian index of manufacturing employment compared to the European average, which is 89, reveals a less important weight of manufacturing activities in the Belgian economy. However, one must stress that this lower performance is compensated for by a higher productivity index of 110. The lower Belgian propensity to patent compared to the European average is explained by the lower R&D expenditures (one third of the gap) and by the repatriation by multinational firms of their research results (two thirds of the gap). Consequently, the question remains whether specifically Belgian firms are less innovative than their European competitors and how the national innovation system depends on foreign decision centres. In the light of the manufacturing employment index, another point deals with the ability of the Belgian S&T policy to valorise efficiently the innovative potential of the country to develop new market niches.[3] To address this question we need to deepen our understanding of the Belgian innovation system in order to identify the particularities that differentiate Belgium from other European countries.

8.2.2.   Patenting activities of firms

Multinational firms largely dominate the Belgian technology infrastructure. The share of large foreign firms in national innovative activities of 54% is by far the largest among the industrialised countries (Patel and Pavitt, 1998). In the 1980s, this share was 40%. This suggests that there have long been strong linkages between the national science and technology base within the Belgian innovation system. Thus, because of its smallness and the ensuing need for a high degree of specialisation, the internationalisation of the Belgian technology base is indisputable. However, this can have had an adverse influence on the innovative effort of domestic firms in terms of the intensity of R&D and its spillover effects. As shown by Veugelers and Vanden Houte (1990) in an analysis of Belgian data on domestic R&D in the presence of multinational enterprises, the higher the presence of multinational firms in an industry, the weaker will be the innovative efforts of domestic firms in that same industry.

---

[2] The use of patent data per applicant leads to an index of patents per capita of 65, to an index of R&D per capita equal to 88 and a R&D productivity index of 74. When the patent data per inventor are used instead of per applicant, the indexes are 87, 88, and 99, respectively.
[3] This question becomes more relevant to our present concern when Belgium is compared with other core countries of the European Union instead of the European average.

Figure 8.1 sheds some light on the patenting activities of the top 50 Belgian firms. As can be observed, this activity is quite concentrated. Indeed, in terms of European patents, the two firms with the highest number of patent applications hold 14% and 7%, respectively, of the total number of patents applied for by Belgian applicants between 1980 and 1996. In terms of US patents, these shares are even higher, being 19% and 11%, respectively. The cumulated share of US patents of the top 50 Belgian firms is about 75% against 60% for European patents. This shows that it is mainly the largest firms that patent outside the European market.

Figure 8.1:   Cumulated distribution of the number of patent applications of the top 50 Belgian firms (EPO and USPTO, 1980-1996)

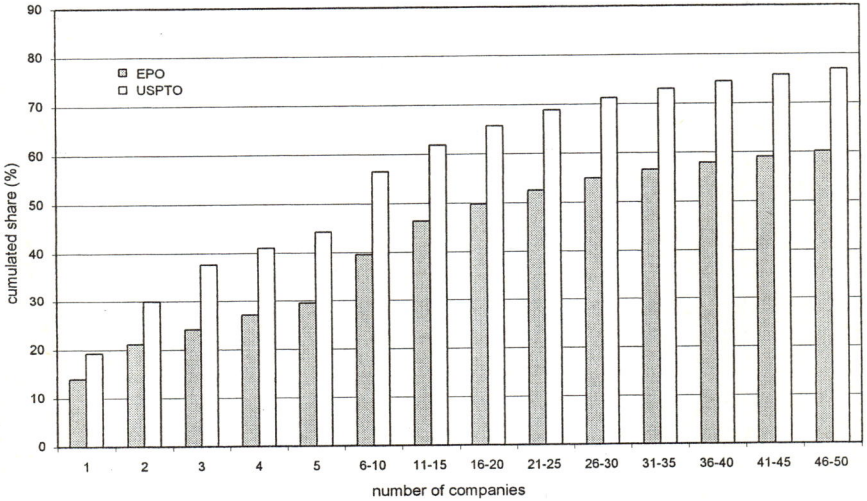

Sources: EPO and USPTO databases; own calculations.

Table 8.1 gives the list of the 20 companies that account for 50% of Belgian patents. As can be seen, three companies (Agfa-Gevaert, Solvay-Interox, and Janssen Pharmaceutica) concentrate 25% and 38% of the patent applications at the EPO and the USPTO, respectively. Globally, Belgian patent activity is highly dependent on a few companies. Another weakness of Belgian patent activity is that a significant number of these companies are subsidiaries of foreign multinationals. This is particularly the case for Agfa-Gevaert, Janssen Pharmaceutica, and Alcatel-Bell, which account for more than 20% of all Belgian applications.

The high dependency of the Belgian innovation system on foreign multinationals could be an important reason for its lower propensity to patent. Indeed, on the one hand, there is the hypothesis that Belgian subsidiaries are specialised in the adaptation to the European market of products and processes developed, in the first place, in foreign headquarters of multinationals. On the other hand, head offices could be hoarding a significant part of their R&D output, the foreign firms taking advantage of the local availability of a highly qualified workforce and knowledge base. These points deserve further consideration.

Table 8.1: The top 20 Belgian firms in terms of European and US patent applications, 1980-1996

Rank	EPO	C%	USPTO	C%
1	Agfa-Gevaert	14.3	Agfa-Gevaert	19.3
2	Solvay-Interox	21.5	Solvay-Interox	29.9
3	Janssen Pharmaceutica	24.5	Janssen Pharmaceutica	37.7
4	*Alcatel/Bell Telephone*	27.5	Picanol	41.1
5	Picanol	30.0	Bekaert	44.3
6	Raychem	32.2	*Glaverbel*	47.3
7	Bekaert	34.3	Raychem	49.6
8	*Ford New Holland*	36.4	*Staar*	51.8
9	Centre de Recherches Métallurgiques Centrum Voor Research in de Metal-lurgie	38.5	Centre de Recherches Métallurgiques Centrum Voor Research in de Metal-lurgie	53.9
10	ACEC	40.3	Fina Research	56.5
11	Fina Research	41.9	UCB	58.0
12	*Procter & Gamble*	43.2	*Metallurgie Hoboken-Overpelt*	59.0
13	*Monsanto Europe*	44.4	*Confiserie Leonidas*	59.9
14	*Pumptech*	45.6	*Dow Corning*	60.9
15	*Cockerill Sambre*	46.4	Fabrique National Herstal	61.8
16	*SmithKline Biologicals*	47.2	ACEC	62.6
17	*GB Boucherie*	47.9	*Champion Spark Plug Europe*	63.4
18	Fabrique National Herstal	48.6	Michel Van de Wiele	64.2
19	Michel Van de Wiele	49.2	*Esselte Dymo*	65.0
20	UCB	49.8	*Texaco Belgium*	65.7

Note: C% = cumulative share; the companies in italics are in only one of the top 20 rankings.
Sources: EPO and USPTO databases; own calculations.

8.2.3. Product- and process-oriented patents at the USPTO

Technological change can be defined in several ways. For instance, it is common to distinguish process innovation from product innovation. The former is related to the discovery of a new production process while the latter is associated with the invention of a new product. This distinction is important because it is often suggested that the private rate of return is higher for processes than for products (Mansfield et al., 1977, Mansfield, 1988), although product innovations are more favourable to job creation than process innovations, which mainly improve pro-

ductivity.[4] In fact, a considerable part of R&D expenditure goes to product innovation (see also Chapter 5, Section 5.2.2).[5]

Innovation counts based on patent data allow one to appraise the orientation of
the Belgian NIS. A logometric analysis of the summary of each patent applied for
from the USPTO was conducted. Each time the word 'process' and/or 'method'
were found, the patent was assigned to a process invention. Figure 8.2 indicates
that, on average, one third of the total number of patents over the period are process patents. This observation can be compared to the orientation of R&D expenditures presented in Chapter 4. The distribution of patents between these two categories does not seem to have changed drastically over time. Note, too, that the
time pattern of both kinds of patents is not synchronised.

**Figure 8.2:   Patent distribution by type of invention (product- and process-oriented
patents at the USPTO (Belgium, 1980-1996)**

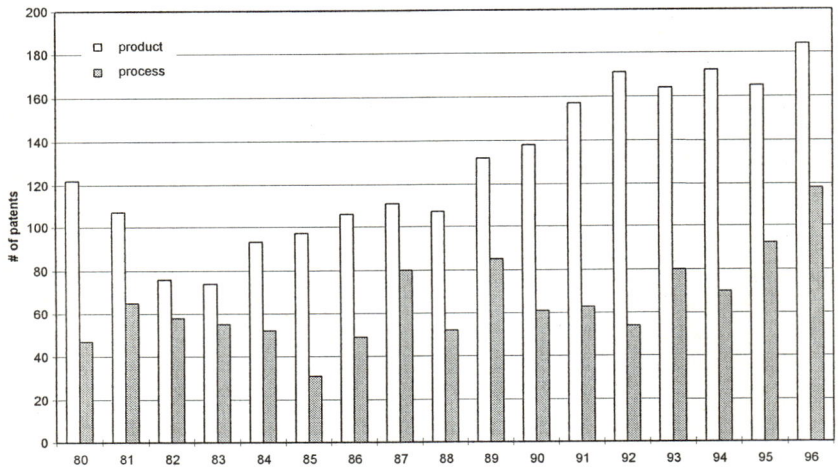

Source: USPTO database; own calculations.

---

[4] See Griliches and Lichtenberg (1984) and Edquist *et al.* (1998).
[5] Cohen *et al.* (1998) observe that 66% of the USA and 81% of the Japanese R&D effort are
devoted to product innovation. In the UK, the proportion of process innovations is equal
around 69% (Pavitt *et al.*, 1987).

8.2.4.   Patenting activities of universities, RTOs, and government agencies

Non-market institutions have a lower propensity to patent than do profit-seeking organisations. Around 80% of all EPO patents applications filed by Belgian applicants come from firms and 15% from individual inventors. Only 5% come from academic institutions, RTOs, and government agencies. Table 8.2 shows the number of EPO patent applications by public research institutes, universities, private non-profit organisations, and government agencies. Once again, the patenting activities of these institutions are quite concentrated.[6] Indeed, three institutions out of 33 hold 52.7% of the total number of patents applied for by these institutions.

Table 8.2:   **EPO patent applications (1980-1996) of Belgian public research institutions, universities, and government agencies**

	Public institutions (I), universities (U), governments (G)	NPA	C%
I	Centre de Recherches Métallurgiques	126	35.3
I	Interuniversitair Microelektronica Centrum (IMEC)	35	45.1
G	La Région Wallonne	27	52.7
I	Leuven Research & Development	23	59.1
I	Stichting REGA	22	65.3
I	S.C.K/C.E.N.	19	70.6
U	Université Catholique de Louvain	16	75.1
I	International Institute of Cellular and Molecular Pathology (ICP)	16	79.6
I	Vlaamse Instelling voor Technologisch Onderzoek (VITO)	14	83.5
G	Etat Belge, Services de Programmation de la Politique Scientifique	13	87.1
U	Rijksuniversiteit Gent	10	89.9
U	Université Libre de Bruxelles	9	92.4
U	Université de Liège	4	93.6
I	Société de Recherches et de Développement Industriel (SOREDI)	2	94.1
I	Institut d'Enseignement Spécial, Atelier Protégé les Erables	2	94.7
I	Institution pour le Développement de la Gazéification Souterraine	2	95.2
I	Wetenschappelijk en Techn. Centrum van de Belg. Textielnijverheid (Centexbel)	2	95.8
I	Miscellaneous	15	100.0
	TOTAL	357	

Notes: NPA = number of patent applications; C% = cumulative share.
Sources: EPO database; own calculations.

Another feature that emerges from the table is the relatively low propensity to patent of universities and public research institutes in comparison with the organisations specifically engaged in R&D activities and to private business firms. Of course, given the more scientific nature as well as the aims and the functions of the research activities undertaken by such institutions, patent statistics are not well

---

[6] A similar observation can be made for private business firms.

suited for assessing their output. Hence, other indicators, such as the number of scientific papers and their citations, may be more appropriate for this purpose.

Until recently, given the missions assigned to them and the academic-reward rules, the institutions of higher education were motivated more to publish scientific papers than patent inventions. As pointed out by Etzkowitz and Webster (1998, p. 21), "today, universities are undergoing a second revolution" that is leading them increasingly to translate "research findings into intellectual property, a marketable commodity, and economic development". The number of university patent applications multiplied by 2.5 from the 1981-1988 period to the 1989-1996 period while the total number of patent applications multiplied only by 1.6. These data are an indication of the increased involvement of universities in economic development over the last years.

8.2.5.   The impact of R&D on patenting and scientific publications

This section investigates the impact of R&D activities on the number of patents as well as of scientific publications for 383 Belgian manufacturing firms in 1995.[7] The analysis is carried out by considering an extended 'knowledge production function' (Griliches, 1979), which is estimated by means of the 'General Event Count' econometric model.[8] This exercise extends previous work on the R&D-patent relationship[9] by considering several components of R&D activities (i.e. its 'R' and its 'D' component, product- versus process-oriented R&D, and intramural and subcontracted R&D) rather than total R&D expenditures of firms. The distinction between the origin of the financing, i.e. internal versus external funding, is also considered. As regards the external funding of R&D, information is available on whether the funds originate from public authorities, other business firms, or research and technology organisations (RTOs) and Higher Education Institutions (HEIs). A similar distinction for extramural R&D activities is made.

The main findings are reported in Table 8.3. On the whole, total R&D activities exhibit slightly decreasing returns to scale with respect to patenting.[10] Nevertheless, when the R&D components are considered in function of the type of activity and the source of financing, the estimates appear much more differentiated. For scientific publications, the returns of total R&D are lower. The higher risks and uncertainties of basic or fundamental research activities could account for this result.

---

[7] The data come from the 1996 biannual survey of R&D activities of Belgian firms organised by the OSTC.

[8] See Winkelmann and Zimmermann (1994) for a discussion of this model. The framework allows one to deal with the discrete non-negative nature of patent and scientific publication counts.

[9] This result corroborates previous findings of related studies. See Cincera (1998), for a survey.

[10] See, among others, Hausman, Hall and Griliches (1984), Hall, Griliches and Hausman (1986), Crépon and Duguet (1997a, 1997b) and Cincera (1997).

The estimates with respect to the impact of R&D activities and its different components on patenting are summarised on the left side of Table 8.3. The distinction between in-house and sub-contracted R&D indicates that it is mainly the former activity that contributes to technological output as measured by patents. One argument to explain the lower 'productivity' of R&D carried out outside the firm is the occurrence of major transaction costs. As emphasised by Geroski (1995a), given these costs, external research facilities will generally provide generic rather than specialised inputs into the R&D programmes of their clients. These generic inputs are less likely to lead to successful inventions and to patent applications.

If we now turn to the composition of the R&D effort, the estimates suggest that the returns are higher for development activities, product-oriented research, and the share of R&D expenses for the salaries of researchers. The result for the last component indicates the importance of human capital in the inventive process with respect to investments in R&D capital. Indeed, as shown in Chapter 4, the share of the R&D personnel expenditures accounts for more than two thirds of the total intramural R&D budget. The high estimated elasticity associated with the share of R&D allocated to product innovation confirms the higher propensity of Belgian firms to apply for product-oriented patents already observed in section 8.2.3. The estimated elasticities associated with the actual research and development components of R&D activities indicate that patenting tends to occur during the stage of the invention process of development of new products and processes. This finding can be related to many patenting firms in Belgium being subsidiaries of foreign companies. These firms may well be more involved in the development of already patented products by the foreign mother company for local or national markets.

While some empirical evidence has been found for a leverage effect of publicly financed R&D on private R&D, there is in general no impact of the former variable on output performances of firms as measured by productivity growth[11] or patenting. The estimates associated with the share of intramural R&D financed by external funds, i.e. firms, government agencies, RTOs, and HEIs, lead to a similar conclusion. Moreover, significant negative elasticity is found for the RTOs and HEIs. The non-commercial orientation of the research financed by such organisations may account for this result. Finally, the higher returns of out-sourced R&D on own patenting come mainly from other business firms and to a lesser extent from RTOs and HEIs. This opposite finding with respect to the external funding is because the decision to sub-contract R&D activities in such organisations comes from the firms themselves.

---

[11] See Capron (1992b) and Hall (1996) for a review.

Table 8.3:   **'Knowledge production functions': estimated impacts of R&D 'components' on scientific publications and patent applications (383 Belgian firms, 1995)**

	Dependent variable: number of patents						Dependent variable: number of scientific publications					
Total R&D	0.9 (.10)*						0.6 (.09)*					
Intramural R&D		0.6 (.08)*						0.5 (.08)*				
Research			0.1 (.03)*						0.1 (.03)*			
Development			0.3 (.06)*						0.2 (.06)*			
Product				0.2 (.05)*						0.1 (.04)*		
Process				0.0 (.04)						0.0 (.03)		
Other				0.1 (.04)*						0.1 (.03)*		
Personnel					0.3 (.19)**						0.5 (.11)	
Investment					0.0 (.08)						0.0 (.07)	
Organisation					0.1 (.05)**						0.0 (.04)	
Own funds						0.4 (.08)*						0.4 (.07)*
Extern. Funds **Firms**						0.0 (.04)						0.0 (.03)
Government						0.0 (.03)						0.1 (.03)*
RTOs and HEIs						-0.2 (.08)**						0.0 (.04)
Extramural R&D		0.2 (.03)*	0.2 (.03)*	0.2 (.04)*	0.2 (.04)*			0.1 (.03)*	0.1 (.03)*	0.2 (.04)*	0.1 (.03)*	
Firms						0.2 (.04)*						0.0 (.03)
Collective research centres						0.0 (.04)						0.0 (.03)
RTOs and HEIs						0.1 (.04)*						0.1 (.03)*
K	1.0 (.13)*	1.0 (.13)*	0.9 (.12)*	0.8 (.10)*	1.0 (.13)*	0.9 (.11)*	0.6 (.16)*	0.5 (.13)*	0.4 (.13)*	0.4 (.15)*	0.5 (.13)*	0.4 (.12)*
s^2	5.6 (1.0)*	5.1 (.91)*	5.4 (.83)*	6.9 (1.2)*	5.2 (.92)*	4.4 (.71)*	8.2 (1.4)*	7.1 (1.4)*	8.2 (1.8)*	8.6 (1.9)*	7.0 (1.4)*	6.6 (1.2)*
Loglikelihood	-332	-327	-328	-337	-330	-318	-417	-402	-407	-414	-402	-397

Notes: a) heteroskedastic-consistent standard errors in parenthesis, *, resp. ** means statistically significant at the 5%, resp. 10% level;

b) RTOs = Research and Technology Organisation, HEIs = Higher Education Institutions.

The right side of Table 8.3 reports the estimated effect of R&D expenditure components on the number of scientific publications by firms. This measure better reflects basic or fundamental output of R&D activities. The pattern of the estimated coefficients does not exhibit drastic differences when compared to the patent variable, but three differences are deserving of mention. First, as discussed above, the overall impact of R&D is lower. Second, as far as external funding is concerned, no impact is observed with respect to funds originating from firms or RTOs and HEIs. However, the opposite holds for public funds. This result does not contradict the argument that public subsidies to R&D are directed to basic and more risky research. Finally, only subcontracted R&D to RTOs and HEIs appear beneficial to scientific output.

8.3. Differences in regional profiles

Increasingly, regional technology initiatives are inducing important changes in national innovation systems, especially in federal countries like Belgium. The adequate targeting of S&T policies at the different spatial decision levels in terms of effectiveness, priorities, and complementarities is vital for reinforcing the capacity to cope with increased technological competition and its economic consequences. Indeed, S&T policies are not spatially neutral.[12] The spatial structures are not only central in the innovation process but innovation is also a spatial process in itself. Innovation appears to be less the product of individual firms than the result of agglomeration of technological infrastructure in specific places. In this regard, the technological infrastructure of a region strengthens the innovation potential and influences the location of firms. Proximity between industries and academic research centres may also be a significant source of productivity benefits.[13] Furthermore, knowledge spillovers are intrinsically linked to location factors. Consequently, in order to assess innovation dynamics properly it is essential to grasp the regional context.

As a federal country, a large part of the Belgian S&T policy is now under the responsibility of the three regions, Flanders, Wallonia, and Brussels-Capital as well as the French Community.[14] The federal government can still take initiatives regarding international agreements or specific scientific fields going beyond the concerns of a single region or community.

---

[12] For a discussion, see Jaffe, Trajtenberg, and Henderson (1993) as well as Audretsch and Feldman (1993).

[13] See, for instance, Jaffe (1989).

[14] Strictly speaking also the Flemish Community can be said to be partly responsible for S&T policy, but on the administrative and political level the Flemish Community is merged with the Flemish Region.

Figure 8.3 gives the distribution of Belgian patents counts at the EPO and the USPTO among the three Belgian regions: Flanders, Brussels-Capital, and Wallonia. On the whole, Flanders, with about 60%, has the highest share in both patent offices over the period 1980-1996. Moreover, this share in terms of European patents has increased from about 41% in 1980 to 58% at the end of the period. For USA patents, this increase is even larger. Conversely, the shares of the two other regions, Brussels and Wallonia, have decreased over the same period. However, these figures have a somewhat different pattern depending on the patent office considered. Indeed, for European patents, the decline is similar in both regions and seems to have stabilised at the end of the period. In terms of USA patents, the share of Brussels has fallen from 40% in 1980 to less than 15% in 1996, while Wallonia's share has been stable over this period.

With regard to the patent distribution at the district level, it appears that the number of patent applications is highly concentrated in a few districts. Antwerp and Brussels, the two most important Belgian districts in terms of economic activity, concentrate together 46.4% and 54.2%, respectively, of the total number of European and USA patents over the period 1980-1996. Consequently, they can be viewed as the most innovative Belgian areas if patents are used as the criterion.

Figure 8.3:   Number of patent applications by region (EPO and USPTO, 1980-1996)

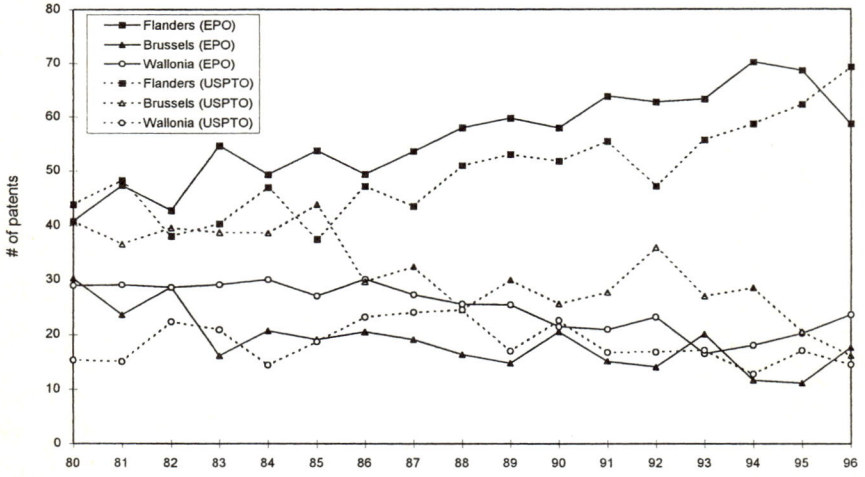

Sources: EPO and USPTO databases; own calculations.

Figure 8.4:   Concentration of innovativeness and wealth at the district level
(Belgium = 100, average 1981-1993)

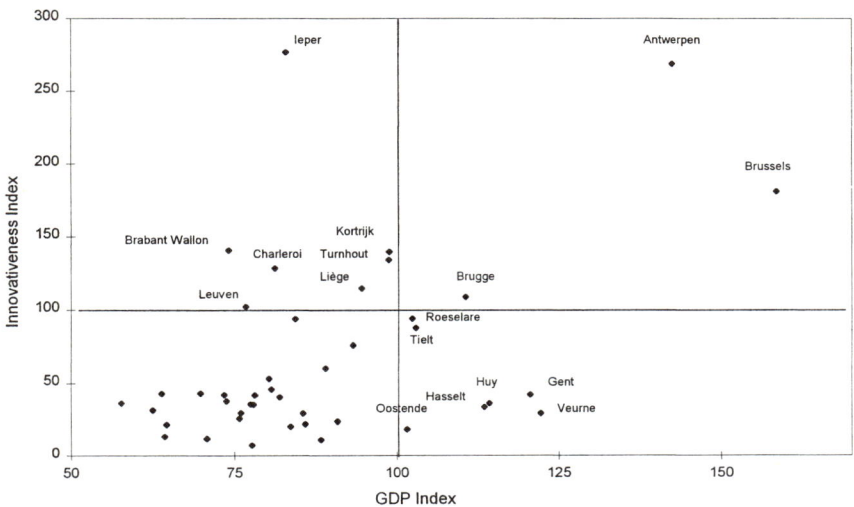

Figure 8.5:   Concentration and diversity of innovativeness at the district level
(Belgium = 100, average 1981-1993)

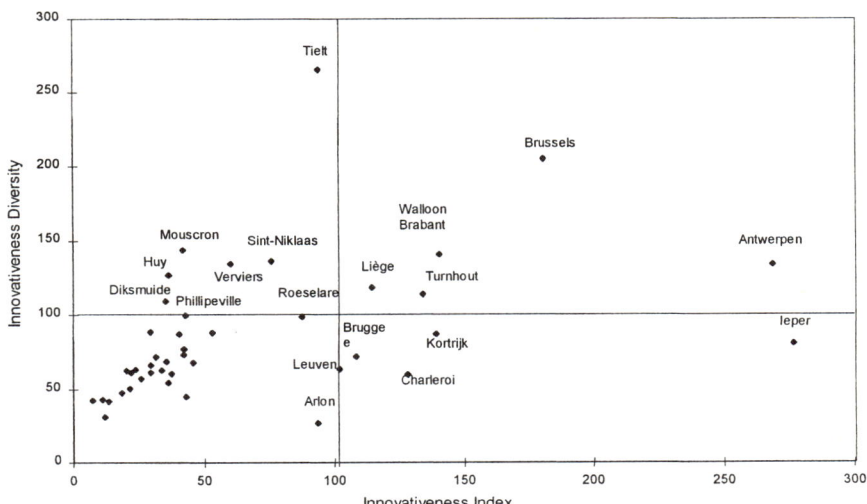

Table 8.4:   **Regional GDP, patents and innovating firms per capita (Belgium = 100) and technological concentration in Belgium, 1981-1993**

District PROVINCE REGION	index of GDP per capita		index of # of patents per capita		index of # of innovating firms per capita		index of technological concentration	
Antwerp		142		269		134		4.2
Mechelen		86		30		61		3.4
Turnhout		99		134		114		4.9
ANTWERP	122		193		116		3.5	
Halle-Vilvoorde		80		53		88		3.3
Leuven		77		102		64		3.0
FLEMISH BRABANT	79		75		77		2.3	
Hasselt		114		34		63		2.8
Maaseik		84		20		62		3.6
Tongeren		63		32		72		3.0
LIMBURG	93		30		65		2.2	
Aalst		70		43		45		3.0
Dendermonde		74		38		60		3.2
Eeklo		73		42		73		5.0
Ghent		121		42		77		3.0
Oudenaarde		91		24		63		3.5
St-Niklaas		93		76		136		3.0
EAST FLANDERS	95		46		77		1.9	
Bruges		111		108		72		7.8
Diksmuide		78		35		109		5.9
Ypres		83		277		81		8.9
Kortrijk		99		139		87		2.6
Ostend		102		18		48		3.3
Roeselare		103		88		99		6.0
Tielt		102		94		265		2.4
Veurne		122		29		89		5.5
WEST FLANDERS	101		110		94		3.6	
WALLOON BRABANT	74		141		141		2.7	
Ath		65		22		50		5.0
Charleroi		81		128		60		3.0
Mons		76		30		66		2.4
Mouscron		78		42		144		2.9
Soignies		71		12		31		4.3
Thuin		58		36		54		5.8
Tournai		77		36		69		3.5
HAINAUT	75		62		62		2.1	
Huy		114		36		127		2.9
Liège		95		114		119		1.7
Verviers		89		60		134		2.3
Waremme		64		13		42		8.6
LIEGE	93		87		119		1.5	
Arlon		84		94		27		5.6
Bastogne		82		41		87		5.7
Marche-en-Famenne		88		11		43		8.1
Neufchâteau		86		22		61		5.1
Virton		76		26		57		4.6
LUXEMBOURG	83		39		54		3.4	
Dinant		78		7		42		4.8
Namur		81		46		68		2.6
Philippeville		64		43		100		5.2
NAMUR	78		37		67		2.3	
Flemish Region	**101**		**102**		**90**		**2.1**	
Brussels-Capital	**158**		**181**		**205**		**2.0**	
Walloon Region	**81**		**72**		**87**		**1.6**	
BELGIUM	**100**		**100**		**100**		**1.4**	

Sources: INS, EPO database, own calculations.

Table 8.4 gives the levels of concentration and diversity of innovativeness in function of European patents in the Belgian districts, provinces, and regions. Figures 8.4 and 8.5 also give some complementary illustrations. It follows from these figures that Antwerp and Brussels are the two main Belgian patenting districts with 25% and 18% of patent applications, respectively, and the two main Walloon innovative districts are Liège and Charleroi with 7% and 6% of the patent applications, respectively.

All the other districts have a share that is less than 5%, except Turnhout (a district contiguous to Antwerp) with 5%. Ypres has an innovativeness index similar to the one obtained for Antwerp. There is, however, no direct link between the wealth of districts and their innovativeness. While Ypres has a high innovativeness index, its GDP per capita (average for the period 1981-1993) is less than that of Ghent and Hasselt, the innovativeness indices of which are low.

If we turn to the link between innovativeness concentration and innovativeness diversity (measured by the number of innovative firms or individuals in function of patents), Brussels has higher innovativeness diversity than Antwerp. Ypres is, to a large extent, dependent on a small number of innovators. Liège, Walloon Brabant, and Turnhout have a balanced distribution of patents among innovators. If we look at the technological concentration measured by the variation coefficients among technological classes,[15] we observe that Antwerp is characterised by a higher concentration of patent applications in some technological classes[16] than is Brussels. The two main Walloon districts, Liège and Charleroi, also show a more diversified technological activity.

8.4. Co-patents

Quoting Archibugi and Pianta (1992, p. 12), "the internationalization of technology and the growing sectoral specialization of the activities of countries and firms have led, over the last decade, to a new pattern of cooperation in innovative activities both across borders and among different institutions, namely research centres, industry and government agencies." The purpose of this section is to look at the behaviour of the Belgian actors with regard to S&T collaborative activities in the field of patents. More precisely, we turn our attention to the output of the Belgian co-operative activities as measured by co-patenting activities. Before examining these figures more carefully, we would recall briefly the main theoretical arguments in favour of S&T collaborations. The main advantages associated with

---

[15] The data on which these figures are based are not corrected for the distinction between headquarters and R&D centres.
[16] The main explanation is the high propensity of Agfa-Gevaert to patent in some technological classes.

technological co-operation[17] are the sharing of the risks of S&T activities, better access to the funds needed to finance them, and the ability to take advantage of economies of scale and of scope. In addition, joint S&T activities allow firms to benefit from complementary knowledge bases and eliminate the duplication of resources allocated to such activities.

Figure 8.6 shows the share of co-patent applications with respect to the total number of patents filed with the EPO from 1980 to 1994. On average, 10% of patents are co-patent applications. Compared to France, whose economy is less open than Belgium, this share is somewhat lower.[18] Hence, the success of Belgian technological collaborations as measured by patents may be questioned. Nevertheless, among the co-patents registered, two out of three on average involve a foreign co-applicant. It should be noted that this proportion tends to be accentuated in time and is higher than in France, where one co-applicant out of two is a foreign one.

Figure 8.7 exhibits the share of foreign co-patent applications with Belgium. The four largest shares represent a total of 71%. With the exception of the United States, these countries – France, the Netherlands, and Germany – are neighbours of Belgium. Hence, technological collaborations in terms of co-patenting appears to be spatially oriented.

---

[17] See Kamien *et al.* (1992) or Geroski (1995).
[18] 15% over the period 1980-1989 (Duguet, 1994).

Figure 8.6:   Share of co-patent applications (1980-1996, EPO)

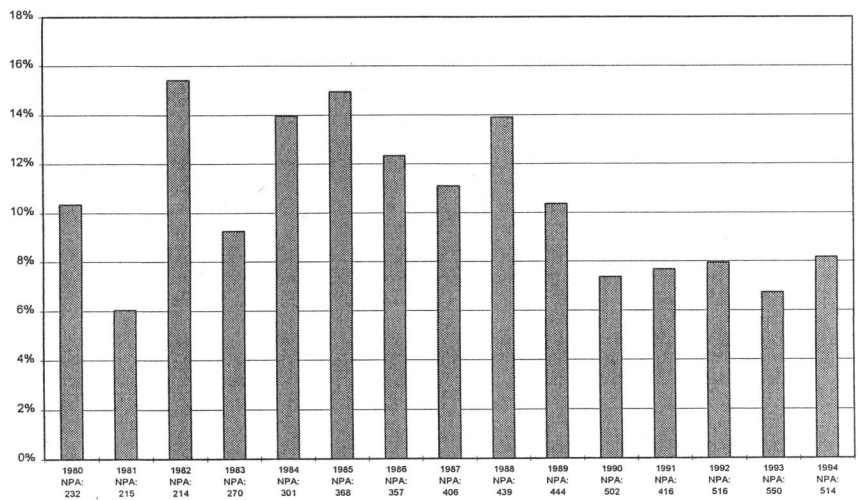

Note: NPA = number of patent applications.
Sources: EPO database; own calculations.

Figure 8.7:   Foreign co-applicants: share by country (1980-1994, EPO)

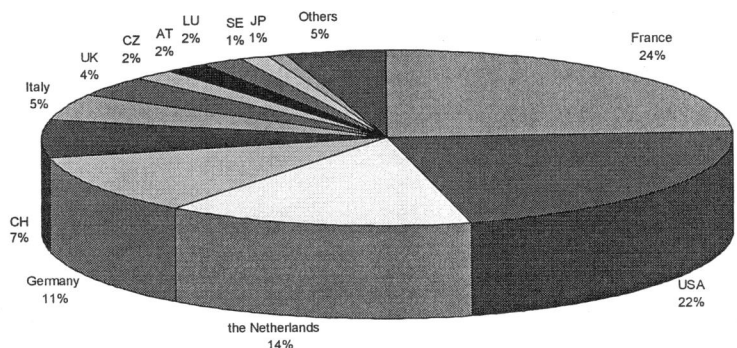

Sources: EPO database; own calculations.

The number of co-patents involving Belgian and foreign public institutes, universities, and governmental agencies represents a small portion of the total patenting, only about 0.9%, and of the total of co-patents, 12%. The *Centre de Recherche Métallurgique* holds the largest number of co-patents: 8 out of the 47.

About one fifth of the co-applicants are universities, and 8 out of the 47 are foreign institutes.

8.5.   Technological specialisation and technological revealed comparative advantage

The evaluation of the technological capacity of a country in terms of its economic performance is becoming increasingly important for political decision-makers. This section analyses the technological fields in which Belgium is specialised or has revealed comparative advantages as compared to the European Union. For this purpose, the European patent statistics are used. Table 8.5 indicates the main technological classes in which Belgium is specialised in terms of EPO patents. We use the International Patent Classification (IPC). On the whole, it appears that innovative activities are quite concentrated in specific technological areas.

Indeed, this concentration has intensified during the recent years: the top IPC-classes represent 40.3% of all the patents over the sub-period 1980-1985 against 52.4% for 1991-1996. Instruments and particularly photography are characterised by the highest shares in all three sub-periods. Furthermore this share has more than doubled in the last sub-period. Over the period, organic compounds and to a lesser extent biochemistry and packing have become more important while agriculture, health, and measurement instruments have declined in relative importance.

Table 8.6 gives the TRCA[19] indexes. A value less than one of this index of specialisation means that Belgium holds a smaller share in its patent distribution for the particular technological class than its world counterpart. The IPC classes have been ranked in decreasing order of the performed value taken by this index for each of the three sub-periods. The TRCA indexes shed some light on the relative advantages of Belgium with respect to its existing technological capability. Over the entire period, personal articles (in particular brushware and textiles (weaving), and ropes) represent the activities for which Belgium has the highest TRCA. In the more recent sub-period, four new IPC classes entered the top 10: instruments (photography), printing, agriculture, and metallurgy (electrolytic processes). In the later sub-period, only three high-tech classes are identified as Belgian specialisations among the first 20 classes: photography, inorganic chemistry, and biochemistry.

---

[19] The IPC classification at the 2-digit level is used to compute the TRCA index. It should be noted that an alternative more aggregated classification has also been retained. The results obtained are along the lines of the findings of Archibugi and Pianta (1992) in their study of the technological specialisation of advanced countries.

The growth of patents in the 118 IPC sub-classes between the two sub-periods 1985-90 and 1991-96 shows that Belgium has higher than average mean annual rates of change of patent applications, relative to the total number of patent applications to the EPO in the corresponding class, in three rapidly growing classes: computing and calculating, basic electronic circuitry, and printing. The other rapidly growing classes in which Belgium has a higher growth rate than the general average, but not higher than the growth rate of the corresponding class, are dyes and paints, photography, engineering elements, packing and storing, physical and chemical processes, electric power, electric technology, electric communication technology, and organic compounds. In other rapidly growing classes that correspond to a high TRCA for Belgium such as biochemistry, the growth rate is less than the general average. In a nutshell, the low growth rate of Belgian patent applications to the EPO can to a large extent be explained by its relative sectoral

Table 8.5:   Relative share of top IPC classes, 1980-1996, EPO

Rank	1980-1985			1986-1990			1991-1996		
	IPC	%	C%	IPC	%	C%	IPC	%	C%
1	Photography	5.6	5.6	Photography	6.6	6.6	Photography	12.6	12.6
2	Agriculture	5.4	11.0	Organic chemistry	6.1	12.7	Printing	6.0	18.6
3	Organic chemistry	5.3	16.3	Weaving	5.0	17.8	Transmission	5.8	24.4
4	Medical and hygiene	4.4	20.7	Agriculture	4.7	22.4	Organic compounds	5.6	30.0
5	Packing and storing	4.1	24.7	Organic compounds	4.6	27.0	Organic chemistry	5.2	35.1
6	Measuring instruments	3.5	28.2	Medical and hygiene	4.1	31.1	Agriculture	4.1	39.2
7	Heating	3.1	31.4	Biochemistry	3.6	34.7	Biochemistry	3.6	42.8
8	Organic compounds	3.1	34.5	Measuring instruments	3.5	38.2	Packing and storing	3.4	46.2
9	Building	3.0	37.5	Packing and storing	3.0	41.2	Medical and hygiene	3.2	49.4
10	Oils, detergents and candles	2.8	40.3	Mining	2.9	44.1	Measuring instruments	3.2	52.6
11	Engineering	2.8	43.1	Building	2.5	46.5	Weaving	3.0	55.6
12	Plastics	2.5	45.6	Electric elements	2.2	48.7	Engineering	2.3	57.9
13	Electric power	2.1	47.7	Plastics	2.0	50.8	Dyes and paints	2.2	60.1
14	Electric elements	2.1	49.8	Engineering	2.0	52.8	Processes and apparatus	2.2	62.4
15	Domestic articles	2.0	51.8	Domestic articles	2.0	54.8	Plastics	2.1	64.5
16	Sports and games	1.9	53.7	Processes and apparatus	2.0	56.8	Electric elements	1.9	66.4
17	Processes and apparatus	1.6	55.2	Heating	1.8	58.6	Building	1.8	68.3
18	Weaving	1.5	56.7	Transmission	1.8	60.3	Computing	1.8	70.1
19	Vehicles	1.5	58.2	Combustion apparatus	1.7	62.0	Domestic articles	1.3	71.5
20	Transmission	1.5	59.7	Oils, detergents and candles	1.7	63.7	Electric power	1.3	72.7

Notes: % = share, C% = cumulated share.
Source: EPO, own calculations.

Table 8.6:   Technological Revealed Comparative Advantage (TRCA), 1980-96, EPO

	1980-1985			1986-1990			1991-1996		
rank	IPC	%	TRCA	IPC	%	TRCA	IPC	%	TRCA
1	Brushware	0.9	11.7	Weaving	5.0	21.0	Ropes and cables	0.4	16.3
2	Ropes; cables	0.2	7.4	Ropes and cables	0.5	20.3	Weaving	3.0	12.3
3	Oils, detergents and candles	2.8	5.6	Brushware	0.7	7.9	Brushware	0.5	8.3
4	Weaving	1.5	5.6	Sugar industry	0.2	6.0	Sugar industry	0.1	6.8
5	Explosives	0.3	5.4	Instruments	0.1	5.1	Photography	13.0	4.8
6	Machines and engines	0.9	4.6	Mining	2.9	4.9	Printing	6.0	3.8
7	Cleaning	0.1	3.9	Metallurgy	1.4	3.9	Metallurgy	0.9	3.7
8	Sugar industry	0.2	3.6	Combustion apparatus	1.7	3.8	Saddlery and upholstery	0.0	3.3
9	Heating	3.1	3.6	Heating	1.8	3.7	Agriculture	4.1	3.0
10	Agriculture	5.4	3.0	Heat exchange	0.9	3.5	Electrolytic processes	0.7	2.7
11	Metallurgy	1.3	2.9	Oils, detergents and candles	1.7	3.1	Mining	1.1	2.3
12	Sport, games	1.9	2.8	Photography	6.6	3.1	Weapons	0.4	2.1
13	Photography	5.6	2.6	Electrolytic processes	1.4	3.1	Butchering	0.3	2.0
14	Building	3.0	2.3	Spraying, atomising	0.1	2.9	Sewing	0.2	2.0
15	Heat exchange	0.8	2.3	Agriculture	4.7	2.9	Building	1.8	1.9
16	Weapons	0.8	2.3	Headwear	0.1	2.8	Inorganic chemistry	1.1	1.9
17	Ammunition	0.5	2.3	Drying	0.2	2.7	Casting	0.8	1.7
18	Life-saving	0.4	2.2	Hydraulic engineering	0.9	2.6	Baking	0.2	1.7
19	Hydraulic engineering	0.9	2.2	Saddlery and upholstery	0.0	2.4	Biochemistry	3.6	1.5
20	Constructions	0.8	2.2	Weapons	0.7	2.4	Dyes and paints	2.2	1.5

Notes: % = share;

$$TRCA_{ij} = \left(n_{ij} / \sum_i n_{ij} \right) / \left(\sum_j n_{ij} / \sum_i \sum_j n_{ij} \right)$$, where n_{ij} is the number of patents of country j

in the i-th technological class, all countries.

Source: EPO, own calculations.

weaknesses in rapidly growing classes. If at the policy level it is reasonable to reinforce advantages in established low-growing technological sectors of strength, there is at the same time a need to promote innovative efforts in new fast-growing technological fields in order to ensure a soft transition in the growth process.

8.6. Scientific publications

If patents can be viewed as a main indicator of innovative output in industry, publications are often considered to be a good indicator of the innovative effectiveness of the higher education system (Patel and Pavitt, 1995). Around 72% of publications originate from the five largest universities (KUL, UCL, ULB, UG, ULG) (European Commission, 1997b). Table 8.7 shows that Belgium is in a favourable position in three scientific fields: clinical medicine, biomedical research and physics. These scientific specialisations roughly correspond to the main technological specialisations found in the analysis of patents. Nevertheless, a slow but real decline in the number of scientific publications is observed in comparison with the European evolution: the Belgian share of international publications at the world level is decreasing while the European one is increasing. In 1993, the index of the number of publications was 7% less than the European average. The main scientific specialisation of Belgium is in biomedical research, a field that corresponds to a revealed advantage in biochemistry as measured by the analysis of the patent data. Nevertheless, although Belgium is specialised in some chemicals-related patent classes, there is no scientific specialisation in this field. Globally, taking into account the observed shortage on the labour market of scientists and engineers in Belgium, the country still appears to perform relatively well. Finally, it is worth noting that, despite its small size, Belgium has a broad distribution of its efforts across fields of science (Archibugi and Pianta (1992)).

Table 8.7:   Scientific publications

Publications by scientific fields (% EUR15)	1981	1985	1990	1993	Index 1981	Index 1993
Clinical Medicine	2.9	2.5	2.8	2.7	103	100
Biomedical Research	3.0	2.9	3.2	3.1	107	115
Biology	2.3	2.7	2.7	2.5	82	93
Chemistry	2.7	2.7	2.1	2.2	96	81
Physics	2.9	2.5	2.6	2.7	103	100
Mathematics	3.3	2.8	2.5	2.5	117	93
Engineering	2.1	2.1	2.5	2.4	75	89
Universe Sciences	2.5	2.9	2.3	2.0	89	74
Total (% EUR15)	2.7	2.7	2.6	2.5	96	93
EUR 15 (% world)	29.2	30.1	30.3	32.5	-	-
Publication index	112	113	110	109		
Citation index	121	128	126	133		
Co-publication index	-	-	-	217		

Notes: Index = 100*value of the variable per inhabitant divided by the EUR15 ratio.
         The indexes by scientific fields are corrected for co-publications.
Source: European Commission (1994, 1997b).

An explanation of the drop in the publication index is the increasing international collaboration in which Belgian teams are involved. When not corrected for co-publications, the Belgian position with respect to the European Union average is around 10% higher than the average. Both the citation and co-publication indexes confirm the increase as well as the scope of the degree of internationalisation of the Belgian scientific research. As shown in Table 8.7 Belgian scientists have a high propensity to collaborate with foreign colleagues. Presently, around 44% of Belgian scientific papers involve collaboration with a foreign scientist. The Belgian propensity to collaborate with a foreign team is twice as great as the European average. Finally, the citation index gives clues as to the quality of Belgian research since the value of the index is increasing over time and about 30% higher than the European average.

8.7. Trademarks

In Sections 8.2 to 8.5, we measured innovative success by looking at patents filed in an international context. Nevertheless, a technologically successful firm might easily fail in its efforts to commercialise its potentially superior goods.

In assessing the importance of innovation, therefore, we tried to improve the traditional measure of innovation by complementing it with an indicator of commercial innovativeness and the efforts of firms in selling their goods abroad. Though potentially suffering from similar drawbacks as the patent measure, we retained the national shares in the foreign trademark applications in the USA as a statistical proxy of commercial innovativeness. The rationale for this is that a firm that is prepared to commence a lengthy and costly procedure to protect a brand name on the USA market will also be willing to spend a considerable amount on marketing to introduce the brand on that market. We also assume that the application for trademarks is linked to the final output of innovative activities to generate new products rather than to upgrade the quality of existing products. This implies that the combined use of patent and trademark statistics could give an indication of the importance of the expansion of product variety and of quality upgrading. We will go further into this subject in Chapter 9 (Section 9.2).

Table 8.8: Trademark shares in OECD context

	Germany	France	The Netherlands	Belgium
1964-69	0.222	0.158	0.040	0.015
1970-79 (1)	0.193	0.163	0.033	0.013
1980-89	0.194	0.174	0.032	0.012
1990-95 (2)	0.153	0.172	0.044	0.013
((2)-(1))/(1) (%)	-21.015	5.579	35.393	1.094

Note: The proportions in the table are in terms of the total number of trademarks deposited by OECD countries (excluding the US) at the USPTO.

The evidence for commercial innovativeness for Belgium in comparison with its main competitors is summarised in Table 8.8 and Figure 8.8 and shows that the position of Belgium in this context is no better than for patents. It is true that the level of trademarking by Belgian firms as measured by the OECD trademark share in the total of trademarks deposited in the US remained more or less constant over the period considered (see Table 8.8). On average, the Belgian share in the total of foreign trademarks deposited in the US was approximately 1.32% in the period from 1990 to 1995. However, in relative terms with respect to the size of the population, Belgian firms deposit fewer than half in comparison with their Dutch neighbours and consistently fewer than the firms in most of the other OECD countries (Figure 8.8).

Figure 8.8: Number of trademarks deposited at the USPTO per million inhabitants

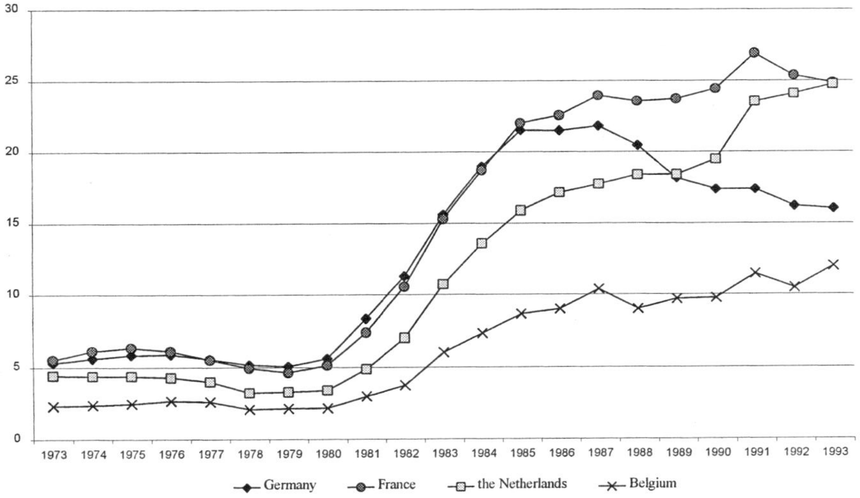

Source: WIPO database.

8.8. Conclusion

Some important conclusions can be drawn from the analysis of patent and trademark applications of Belgian firms and from the number of publications by Belgian scientists as first-level output indicators of its national innovation system. They can be summarised as follows:
- The Belgian patent propensity and patent productivity are considerably inferior to the European average. The specific industrial base and the high degree of dependence of the Belgian NIS on foreign companies could largely account

for this weak performance. Indeed, a more thorough analysis of the patent applications has shown that Belgian R&D centres that are part of domestic branches of foreign multinationals operate in the context of the research policy of these companies, which results in the 'repatriation' of the 'Belgian fruits' of their R&D activities.

- The Belgian technological revealed advantages are mainly concentrated in technological classes linked to medium- and low-tech manufacturing industries (except for instruments). About 50% of the patents are concentrated in about 10 technological classes out of 118.

- The Belgian R&D system is to a large extent oriented towards product innovation. About two thirds of the patents are mainly associated with new products, a ratio that is compatible with the CIS data.

- At the regional level, two districts concentrate a large part of Belgian patent applications: Antwerp and Brussels. Among the Walloon districts, Charleroi and Liège, the major industrial districts, as well as Walloon Brabant appear the most innovative ones in patent terms. Still, there is a significant gap of innovativeness between these three Walloon districts and the two main Belgian innovative areas. However, this gap should not be made too much of since the data for Antwerp are affected by the very high propensity to patent of the Agfa establishment there.

- With regard to the scientific position of Belgium, the indicators reveal a number of publications and co-publications higher than the European average and an increase in the internationalisation of teams. The main fields of specialisation are clinical medicine, biomedical research, and physics. Furthermore, despite its small size, Belgium is characterised by a broad distribution of its efforts across the fields of science.

- The trademark statistic suggests that, in terms of commercial innovativeness, Belgium performs significantly less well than does its main competitors.

Chapter 9. Technological Performance and Performance in International Trade

Wim Meeusen and Glenn Rayp

9.1. Introduction

In the previous chapter, we examined the technological performance of Belgium in the strict sense. But technological performance of a nation is, of course, not a goal in itself. A strong technological position should be instrumental in terms of higher rates of economic growth, welfare, etc. Indeed, the performance of countries is measured in the first place by very basic economic indicators like the level and evolution of per capita income, the relative inequality of the distribution of income, the unemployment rate, and the degree of indebtedness to the rest of the world. For very open economies like Belgium, one of the main determinants of these basic variables is its share in world trade and the evolution of that share. As it happens, the Belgian market share in OECD exports of manufactured goods, although still high relative to the size of the country, has shown a marked decline since the beginning of the 1970s: from about 6.0% in the early 1970s to about 5.5% in the early 1990s (see Figure 9.1). This is a drop of more than 8% in relative terms.

Figure 9.1: OECD export share in the manufacturing industry, Belgium 1970-1995

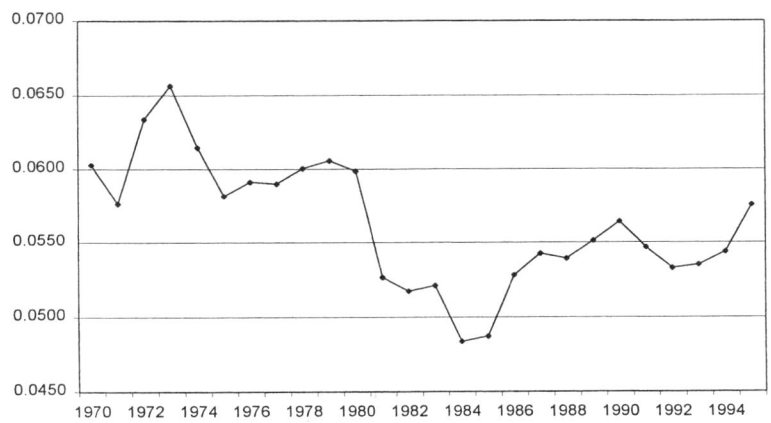

Source: OECD-ISDB databank

In this chapter, we will gauge the determinants of this evolution and evaluate the relative importance of changes in the technological position. We will conduct the analysis in the context of the main OECD competitors of Belgium. In Section 9.2, we will present the stylised facts with respect to international competitiveness in the OECD context and identify and discuss the main variables that come into play. In Section 9.3, the results of a hysteresis estimation of export share equations is presented. We conclude in Section 9.4.

9.2.   The stylised facts

There are, in principle, five potential candidate determinants of the evolution of the export share:

  1) relative price or cost according to whether firms operate as price-makers or price-takers; relative unit-labour cost can be used as a proxy for the price variable (in the first case) or as an indicator of gross profit margins (in the second);
  2) relative quality;
  3) relative marketing efforts;
  4) relative 'capacity to deliver';
  5) 'reputation'.

We will limit ourselves here to the consideration of data for the aggregate manufacturing industry sector. Therefore, we implicitly treat this sector as being homogeneous and discard possible composition effects in the evolution of global export shares.

We define relative unit-labour costs as follows:

$$RelULC_{it} = \frac{(1-\omega_{it})\,ULC_{it}}{\displaystyle\sum_{\substack{j=1 \\ j\neq i}}^{n} \omega_{jt}\,ULC_{jt}} \qquad\qquad [1]$$

where

$$ULC_{it} = \frac{W_{it}\,L_{it}/e_{it}}{y_{it}/\hat{e}_{i0}}\cdot\frac{N_{it}}{L_{it}}\ , \qquad\qquad [2]$$

and where W_i is the nominal wage cost per worker in the currency of country i ; L_i is the number of workers; N_i is total employment (including the self-employed); y_i is real output at constant domestic prices of 1985; e_{it} is the current exchange rate for the currency of country i with respect to a reference currency; $\hat{e}_{i0}$ is the purchasing power parity exchange rate of the currency of country i in 1985; and ω_t is the OECD export share (Xsh), used as weights for converting ULC's into relative unit labour costs. Equation [2] makes it clear that due account is taken of part of the industry output being attributable to non-salaried employment (we assume that the self-employed operate at the same average productivity as do wage-earners).

Lack of precision in the definition of the 'non-price' product-quality component of competitiveness explains why it is commonly reduced to production-cost considerations. Direct measures of product quality are, indeed, hardly at all available, so they are proxied by indicators for the efforts that result in product-quality differences, innovation efforts in the first place. We can get an idea of the latter, e.g., by determining the proportion of R&D outlays to output (*RelRDY*) relative to the average proportion in the other countries (using again export shares as weights), or through the share of patent applications in the US (*PATsh*).

Measurement problems of the same kind and order as with product quality arise concerning marketing efforts: it is not easy to compile internationally comparable data series for a sufficiently long period of time.[1] However, disregarding the matter by assuming a priori that there is a good correlation between marketing and technical innovation efforts might also be rather hazardous. First, even if this correlation were high, the innovation indicators one has are imperfect and biased. R&D expenditures constitute an indicator of innovation effort, not of its result, and are generally considered to underestimate innovation outside formal research departments. Patenting decisions are conditioned by commercial considerations about the costs and expected benefits of the protection of an innovation offered by the patent, i.e. its adequacy as a strategy against imitation. This is generally regarded as being sector and country specific. Geroski (1995b), who found a rather weak relationship between directly measured innovation and patenting in the UK, confirms this. Second, how well should marketing efforts and technological innovation be correlated in order to be able to neglect relative marketing efforts altogether in the list of determinants to be included in the right-hand side of a market-share equation?

Technological innovation is not identical with commercial innovation and excelling in the former does not imply straightforward success in the latter. Patenting may be considered an aspect of commercial strategy, but it reflects more the intention of the commercial exploitation of an innovation rather than the extent to which this is effectively done: a technologically successful firm might easily fail in its efforts to commercialise its potentially superior goods. Moreover, commercial innovation does not necessarily require a technological breakthrough.

Ideally, one would like to have data for the commercial efforts of firms on their foreign markets, but these are not readily available. The usual breakdowns of marketing data (which in any event are of rather recent date) neither include the nationality of the spending firms nor the origin of the amounts spent. As a substi-

---

[1] To our knowledge, the only attempt to include marketing efforts in explaining international trade flows (import penetration in this case) was by Tharakan *et al.* (1978), who used advertising expenditures from national data sources.

tute, we could turn to the importance of the national advertising market as an indicator of the global commercial dynamism of firms. One might indeed assume that firms that are compelled to invest in major advertising efforts on their home markets will be more sensitive to the marketing issue and will pay more attention to their marketing mix in general. Internationally comparable figures on national advertising expenditures exist for a large number of countries, but they have been systematically compiled only since the beginning of the 1980s (Euromonitor, 1983a,b to 1993a,b). For previous periods, the data are only sporadic and in diverse forms and for different aggregates.

However, we do have a rather long and complete set of data on trademark applications to the various national patent and trademark offices, including the US Patent and Trademark Office. A foreign firm that takes the trouble to engage in the lengthy and costly procedure of applying for, say, a US trademark, may also reasonably be assumed to invest seriously in marketing efforts on international markets. In this sense, trademark applications could serve as an indicator of commercial effort. We are well aware of its shortcomings, however, the first and foremost one being that marketing efforts for the promotion of existing brand names are ignored. Next, as with patents, not all traded goods qualify for potential protection by trademarks. Trademark protection is mainly relevant for consumer goods and much less so for investment goods.

The high values of the Pearson correlation coefficient that we found between patent and trademark shares in the US (contemporaneously, for different lag specifications, and for different countries) come as no surprise. On the other hand, we also noticed a rather important correlation of annual trademark application shares in the US with national advertising expenditures. Especially when Japan was discarded, the Pearson correlation coefficient were in a range from 0.7 to 0.8.[2,3] Apparently, the trademark share variable contains sufficient information when it comes to measuring marketing efforts and, therefore, though potentially affected by similar defects as the patent measure, we decided to use the national shares in the foreign trademark applications in the US (*TMsh*) as a statistical proxy of commercial innovativity.

Concerning the fourth and fifth determinants of competitiveness that we distinguished, we used relative capacity use in industry and the lagged value of the market share as their respective empirical measures.

The data used are mainly from OECD sources: the *International Sectoral Database* (ISDB), which contains data for internationally comparable sector definitions (Meyer zu Schlochtern and Meyer zu Schlochtern, 1994), was used for trade,

---

[2] Correlation coefficients including Japan have a comparable value for the beginning of the 1980s but show a gradual decline over the decade to a range from 0.4 to 0.5. The same phenomenon is present in the correlations of trademark and patent shares.
[3] Surprisingly, however, Allegrezza and Guarda-Rauchs (1998), using firm-level data from a survey of SMEs conducted by the Benelux Trademark Office, did not find a significant relation between trademark applications and the size of the advertising budget.

production and labour rewards, and the *Basic Science and Technology Statistics* (BSTS) provided the R&D expenditures and patent applications data. Trademark applications data are to be found in the databank of the World Intellectual Property Organisation (WIPO).

Table 9.1 summarises the observed relationship between OECD competitiveness and its main determinants. We omitted the summary statistics in the table on relative 'capacity to deliver' as no clear causal pattern emerged from these data. Neither did we find evidence of the role of this variable in the econometric exercises on which we will report in Section 9.3. For the manufacturing industry taken as a whole, international goods markets do not seem to be supply constrained. The situation may, of course, differ in specific sectors (see Greenhalgh, 1990 and Greenhalgh *et al.*, 1994).

We note first that the relation between movements in the export share and movements in relative unit labour cost is 'perverse' in 6 of the 12 countries examined. In Belgium, France, the Netherlands, Sweden, and the US, a loss of export shares in the period considered coincided with a gain in cost competitiveness. The opposite holds for Japan. Only Germany, Italy, Denmark, the UK, Finland, and Canada confirm the expectations generated by traditional economic theory, albeit often only marginally. This is particularly true in the two most important cases. Germany lost market share only slightly although in the same period labour cost competitivity deteriorated by more than 28%.

This impression is confirmed when we consider the time series themselves rather than the averages over longer periods. Correlations of the market share with contemporaneous and lagged values of relative unit-labour cost never turn out to have a negative sign that is statistically significant. The majority of the correlations (for the different countries and for different lags) are positive and significant (see Meeusen and Rayp, 1995). A comparison of Figures 9.1 and 9.2 further illustrates, for the case of Belgium, the 'perversity' of the relation between export shares and relative unit-labour cost.

The reason for the apparent lack of influence of wage costs, as we shall see in the next section, is that, although – in terms of partial rather than simple correlations – the relation between labour costs and export shares often carries the right sign (negative), the influence of labour costs is relatively weak and in most cases submerged by the influence of technology shifts. The picture of this negative net influence of labour costs is, for that matter, probably also blurred by reverse causation of opposite sign: as countries grow more competitive (because of technology reasons) and their wealth increases, more room is created for wage increases (cf. the so-called Kaldor paradox).[4] Although Granger causality tests did not turn

---

[4] Carlin, Glyn, and Van Reenen (1998) stumble on the same problem. However, by using a long panel of 12 industries across 14 OECD countries, they were able to find some evidence for cost-competitiveness effects with the 'right' sign, albeit this seemed to be far less the case for countries that are closely associated in a monetary context and for high-tech industrial sectors.

out to be conclusive one way or the other, Meeusen and Rayp (1998a and 1998b) showed, by means of the estimation of a vector autoregression error-correction model, that this last argument is more than a conjecture.

Figure 9.2: Relative unit labour cost in the manufacturing industry, Belgium 1970-1995

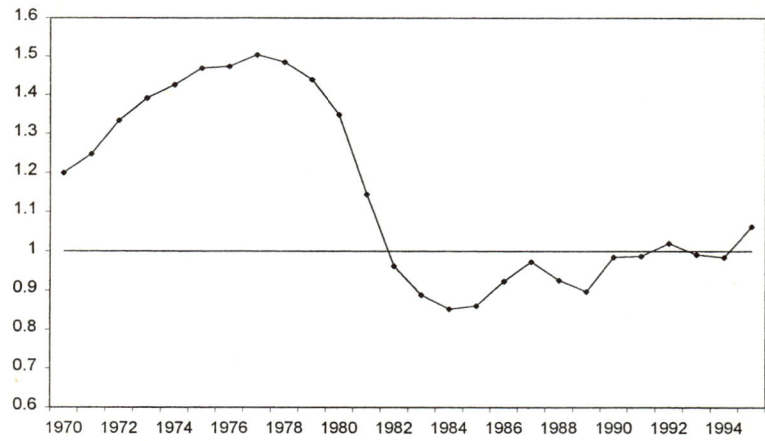

Source: OECD-ISDB databank

While the cost factor does not seem to be decisive in the struggle for market shares, quality and marketing factors apparently do. Most of the countries that lost market share in the period also saw their relative share of R&D expenditures in GDP decrease and/or lost patent- or trademark share. This seems to be the case particularly for Germany, Italy, The UK, Finland, the US, Canada, and Japan. Obviously, the picture that emerges is not sufficiently clear when it comes to distinguishing the relative importance of each of these factors. For this, we need to turn to an econometric analysis.

Table 9.1: Export shares, relative unit-labour cost, relative R&D intensities, patent shares, and trademark shares in the manufacturing industry in 12 OECD countries (average shares and proportions per period and relative differences)

	BE	DE	FR	IT	NL	DK	UK	SE	FIN	US	CAN	JAP
Export shares,(Xsh)												
1970-79 (1)	0.0610	0.1889	0.0967	0.0723	0.0610	0.0158	0.0899	0.0333	0.0119	0.1693	0.0547	0.1211
1980-89 (2)	0.0580	0.1826	0.0919	0.0768	0.0580	0.0148	0.0805	0.0292	0.0134	0.1672	0.0562	0.1579
1988-95 (3)	0.0575	0.1872	0.0952	0.0800	0.0575	0.0150	0.0804	0.0270	0.0122	0.1701	0.0514	0.1577
(3)-(1) (%)	-5.74	-0.90	-1.55	10.65	-5.74	-5.06	-10.57	-18.92	2.52	0.47	-6.03	30.22
Relative unit-labour cost (RelULC)												
1970-79 (1)	1.3970	0.9432	0.9102	0.9150	1.0813	1.2955	0.8161	1.5794	1.1174	1.0401	1.0369	0.7999
1980-89 (2)	0.9777	0.9917	0.8994	0.8399	0.9188	1.1457	1.0482	1.3179	1.1344	1.0746	1.0051	0.9888
1990-95 (3)	1.0045	1.2091	0.9054	0.8402	0.8771	1.3247	0.9748	1.2579	0.9949	0.8001	0.8364	1.2010
(3)-(1) (%)	-28.10	28.19	-0.53	-8.17	-18.88	2.25	19.45	-20.36	-10.96	-23.07	-19.34	50.14
Relative share of R&D expenditures in GDP (BERD)												
1970-79 (1)	0.8508	1.4594	1.0875	0.4346	1.0717	0.4489	1.4026	1.1723	0.4952	1.6432	0.4021	1.2201
1980-89 (2)	0.8663	1.5169	0.9922	0.4461	0.8854	0.5187	1.1702	1.3952	0.6771	1.5296	0.5020	1.4298
1990-95 (3)	0.8166	1.2402	1.0551	0.4899	0.7279	0.7193	1.0100	1.6486	0.9319	1.3808	0.5941	1.5667
(3)-(1) (%)	-4.02	-15.02	-2.98	12.73	-32.08	60.22	-27.99	40.63	88.19	-15.97	47.74	28.40
Patent share, average over the periods t-5 to t-1 [1]												
1970-79 (1)	0.0183	0.3638	0.1363	0.0527	0.0432	0.0110	0.2257	0.0526	0.0066	*0.7130*	0.0898	*0.2370*
1980-89 (2)	0.0166	0.3885	0.1386	0.0592	0.0443	0.0131	0.1811	0.0591	0.0137	*0.6057*	0.0859	*0.3739*
1990-95 (3)	0.0186	0.3648	0.1481	0.0609	0.0461	0.0167	0.1771	0.0505	0.0221	*0.5467*	0.0950	*0.4771*
(3)-(1) (%)	1.39	0.28	8.66	15.57	6.84	52.05	-21.55	-3.89	236.39	*-23.32*	5.79	*101.28*
Trademark share, average over the periods t-3 tot t [2]												
1970-79 (1)	0.0126	0.1925	0.1598	0.0668	0.0333	0.0179	0.1886	0.0369	0.0061	*0.9311*	0.1403	0.1452
1980-89 (2)	0.0125	0.1993	0.1716	0.0990	0.0315	0.0137	0.1211	0.0367	0.0098	*0.9021*	0.1659	0.1390
1990-95 (3)	0.0133	0.1540	0.1786	0.1130	0.0412	0.0135	0.1362	0.0261	0.0094	*0.8694*	0.1954	0.1194
(3)-(1) (%)	5.56	-20.00	11.76	69.16	23.72	-24.58	-27.78	-29.27	54.10	*-6.63*	39.27	-17.77

Notes: [1] The patent shares are national shares in the total number of applications of foreign origin in the US. Japan not included. The figures for the US are the share of domestic applications in the total number of applications, regardless of origin; the figures for Japan are the share of Japanese applications in the total number of foreign applications (both in italic).
[2] The trademark shares are computed as the national shares in the total number of applications of foreign origin in the US. The figures for the US are the share of domestic applications in the total number of applications, regardless of origin (in italic).

Source: Own computations on the basis of ISDB-OECD, International Labor Statistics (Bureau of Labor Statistics), Basic Science and Technology Statistics (OECD) and World Organisation for Industrial Property (WIPO).

9.3. Estimation of a hysteresis model of OECD export shares

The choice of an appropriate theoretical framework for modelling exports is not obvious. The first decision concerns the degree of detail of the model. A complete structural model of international competitiveness would require that the variables that determine cost factors, product quality etc., or their proxies are taken into account, together with the feedbacks generated. This would mean that the determinants of economic growth, the balance of payments, the exchange rate, the government budget constraints and other factors in each of the countries considered would have to be included. Nevertheless, for the purpose of identifying the respective weights of the determinants of competitiveness, shortcuts in modelisation using a reduced form composed of export shares and its final intervening determinants seem justified. A second choice relates to the possible existence of long-run equilibrium export shares. If such is thought to be the case, an error-correction model (ECM or VAR) specification is warranted (Greenhalgh, 1990 and Greenhalgh *et al.*, 1994; see also Meeusen and Rayp, 1995 and 1998b).

Although the ECM or VAR approach, which assume a stable, long-term relationship between competitiveness and its determinants – particularly product quality and relative costs – did seem to lead to some meaningful results for a few countries in a previous study (Meeusen and Rayp, 1998b), we could not ignore that the indications of long-run equilibrium (be it determined by relative costs, innovation or both) are not very strong. How reasonable then is a long-run equilibrium-share approach at all?

Suppose that trade hegemonies are continuously shifting and world trade would, therefore, always be seen to be adjusting to new targets, then international markets would show permanent disequilibrium conditions that econometric specifications should reflect (for an econometric approach in this context see Amendola *et al.*, 1993). An increasing number of trade theorists believe indeed that technological change is the main driving force behind these shifts in trade positions, at least within an OECD context, given that there obviously is diversity in the rate of change of technological innovation. The leads from which innovating firms, sectors, and, indeed, countries can profit gives them a competitive edge that very often will have durable effects. The following equation provides a natural modelisation of these 'persistence' effects:

$$Xsh_t = \lambda Xsh_{t-1} + B(L)Z_t + u_t \qquad\qquad [3]$$

where Z is a vector of exogenous variables; $B(L)$ is the corresponding vector polynomial in the lag operator L; and λ (with $0 < \lambda \leq 1$) is the parameter expressing the 'persistence' effect. In the case that $\lambda = 1$, we obtain a model of hysteresis. The long-run equilibrium is then no longer unambiguously defined, and, loosely speaking, 'where you get will depend on how you get there'.[5]

Baldwin (1990) is one of the authors who makes a convincing theoretical case for hysteresis in trade (see also Dixit, 1989). He cites three possible mechanisms: fixed selling costs that are sunk and durable; consumers who are imperfectly informed about the quality of the goods, and multiple equilibria in the presence of increasing returns to scale. He illustrates the first mechanism by considering the effect of a prolonged overvaluation of the currency of a country. Profits and market shares of foreign firms will increase, and this in turn may induce these firms to make the necessary investment in the country to increase selling there. Since, however, the investment costs are sunk, not all new entrants will exit when the exchange rate returns to its 'fundamental'.

A similar of mechanism may presumably be at work when a country enjoys the benefits of a market lead due to technological innovation. After the diffusion phase, the gain in market share may easily remain. Grossman and Helpman show, under conditions of strictly national technological spillovers, how a temporary head start in R&D results in a permanent advantage in the production and export of technology-intensive commodities (1991a, Chapter 8, and 1993). Exchange-rate or production-cost considerations could be combined with the acquisition of a technological lead, for example, along the lines of Brezis *et al.* (1993), for whom technological 'leapfrogging' is caused by a sufficiently low wage level that makes a new technology profitable.

The second mechanism is related to the risk-reducing strategy of the representative consumer: confronted with the choice between tried and untried products of the same perceived quality, he will be willing to pay more for the known brand since it involves no uncertainty. Clearly this mechanism refers to the last determinant of export share ('reputation'), to which we have thus far paid no explicit attention.

If, as it turned out, λ is not significantly different from unity in regressions like [3], and if *RelULC*, *PATsh* and *TMsh* are integrated of order 1, as indeed it appears, then [3] can be reduced to the following hysteresis model:

$$\Delta Xsh_t = B_1(L)\Delta RelULC_t + B_2(L)\Delta PATsh_t + B_3(L)\Delta TMsh_t + u_t \qquad [4]$$

with $B_1(L)$, $B_2(L)$ and $B_3(L)$ being lag polynomials.

One may object that, by allowing for hysteresis in our approach, we grant too much weight to 'history', i.e. temporary occurrences with lasting consequences, in the determination of competitiveness. After all, while it is true that hysteresis has

---

[5] We use the term 'hysteresis' in the usual, somewhat loose, sense. Hysteresis in the strict sense as it is applied in the physical sciences implies not only 'persistence', but also 'remanence', meaning that there are permanent output effects following a transitory change of inputs in the process considered. Remanence is always a result of some form of non-linearity. See Amable *et al.* (1995).

so far been much neglected in this context, comparative advantage may form an equally important element of competitiveness and specialisation, and natural feed-back effects from the current-account position may be present. Hence, one might be more inclined to take an intermediate modelling position that accounts for hysteresis phenomena as well as factors that influence a possible long-run equilibrium position. This is the approach followed in Meeusen and Rayp (1998b). In the following we limit ourselves to the hysteresis alternative, i.e. to what turned out to be the most satisfying model from a 'goodness-of-fit' point of view.

Equation [4] was estimated for each country by OLS in a general-to-specific framework, starting with orders 3, 7, and 4, respectively, for the polynomials B_i. No attempts were made at this stage to account for the inherently simultaneous nature of the equations: the implicit cross-equation restrictions on the parameters turn out to be data-dependent and some of them are highly non-linear. Moreover, an intuitively appealing 'general-to-specific' strategy to be pursued in the case of the application of a SURE method is not readily available.

The reduction strategy used was as follows: first, we eliminated the terms, one by one, that had the wrong signs, beginning with those that were statistically most 'significant'; then we eliminated, again one by one, the terms for which the coefficients had t-values less than unity in absolute value. Finally, we accepted those resulting equations that passed the unit root tests on the regression errors and that were significant as a whole (the Wald χ^2 test). We failed to arrive at a meaningful result only in the case of the Netherlands and Canada. Table 9.2 summarises our findings.

As can be seen, the earlier impression that labour costs play only a minor role has to be qualified: for Denmark, the US, Japan, Finland, and the UK, the coefficient for the labour cost variable carries a significantly negative sign, although only marginally so for the last country. But equally important is the result that for all countries, except Germany (where the influence of labour costs was not significant anyway) and the UK, the patent share and/or the trademark-share variables turned out to be statistically significant. For Italy, Belgium, and Denmark even both variables were significant.

It should be noted, too, that there is a remarkable consistency with respect to the lag structure of the *PATsh* and *TMsh* variables. The patent lag is nearly always between 5 and 7 years for the countries where this variable was significant. Exceptions are Italy and Finland, where the lags are less important. The same consistency holds for the trademark lag, which is nearly always between 2 and 4 years.

When we compare with the results of alternative models (see Meeusen and Rayp, 1998b), the parameter estimates for *RelULC* show the highest variability in sign and significance. Nevertheless, there is a good general consistency between the results of both models with respect to the parameter estimates (in sign and size) of the product-quality component of competitiveness (technological innovation and commercial efforts), except for the somewhat lesser extent to which the two components of product quality are both individually significant in the hysteresis model. Despite these differences, the conclusions remain qualitatively identical for the two approaches: in the VAR as well as in the hysteresis model one would conclude to the dominance of the product-quality component of competitiveness over the cost-competitiveness competitiveness, either technological or commercial or both. This is especially true for Belgium.

The findings for Belgium reported here corroborate earlier results obtained by Meeusen and Rayp (1995) using a 'non-VAR' ECM approach. They demonstrated that, for the period from 1971 to 1992, 80% of the explained variance of the Belgian export share variable could be traced back, directly or indirectly to technological determinants.

9.4. Conclusion

We reported the results of the estimation of a hysteresis model of OECD export shares of the manufacturing sector for different OECD countries, and concluded that labour cost per unit of output plays only a relatively minor role for most of the countries studied. For Belgium, the labour-cost variable does not even appear in the specification that is finally estimated. For all the countries, but especially for Belgium, the technological proxy variables (patents and trademarks) were shown to be the most decisive ones: the patent-share and/or the trademark-share variables turned out to be statistically significant. For Belgium, Italy, and Denmark, even both of these variables are significant. We also showed that there is a remarkable consistency with respect to the lag structure of the patent-share and trademark-share variables. The patent lag with respect to export shares is nearly always between 5 and 7 years for the countries where this variable was significant. The same consistency holds for the trademark lag: the lag is nearly always between 2 and 4 years.

The results that were obtained in our view corroborate the 'technology gap' interpretation of international trade flows, and implicitly therefore also the view that technology factors are one of the final important determinants of the wealth of nations. In comparison with other OECD countries this seems to be particularly true for Belgium.

Table 9.2: First difference regression results for OECD export shares (1970-1995)

	t-adf(0) Xsh	t-adf(0) ΔXsh	RelULC	PATsh	TMsh	Wald χ^2	LM AR F-test	t-adf(0) u
D	-2.149	-4.931***	-0.042 (1) (0.028)	-	0.317 (3,4) (0.156)	7.096*	2.5373	-4.165**
F	-2.010	-5.829***	-0.025 (1) (0.017)	0.238 (7) (0.180)	**0.075** (3) (0.038)*	8.113**	1.0285	-6.172***
I	-2.038	-5.979***	-0.013 (1) (0.011)	**0.525** (3) (0.289)*	**0.125** (1) (0.054)**	11.283**	1.2643	-7.266***
B	-1.920	-3.822***	-	**1.709** (5,6) (0.675)**	**0.918** (1,2,4) (0.280)**	12.712***	0.9482	-9.057***
UK	-2.685	-6.559***	**-0.021** (1) (0.012)*	-	0.205 (1,2,3) (0.084)	8.862**	0.9515	-7.973***
DK	-2.676	-7.452***	**-0.0035** (3) (0.0012)**	**0.422** (7) (0.153)**	**0.164** (1,2) (0.055)***	18.859***	0.0747	-6.668***
US	-2.015	-3.409**	**-.058** (1,2) (0.016)***	0.189 (5,6) (0.109)	**0.319** (3,4) (0.140)**	16.470***	2.5473	-4.134**
CAN	-2.282	-3.158**	-	**0.441** (7) (0.185)**	0.052 (2) (0.048)	5.861	1.1712	-2.962*
JAP	-1.778	-5.024***	**-0.090** (1,2) (0.027)**	**0.265** (7) (0.108)**	0.618 (2,3,4) (0.287)	13.426***	0.2248	-6.456***
FIN	-1.931	-3.428**	**-0.0051** (2) (0.0012)***	**0.258** (2,3) (0.110)*	0.031 (2) (0.029)	30.790***	0.6037	-3.865*

Notes: Own computations, using ISDB (OECD) and WIPO. Standard errors of estimates between brackets; ***, **, * means 99%, 95%, and 90% statistical significance, respectively. The estimates are the sums $B_i(1)$ over the different lags of the coefficients in the final form of Equation [4]; the lags are given between brackets. The unit-root tests on *Xsh* and *ΔXsh* were performed in a model with intercept.

Chapter 10.   Conclusions

Henri Capron and Wim Meeusen

This book has a linear structure even though it focuses on the systemic as opposed to the classical approach of the relations between science, technology, R&D, innovation, and economic performance. After a review of the theoretical aspects of the systemic approach, the historical background of the Belgian economic structure was discussed. We then studied the institutional setting, continued with the 'inputs' in the technological system, and concluded with an examination of the identifiable technological 'outputs'. We will structure this concluding chapter accordingly and look in turn at the historical background and institutional setting (Section 10.1), the NIS inputs (10.2), co-operation and diffusion aspects (10.3), and the NIS outputs (10.4). In Section 10.5 we draw conclusions with respect to technological policy. Section 10.6 asks 'What next?'

10.1. The historical background and the institutional setting

Belgium is a country with a highly educated and industrious population and is located at the economic centre of Europe. These are important advantages. In order to understand properly the specificity of its NIS, however, one also has to take account of three major characteristics that cannot be considered beneficial in every respect: its early industrial development, following the lead of Great Britain, its geographical location at the juncture of the Latin and the Germanic cultures, and its smallness.

The first factor explains why the technological orientation of the national innovation system has until relatively recently been mainly toward traditional industrial activities: metallurgy, chemicals, and textiles. Belgium turned to R&D activities in the new high-tech fields after other countries, which had started their industrial revolution with some delay, had already gained, through the 'dialectics of progress', a perhaps decisive head start. The same industrial mismatch explains in part why the government has had great difficulties in making corrections and in modernising the NIS. At the end of the 1970s, when many West European countries, as a result of a number of concurring adverse circumstances, were forced to start coping with the consequences of excessive government indebtedness, Belgium was more affected than its neighbours because, among other things, it was in the process of 'restructuring' its traditional industries. Unfortunately, this 'restructuring' was not very effective since it mainly took the form of subsidising failing enterprises that had few future prospects. The ensuing snowball effect of debt service on the government budget made it impossible to provide the funds for re-orienting the technological bias of the NIS. The particular circumstance that the industrial crisis hit the South of the country harder than the North only aggravated the situation. This brings us to the second factor.

It is fair to say that in Europe, where quarrels and wars between the nations have dominated history for as long as one cares to remember and continue to do so until this day, the cultural and linguistic differences between the Dutch speaking part of the population in the North of Belgium and the French speaking part in the South have remained manageable. But, at the same time, the management of these differences has proven to be far from easy and has deflected the attention of politicians for too long, at the expense of other urgent needs like the implementation of an adequate S&T policy.

In 1989 and again in 1993, in an effort to solve the problems between the two linguistic 'communities' once and for all, the country was reshaped into a federation in which authority in large areas of policy was given to the regions (Flanders, Wallonia, and Brussels) and the communities (Dutch-speaking, French-speaking, and German-speaking). S&T policy was one of these matters, the authority on education having already been regionalised at an earlier stage. It is probably more than a coincidence that regions in other countries also gained more authority in various matters around the same time.

The implications of this regionalisation for the adequacy of the NIS have been twofold. On the one hand, the implicit decentralisation has undeniably had an activating effect. Freed from the burden of servicing the debt, which continues to be carried by the federal government, the regional governments are now in a position to set out clear targets in the S&T field and to make available the necessary funds. In relative terms, the Flemish government, also as a result of less strict budgetary constraints, has placed a higher priority on S&T policy objectives and formulated them in a clearer way (e.g. the creation of a number of interuniversity research labs in high-tech disciplines, the establishment of new, largely autonomous, bridging institutions like the IWT) than have the other regions. However, there are clear signs that the Walloon regional government is now moving in the same direction and a catching-up process is underway.

On the other hand, as activating as the regionalisation of R&D policy may have been, it might be argued that it runs contrary to what is happening on a broader European scale where centralisation, the knitting together of R&D initiatives, the merging of national into supranational financial funds, scale enhancement, and so on are on the agenda. In other words, *if* (but of course *only if*) being a small country constitutes a handicap on the international technological scene, then regionalisation only aggravates the situation. This brings us to the third factor.

The question of the economic advantages and disadvantages of small countries on world markets is an intricate one. But if we confine ourselves to technological aspects, it can scarcely be denied that the disadvantages dominate the advantages.

Small countries acting on their own cannot reach the minimum scale in terms of the financial means needed to initiate major research projects in many high-tech disciplines, in terms of the volume of human capital required, in terms of the markets that one must have access to for the final output of the R&D project, etc.

Small countries, therefore, have no other option than to specialise in a few technological disciplines and to accept the inherent risks of such specialisation, or to open their borders to allow foreign multinational corporations to dominate the domestic technological scene through inward FDI and takeovers of domestic firms. Both scenarios were followed in Belgium. The latter strategy, in particular, seems to a certain extent to have mortgaged the development of the NIS in the high-tech disciplines, since there is evidence that the R&D in many Belgian laboratories is confined to narrow niches and/or that the results are for a large part 'repatriated' to foreign headquarters of multinational corporations.

However, a 'modern' alternative to minimum efficient scale, in principle at least, is technological networking. When the European Commission started its Framework Programmes in the 1980s, small countries, among them Belgium, engaged proportionally more in international R&D co-operation than did larger ones. Time will tell if networking in actual practice constitutes an adequate substitute for minimum efficient scale and, more in particular, if entering pre-competitive R&D networks by firms of small countries will ultimately be translated into forms of market-oriented technological co-operation in which partners from small countries play a significant role.

10.2. Inputs in the NIS

First, we will consider Belgian R&D efforts and the creation of human capital at the global (i.e. macro-economic) and the industrial levels and after that discuss the R&D intensities observed at firm level.

At the global and industrial levels the following conclusions can be drawn:
- The R&D efforts in Belgium are relatively low in comparison with those of most other OECD countries. In particular, the share of government R&D in the total R&D outlays has been insufficiently high in the recent past. A catch-up process is underway, particularly in the Flemish Region. The business sector is by far the largest source of financing and the largest R&D-active sector in the Belgian economy. The services industry relies much more than the manufacturing industry on outside funding of intramural expenditures and, more precisely, on funds from abroad and from the government. The services industry has also a higher propensity to finance extramural R&D.
- High-tech and medium high-tech industries account for only 8% of the total added value created by the business sector as a whole (including services) but use 71% of total business R&D resources. The level of the qualifications of the R&D personnel is much higher in the services industry than in the manu-

facturing industry. However, the manufacturing industry relies ten times more on R&D personnel than does the services industry.

- There is a marked trend towards the regionalisation of S&T policies and a reduction of the role of the federal authorities. Furthermore, the functional distribution of public budget allocations varies substantially among regional authorities, which implies a different regional behaviour in the organisation of their respective innovation systems.

- Despite a favourable positioning with regard to the total number of graduates, Belgium is suffering from an insufficient number of graduates in natural and applied sciences. This deficit can be considered as a mismatch on the part of the higher education system. The important role played by Belgians in international human capital mobility reflects the high degree of openness of Belgium relative to that of other European countries.

At the level of the individual firms, the following conclusions can be drawn:

- On the basis of a sample of R&D-active firms, we found that three-quarters of the intramural R&D budget is spent on the 'development' of new products and processes and only one quarter on 'research' in the strict sense. About two thirds of the total R&D effort is allocated to the innovation of new products, and R&D activity is found to be rather labour intensive. With regard to 'firm size', we found that the smallest and largest firms of R&D-active firms are relatively more research-oriented, the latter also being more product-oriented. For the distinctions 'research vs. development' and 'product vs. process', we found relatively large interindustry differences. Both the chemicals and the iron and steel ferrous metals industry were, relatively speaking, much more research-oriented, the latter being also predominantly process-oriented. Rather surprisingly, we found that the high-tech industries spend the smallest percentage of their total intramural R&D budget on research relative to development. They are also strikingly product-oriented.

- In global terms, and again within the set of the R&D-active firms, the quantitative approach gives evidence of a less-than-proportional relationship between R&D efforts (and therefore, indirectly, innovativeness) and firm size, which stresses the importance of R&D-active SMEs within the National Innovation System.

10.3. Diffusion and co-operation

International trade, inward and outward FDI flows, and technology payments are three important channels that may foster the international diffusion of technology. The most salient observations for Belgium can be summarised as follows:

- The analysis of all three indicators has shown that Belgium relies substantially on research activities from abroad.
- Technology payments, i.e. the extent to which Belgium takes advantage of foreign technology, have increased during the 1980s and stayed quite stable in the early 1990s. During the entire period, the US was the main destination of technology payments. Next in order of importance come four neighbouring countries: the UK, the Netherlands, Germany, and France, which received about half of the technology payments to foreign countries. Technology receipts and inward and outward FDI have also substantially risen in the late 1990s, and their geographical distribution is comparable to that of technology payments. From the early 1980s to the early 1990s, the most noticeable change in their geographical distribution was the strong reduction of the share of the US to the advantage of neighbouring countries.
- The geographical distribution of the various channels of technology diffusion shows that there is a positive relation between geographical proximity, technological endowments, and the size of the countries from which the technology originates on the one hand and technology transfers on the other.
- The analysis of its trade specialisation pattern shows that Belgium, statically speaking, is specialised in declining commodity classes. Nevertheless, in a dynamic sense, companies are generally moving into classes of growing importance. With regard specifically to high-level technology commodities, however, the position of Belgian firms is weakening. This is caused, simultaneously, by share losses, 'wrong' specialisation patterns, and a 'wrong' adaptation patterns.

Co-operation in the field of R&D has received particular attention because of its diffusion implications. The following conclusions emerged:

- Among the main actors involved in R&D collaboration with Belgian firms, Belgian universities, foreign firms, and customers account for more than 45% of the activity. This collaboration predominates in the chemical and electrical industries as well as in the technology services supplied to firms. The R&D collaborative pattern is rather different in the Belgian regions: Flemish firms are oriented more to other foreign and domestic firms and suppliers, while Walloon firms co-operate more with institutions located upstream in the innovation process, i.e. universities and public RTOs.
- The network of R&D collaboration involving Belgian actors (firms, research laboratories, and institutions of higher education) turned out to be highly interconnected. Two interlinked subsets of domestic actors with the highest

(weighted) degree centrality could be distinguished: firms active in IT and universities and interuniversity research laboratories also active in IT disciplines. Another important central subset consisted of foreign multinationals active in IT and telecommunications. This feature of the network was confirmed by the analysis of clique configurations.

- Simple cross-tabulations revealed that the R&D-active firms that participate in international R&D projects or agreements were not significantly more innovative than those that did not participate in such projects or agreements.
- The study of the coincidence of project lines indicated that partnerships between firms in the pre-competitive sphere continued in more near-market projects only to a limited extent.
- The matrix of intra- and interregional and international knowledge flows, implicit in R&D partnerships, reveals that scale effects are as relevant at the regional as at the international level: the largest Belgian region, Flanders, is more 'self-reliant' in this particular respect than are Brussels and Wallonia.
- A hierarchical cluster analysis with data on prime contractors for 10 major RTD subject index codes for a group of 11 countries yielded three important clusters. The first cluster consists of the UK, France, the Netherlands, and Belgium with Belgium and the UK, in particular, having very similar distributions over the subject codes. The countries of the first cluster, relative to other countries, participate highly in agriculture, biotechnology, and medicine. The second cluster is composed of Germany, Italy, and Spain, and has relative strength in materials technology, aerospace technology, and electronics. The third cluster is composed of Greece, Denmark, Portugal, and Ireland, with relative strength in environmental protection and renewable energy sources.
- The closer to the market, we found, the more outspoken the preference of Belgian companies for partners from certain countries.

10.4. Outputs of the NIS

Some important conclusions can be drawn from the analysis of patent and trademark applications of Belgian firms and from the number of publications by Belgian scientists, as 'first level' output indicators of its national innovation system. They can be summarised as follows:

- The Belgian patenting propensity and patent productivity are considerably lower than the European average. The specific industrial base and the high degree of dependence of the Belgian NIS on foreign companies could to a large extent account for this weak performance. Indeed, a more thorough analysis of patent applications has shown that Belgian R&D centres that are part of domestic branches of foreign multinationals operate in the context of the broader research policy of these companies, which often results in the 're-patriation' of the 'Belgian fruits' of their R&D activities.

- The Belgian technological revealed advantages, computed by means of patent data, are mainly concentrated in technological classes linked to medium- and low-tech manufacturing industries (except for instruments). About 50% of the patents are concentrated in about 10 of the 118 technological classes.
- The Belgian R&D system is to a large extent oriented to product innovation. About two thirds of the patents are mainly associated with new products, a ratio that is compatible with the observations from CIS data.
- At the regional level, two districts concentrate a large part of Belgian patent applications: Antwerp and Brussels. Among the Walloon districts, Charleroi and Liège, the main industrial districts, as well as the Walloon part of the Province of Brabant appear to be the most innovative in patent terms. Nevertheless, there is a significant gap of innovativeness between these three Walloon districts and the two main Belgian innovative areas. The significance of this gap should however not be exaggerated since the data for Antwerp are influenced by the very high propensity to patent of the Agfa establishment in that city.
- With regard to the scientific position of Belgium, the indicators reveal a number of publications and co-publications higher than the European average and an increase in the internationalisation of the teams. The main fields of specialisation are clinical medicine, biomedical research, and physics. Furthermore, despite its smallness, Belgium is characterised by a broad distribution of its efforts across the fields of science.
- Trademark shares may be regarded as a measure of commercial innovation in the narrow sense and reflect commercial dynamism. In relative terms with respect to the size of the population, Belgian firms register only about half of what their Dutch neighbours register and consistently less than the other OECD countries.

On the 'second level' of results, i.e. with respect to the relation between technological and economic performance, econometric evidence, based on the estimation of a hysteresis model, shows that the economic performance of Belgium as expressed in the adverse evolution of the OECD trade share of the manufacturing sector can be accounted for mainly by technological determinants. The evolution of unit labour costs does not appear to have played a significant role.

10.5. Policy implications

The efficiency of the Belgian NIS could be improved by targeted action in several complementary directions. The proposals fall in three main categories: first, maintaining and expanding the knowledge base as the main support to economic growth; second, ensuring the adequacy of S&T policy instruments in terms of the socio-economic choices made, and other policies implemented in function of these choices; third, looking for ways to build efficient bridges between the absorptive capacity, the transfer capacity, and the creative capacity in order to improve the socio-economic returns of the knowledge base.

If we turn to the first type of actions that concern the maintenance and expansion of the knowledge base, the following points should be stressed:

- In the medium term, the gap in public R&D expenditures might lead to a weakening of the Belgian technological base. Considerable effort should continue to be devoted to raising the R&D intensity to the European average. As technology is at the root of absolute advantage, it is of primary importance to anticipate any deterioration of the technological base. A high level of university research (which is of itself conducive to high-level teaching) and an efficient public technology infrastructure are prerequisites for efficient business R&D. Any disturbance of the equilibrium could produce cumulated negative effects that will be difficult to correct afterwards (hysteresis effects).
- The low participation of Belgian enterprises in international strategic alliances, as opposed to pre-competitive joint R&D projects, contrasts with the dynamism of Belgian organisations in European R&D networks. In other words, there seems to be insufficient valorisation of the S&T potential in economic terms. Public authorities should design programmes aimed at deepening and completing the acquired knowledge with a special emphasis on downstream capabilities such as manufacturing and commercialisation capabilities.
- The difference of patenting activities as shown by the distinction between applicants and inventors suggests that there might be a significant leaking-out of the fruits of innovative outcomes. This calls for specific public action in order to better internalise them. The inability of the government to reap the economic returns of domestic R&D leads to an indigenous brain drain. In a world of increased international interdependence, both federal and regional governments should think about the best way of stimulating national spillovers.
- As shown by the measures of revealed technological advantage, the country remains strongly dependent on low- and medium-tech industries. Public effort, therefore, should be targeted at high-growth market niches. What is at least as important, however, is the ability of mature industries to adopt and to assimilate the products of R&D-intensive industries. Once more, investments in the public research infrastructure and human capital are likely to be more profitable than subsidies to industrial R&D.

With regard to the second type of action that deals with the formulation and implementation of S&T policies:

- There are certainly some important grounds for strengthening the complementarity between actions implemented by the Federal State and those of the 'federated' entities as well as for better co-operation among 'federated' entities in order to achieve the necessary critical mass in research fields and to avoid duplication of research projects and the perverse effects of unnecessary technological competition. More in particular, the redistribution of responsibilities with respect to technological policy should no longer take place – as in the recent past – in terms of a one-way transfer from the federal to the regional level, but should be placed in a broader efficiency perspective in which shifts can occur in both directions.
- It would be useful to improve the fine-tuning of the S&T policy mix (e.g. direct subsidies vs. favourable fiscal regimes, diffusion and adoption policies in addition to supply policies) in order to boost the leverage effect of public intervention. The emphasis should be placed at least as much on technological assimilation and adaptation as on technological advance.
- There is also a need to develop efficient tools for assessing the effectiveness of S&T instruments as well as the results of S&T policies. Public interventions have to be adapted to the needs of research institutions. It is vital to apprehend correctly what disables the innovation propensity and the valorisation process of innovativeness and to concentrate efforts on the resolving of bottlenecks.

Last but not least, the mismatches between the components of the distribution capacity draw attention to the need to improve the links between the creative, transfer, and absorptive capacities in the following fields:

- Even though Belgium benefits from a favourable positioning for some scientific and technological indicators (patents as measured by inventors, precompetitive research, publications in some scientific fields), there appears to be major difficulties in bridging the gap between its technological performance and the economic valorisation of results (patents as measured by applicants, strategic technological alliances, publications in applied sciences, trademarks). Existing and to-be-created bridging institutions operating as technology-transfer and diffusion centres and interweaving institutions should strive to correct these institutional defects.
- The significant deficit of Belgium in the number of graduates in natural and applied sciences and the poor scores revealed by OECD studies on interest-in-science studies in Belgian schools is a clear signal that something goes wrong in the absorptive process of knowledge. Appropriate measures should be implemented to improve both the accessibility and the receptivity to knowledge. More fundamentally, one should recognise the signs that an adverse process of lagging behind in the technological field is commencing.

10.6. What next?

In this study, our efforts have been concentrated on the more prominent characteristics of the Belgian NIS. The hope is that the analytical background given here can serve to deepen some specific points in future studies. Indeed, some important questions remain unanswered that merit further investigations. Among them, we can point to the following:

- To what extent is the institutional setting that has been described able to confront the challenge of the knowledge-based economy? Is the policy mix of instruments well adapted to the new chain-linked model of innovation or is it still based too much on a linear system?
- Why does the country have a good scientific base but at the same time suffer from disadvantages when compared to its technological base and economic performance in the manufacturing industry? The fact that the position of Belgium gets weaker as we go downstream from the channels of its participation in pre-competitive research networks to near-market research and strategic alliances indicates that there are bottlenecks that should be identified and removed.
- In the present study, the stress has been essentially on the components of the creative and the transfer capacities of the knowledge base. Nevertheless, some of the mismatches have their roots in the deficiencies of the absorptive capacity. Among other things, we must improve our understanding of institutions, extend the analysis of R&D data in the direction of data on innovation in the strict sense, and identify the most appropriate means for improving the absorptive capacity.
- An important dimension insufficiently covered in the analysis is the development of human resources. Education and training are the main channels of knowledge transmission and are the main components of the NIS, not only as input to the R&D process but also as means to convert technological change into economic growth and job creation. In the framework of the present study, the education and training system has been considered as exogenous but, in the future, efforts should certainly be devoted to examine more closely its interconnections with the NIS.

***

On the eve of the 21st century, the regional governance of the Belgian NIS is radically changing the institutional characteristics of the country. However, even if the regions and the communities might be evolving in different directions, they remain largely conditioned by the Belgian historical background. There are definitely a number of tasks that 'federated' entities are able to accomplish more efficiently than the federal state, just as there are other tasks that the federal state can perform more appropriately as these tasks transcend regional spaces. Science and technology, and more generally knowledge, have no frontiers.

List of Tables

List of Figures and Maps

References

Acs, Z.J. and D.B. Audretsch (1991), 'R&D, firm size and innovative activity', in: Z.J. Acs and D.B. Audretsch (eds), *Innovation and Technological Change: An international comparison*, Harvester Wheatsheaf, New York, pp. 39-59.

Acs, Z.J., and D.B. Audretsch (1987), 'Innovation, market structure and firm size', *Review of Economics and Statistics*, 69: 567-574.

Allegrezza, S. and A. Guarda-Rauchs (1998), 'Trademarks and innovation', paper presented at the AEA conference 'Innovations and Patents: Industrial Property Econometrics', Lyon, 14-15 May.

Amable, B., J. Henry, F. Lordon and R. Topol (1995), 'Hysteresis revisited: a methodological approach', in: R. Cross (ed.), *The Natural Rate of Unemployment: Reflections on 25 Years of the Hypothesis*, Cambridge University Press, Cambridge, UK, pp. 153-180.

Amendola, G., G. Dosi and E. Papagni (1993), 'The dynamics of international competitiveness', *Weltwirtschaftliches Archiv*, 129: 451-471.

Archibugi, D. and M. Pianta (1992), *The Technological Specialization of Advanced Countries*, Kluwer, Dordrecht.

Arrow, K.J. (1962), 'Economic welfare and the allocation of resources for invention', in: R.R. Nelson (ed.), *The Rate and Direction of Inventive Activity: Economic and Social Factors*, NBER, Princeton University Press, Princeton, pp. 609-624.

Audretsch, D. and M.P. Feldman (1993), 'The geography of innovation and production', CEPR Working Paper.

Baldwin, R. (1990), 'Hysteresis in trade', *Empirical Economics*, 15: 127-142.

Barro, R.J. and X. Sala-i-Martin (1995), *Economic Growth*, McGraw Hill, New York.

Basberg, B.L. (1987), 'Patents and the measurement of technological change: a survey of the literature', *Research Policy*, 16: 131-141.

Baudhuin, F. (1945), *Histoire Economique de la Belgique, 1914-1939*, Bruylant, Brussels.

Baudhuin, F. (1970), *Histoire Economique de la Belgique, 1957-1968*, Bruylant, Brussels.

Belgian Bio-industries Association (1998), *Biotech in Belgium*, Brussels.

Bidault, F. and A. Fischer (1994), 'Technology transactions: networks over markets', *R&D Management*, 24: 373-386.

Bound, J.C., C. Cummins, Z. Griliches, B.H. Hall and A.B. Jaffe (1984), 'Who does R&D and who patents?', in: Z. Griliches (ed.), *R&D, Patents and Productivity*, University of Chicago Press, Chicago, pp. 21-54.

Brezis, E.S., P. Krugman and D. Tsiddon (1993), 'Leapfrogging in international competition: a theory of cycles in national technological leadership', *American Economic Review*, 83: 1211-1219.

Cabo, P.G. (1997), *The Knowledge Network. European Subsidized Research and Development Cooperation*, Labyrint Publications, Capelle a/d Ijssel.

Capron H. (1992), 'International Outlook in R&D and Patenting Activities', in: T. Khalil and B. Bayraktar, *Management of Technology III, The Key To Global Competitiveness*, Industrial and Engineering Management Press, Georgia, pp. 1143-52.

Capron, H. *et al.* (1992), 'Economic quantitative methods for the evaluation of the impact of R&D programmes - A state of the art', Commission of the European Communities.

Capron, H. (1997), 'The regional technology gap: R&D concentration and technological bases', in: European Commission, *European Report on S&T Indicators*, Brussels, pp. 367-74.

Capron, H. (1998), 'Structuration territoriale, universités et recherche scientifique', in: CIFOP (ed.), *Wallonie et Bruxelles: Evolution et Perspectives*, 13ème Congrès des Economistes Belges de Langue Française, Charleroi.

Capron, H. and M. Cincera (1999), 'The Flemish Innovation System: an external viewpoint', *IWT-Observatorium Paper* 28, Brussels.

Capron, H., W. Meeusen, *et al.* (1998), 'National Innovation Systems: Pilot Study of the Belgian Innovation System', report for the Belgian Federal Office for Scientific, Technical and Cultural Affairs (OSTC) and OECD, Brussels.

Capron, H., W. Meeusen *et al.* (1999), 'ANBERD – Harmonisation of the Belgian industrial R&D expenditure statistic', study carried out for the OSTC, Brussels.

Caracostas, P. and L. Soete (1997), 'The building of cross-border institutions in Europe: towards a European system of innovation?', in: C. Edquist (ed.), *Systems of Innovation*, Pinter, London, pp. 395-419.

Carlin, W., A. Glyn and J. Van Reenen (1998), 'Export market performance of OECD countries: an empirical examination of the role of cost competitiveness', mimeo.

Carlsson, B. (ed.) (1995), *Technological Systems and Economic Performance: the Case of Factory Automation*, Dordrecht: Kluwer.

Carlsson, B. and S. Jacobsson (1997), 'Diversity creation and technology systems: a technology policy perspective', in: C. Edquist (ed.), *Systems of Innovation*, Pinter, London, pp. 266-294.

Castells, M. and P. Hall (1994), *Technopoles of the World - The making of 21st Century Industrial Complexes*, Routledge, London.

Caves, R.E. (1974), 'Multinational frms, competition and productivity in host-country markets', *Economica*, 41: 176-193.

Chesnais, F. (1986), 'Science, technology and competitiveness', *OECD-STI Review*, no. 1, OECD, pp. 86-124.

Chesnais, F. (1988), 'Multinational enterprises and the international diffusion of technology', in: G. Dosi *et al.* (eds), *Technological Change and Economic Theory*, Pinter, London, pp. 496-526.

Chesnais, F. (1993), 'The French national system of innovation', in: R.R. Nelson (ed.), *National Systems of Innovation. A Comparative Analysis*, Oxford University Press, Oxford, pp. 192-229.

Cincera, M. (1997), 'Patents, R&D and technological spillovers at the firm level: some evidence from econometric count models for panel data', *Journal of Applied Econometrics*, 12: 265-280.

Cincera, M. (1998), 'Technological and Economic Performances of International firms', Ph.D. Thesis, Université Libre de Bruxelles.

Cohen, W.M., R.C. Levin and D.C. Mowery (1987), 'Firm size and R&D intensity: a re-examination', *Quarterly Journal of Economics*, 81: 639-657.

Cohen, W.M., A. Goto, A. Nagata, R. Nelson and J. Walsh (1998), 'R&D spillovers, patents and the incentives to innovate in Japan and the United States', Carnegie Mellon University Working Paper.

COPOL (1993), *Belgian Authorities for Science Policy*, EUR#55035.

Cortese, V., G. Steurs and K. Kesteloot (1990), *De Belgische Deelname aan de EG-onderzoeksprogramma's*, DPWB, Brussels.

CRef, (1998), 'Les étudiants et le personnel des institutions universitaires francophones de Belgique', Commission 'Statistique universitaires'.

Crépon, B. and E. Duguet (1997a), 'Estimating the innovation function from patent numbers: GMM on count panel data', *Journal of Applied Econometrics*, 12: 243-263.

Crépon, B. and E. Duguet (1997b), 'Research and Development, competition and innovation: pseudo-maximum likelihood and simulated maximum likelihood methods applied to count data models with heterogeneity', *Journal of Econometrics*, 79: 355-378.

d'Aspremont, C. and A. Jacquemin (1988), 'Cooperative and noncooperative R&D in duopoly with spillovers', *American Economic Review*, 78: 1133-1137.

Dalum, B. (1989), 'Export specialisation, competitiveness and national systems of innovation', Institute for Production, Aalborg, mimeo.

Dalum, B., K. Laursen and B. Verspagen (1997), 'Does specialisation matter for growth?', *MERIT paper* 2/97-007.

Daniels, P. (1993), 'Research and development, human capital and trade performance in technology-intensive manufactures: a cross-country analysis', *Research Policy*, 22: 207-241.

David, P. and D. Foray (1995), 'Assessing and expanding the science and technology knowledge base', *OECD-STI Review*, no. 14, OECD, Paris, pp. 13-68.

Dasgupta, P. and J. Stiglitz (1980), 'Industrial structure and the nature of innovative activity', *Economic Journal*, 90: 266-293.

Debackere, K. and H. Vermeulen (1997), 'Een analyse van de betekenis van clusterbeleid ter stimulering van innovatie, met een toepassing op Vlaanderen', DTEW Onderzoeksrapport 9714, KUL.

Debresson, C. *et al.* (1997), 'Innovative Activity in the Learning Economy', draft report to the OCDE.

Den Hertog, P. *et al.* (1995), 'Assessing the Distribution Power of National Innovation Systems: Pilot Study of the Netherlands', TNO, Apeldoorn.

Descheemaeker, K., M. Oleo and D. Raspoet (eds) (1995), *Valorisatie van Onderzoek*, Garant, Leuven/Apeldoorn.

Dixit, A. (1989), 'Hysteresis, import penetration and exchange rate pass-through', *Quarterly Journal of Economics*, 105: 205-228.

Dodgson, M. (1991), *The Management of Technological Learning: Lessons from a Biotechnology Company*, De Gruyter, Berlin.

Dodgson, M., and R. Rothwell (1994), 'Innovation and size of the firm', in: M. Dodgson and R. Rothwell (eds), *The Handbook of Industrial Innovation*, Edward Elgar, Brookfield, pp. 310-324.

Dosi G., C. Freeman, R. Nelson and G. Silverberg (eds) (1988), *Technical Change and Economic Theory*, Pinter, London and New York.

DPWB (1996), *Overzicht van de Budgettaire Kredieten van de Federale Overheid voor Wetenschapsbeleid en Onderzoek & Ontwikkeling*, Brussels.

Drandakis, E.M. and E.S. Phelps (1966), 'A model of induced innovation, growth and distribution', *Economic Journal*, 76: 823-840.

Duguet, E. (1994), 'La coopération technique au travers des co-brevets européens - près d'un brevet sur six déposés par une entreprise française fait l'objet d'un co-dépôt', *Economie et Statistique*, 275-276: 135-149.

Dumont, M. and W. Meeusen (1999a), 'Samenwerking in O&O: netwerken met Vlaamse actoren in specifieke technologiegebieden', *VTO-paper* 20, IWT, Brussels.

Dumont, M. and W. Meeusen (1999b), 'The Impact of the RTD Policy of the EU on Technological Collaboration: A case study of the European Telecommunications Industry', in: W. Meeusen (ed.), *Economic Policy in the European Union: Current Perspectives*, Edward Elgar, Cheltenham, UK, pp. 135-156.

Dunning, J.H. (1981), *International Production and the Multinational Enterprise*, George Allen and Unwin, London.

Dunning, J.H. (1994), 'Multinational enterprises and the globalization of innovatory capacity', *Research Policy*, 23: 67-88.

Dunning, J.H. (1997), 'Reconfiguring the boundaries of international business activity', paper presented at the International Seminar on the Changing Nature of the Firm, Stockholm, 19 February.

Duysters, G. (1996), *The Dynamics of Technical Innovation - The Evolution and Development of Information Technology*, Edward Elgar, Cheltenham, UK.

Duysters, G. and J. Hagedoorn (1993), *The Co-operative Agreements and Technology Indicators (CATI) Information System*, MERIT, Maastricht.

DWTC (1999), *Heeft België nog een Federaal Wetenschapsbeleid Nodig?*, Brussels.

Edquist, C. (1997), 'Systems of innovation approaches – their emergence and characteristics', in: C. Edquist (ed.), *Systems of Innovation. Technologies, Institutions and Organizations*, Pinter, London and Washington, DC, pp. 1-35.

Edquist, C. (ed.) (1997), *Systems of Innovation. Technologies, Institutions and Organizations*, Pinter, London and Washington, DC.

Edquist, C. and B.-Å. Lundvall (1993), 'Comparing the Danish and Swedish systems of innovation', in: R.R. Nelson (ed.), *National Systems of Innovation*, Oxford University Press, NY/Oxford, pp. 265-298.

EGOR (1990), *Training and Employment of Engineers in Europe*, Paris.

Elam, M. (1997), 'National imagination and systems of innovation', in: C. Edquist (ed.), *Systems of Innovation*, Pinter, London, pp. 157-173.

Ergas, H. (1987), 'The Importance of Technology Policy', in: P. Dasgupta and P. Stoneman (eds), *Economic Policy and Technological Performance*, Cambridge University Press, Cambridge, pp. 51-96.

Etzkowitz, H. and A. Webster (1998), 'Entrepreneurial Science: The Second Academic Revolution', in: H. Etzkowitz, A. Webster and P. Healey (eds), *New Intersections of Industry and Academia*, State University of New York Press, New York.

EUREKA (1998), Project database (http://Eureka.belspo.be).

Euromonitor (1983 to 1993a), *European Marketing Data and Statistics*, London.

Euromonitor (1983 to 1993b), *International Marketing Data and Statistics*, London.

European Commission (1994 and 1997a), *European Report on S&T Indicators*, Brussels.

European Commission (1995), *Green Paper on Innovations*, Suppl. 95/5 of the Bulletin of the European Union, Brussels.

European Commission (1997b), *CORDIS: Community R&D Information Service*, Brussels/ Luxembourg.

Fagerberg, J. and G. Sollie (1987), 'The method of constant market shares analysis reconsidered', *Applied Economics*, 19: 1571-1583.

Fagianelli, D.J. (1994), *Comparison of Scientific and Technological Policies of Member-states*, COPOL, DG12, CEC, Brussels.

Federal Information Services (1999), http://belgium.fgov.be/Engels/417/41708.html.

Feldman, M. (1994), *The Geography of Innovation*, Kluwer Academic Publishers, London.

Fondation Roi Baudouin (1985), *La Recherche Scientifique au Service du Pays*, Bruxelles.

Freeman, C. (1974), *The Economics of Industrial Innovation*, Penguin Books, London.

Freeman, C. (1987), *Technology Policy and Economic Performance: Lessons from Japan*, Pinter, London.

Freeman, L.C. (1979), 'Centrality in social networks: a conceptual clarification', *Social Networks*, 1: 215-239.

Galli, R. and M. Teubal (1997), 'Paradigmatic shifts in national innovation systems', in: C. Edquist (ed.), *Systems of Innovation. Technologies, Institutions and Organizations*, Pinter, London and Washington, DC, pp. 342-370.

Gambardella, A. and W. Garcia-Fontes (1994), 'Regional linkages through European research funding', *MERIT paper* 2/94-034.

Garcia-Fontes, W. and A. Geuna (1995), 'The dynamics of research networks in Brite-Euram', *MERIT paper* 2/95-020.

Geroski, P. (1995a), 'Markets for technology: knowledge, innovation and appropriability', in: P. Stoneman (ed.), *Handbook of the Economics of Innovation and Technological Change*, Blackwell Publishers Ltd, Oxford, pp. 90-131.

Geroski, P. (1995b), 'Innovation and competitive advantage', *Economics Department Working Papers*, 159, OECD.

Geuna, A. (1996), 'Determinants of university participation in EU R&D cooperative projects', *MERIT paper* 2/96-011.

Glismann, H.H. and E.J. Horn (1988), 'Comparative invention performance of major industrial countries: patterns and explanations', *Management Science*, 34: 1169-1187.

Greenhalgh, C. (1990), 'Innovation and trade performance in the United Kingdom', *Economic Journal*, 100: 105-118.

Greenhalgh, C., P. Taylor and R. Wilson (1994), 'Innovation and export volumes and prices - a disaggregated study', *Oxford Economic Papers*, 46: 102-135.

Griliches, Z. (1979), 'Issues in assessing the contribution of R&D in productivity growth', *Bell Journal of Economics*, 10: 92-116.

Griliches, Z. (1986), 'Productivity, R&D, and basic research at the firm level in the 70's', *American Economic Review*, 76: 141-154.

Griliches, Z. (1990), 'Patent statistics as economic indicators: a survey', *Journal of Economic Literature*, 28: 1661-707.

Griliches, Z. (1992), 'The search for R&D spillovers', *Scandinavian Journal of Economics*, 94(Supplement): 29-47.

Griliches, Z. and F. Lichtenberg (1984), 'Interuniversity technology flows and productivity growth: a re-examination', *Review of Economics and Statistics*, 66(2): 325-29.

Grossman, G.M. and E. Helpman (1991a), *Innovation and Growth in the Global Economy*, MIT Press, Cambridge, Mass.

Grossman, G.M. and E. Helpman (1991b), 'Quality ladders in the theory of economic growth', *Review of Economic Studies*, 58: 43-61.

Grossman, G.M. and E. Helpman (1993), 'Hysteresis in the trade pattern', in: W. Ethier, E. Helpman and P. Neary (eds), *Theory, Policy and Dynamics in International Trade. Essays in honour of Ronald W. Jones*, Cambridge University Press, Cambridge, pp. 268-290.

Grupp, H. (1992), 'Competitive advantage of EC nations as a function of their science and technology production?', in: A.F.J. van Raan *et al.* (eds), *Science and Technology in a Policy Context*, DSWO Press, Leiden, pp. 327-355.

Hagedoorn, J. (1990), 'Samenwerking bij productie en innovatie', *Tijdschrift voor Politieke Economie*, 13: 17-39.

Hagedoorn, J. (1995), 'Strategic technology partnering during the 1980s: trends, networks and corporate patterns in non-core technologies', *Research Policy*, 24: 207-231.

Hagedoorn, J. and R. Narula (1996), 'Choosing organizational modes of strategic technology partnering: international and sectoral differences', *Journal of International Business Studies*, 27: 265-284.

Hagedoorn, J. and J. Schakenraad (1990), 'Inter-firm partnerships and cooperative strategies in core technologies?', in: C. Freeman and L. Soete (eds), *New Explorations in the Economics of Technical Changes*, Pinter, London and New York, pp. 3-37.

Hagedoorn, J. and J. Schakenraad (1993), 'A comparison of private and subsidized inter-firm linkages in the European information technology industry', *Journal of Common Market Studies*, 31: 373-390.

Håkansson, H. (1989), *Corporate Technological Behaviour: Cooperation and Networks*, Routledge, London.

Hall, B.H. (1996), 'The Private and social returns to research and development', in: B. Smith and C. Barfield (eds), *Technology, R&D and the Economy*, Brookings Institute, Wash. DC.

Hall, B.H., Z. Griliches and J.A. Hausman (1986), 'Patents and R&D: is there a lag?', *International Economic Review*, 27: 265-283.

Hausman, J.A., B.H. Hall and Z. Griliches (1984), 'Econometric models for count data with an application to the patents-R&D relationship', *Econometrica*, 52: 909-938.

Imai, K. and Y. Baba (1991), 'Systemic innovation and cross border networks. Transcending markets and hierarchies to create a new techno-economic system', in: OECD, *Technology and Productivity - The Challenge for Economic Policy*, Paris, pp. 389-405.

Jaffe, A. (1986), 'Technological opportunity and spillovers of R&D: evidence from firms' patents, profits and market value', *American Economic Review*, 76: 984-1001.

Jaffe, A. (1989), 'Real effects of academic research', *American Economic Review*, 79: 957-970.

Jaffe, A., M. Trajtenberg and R. Henderson (1993), 'Geographical localization of knowledge spillovers as evidenced by patent citations', *Quarterly Journal of Economics*, 108: 577-578.

Johnson, B. (1988), 'An institutional approach to the small country problem', in: C. Freeman and B.-Å. Lundvall (eds), *Small Countries Facing the Technological Revolution*, Pinter Publishers, London, pp. 279-97.

Kamien, M., E. Muller and I. Zang (1992), 'Research joint-venture and R&D cartels', *American Economic Review*, 82: 1293-1306.

Katz, M.L. (1986), 'An analysis of cooperative research and development', *Rand Journal of Economics*, 17: 527-543.

Kennedy, C. (1964), 'Induced bias in innovation and the theory of distribution', *Economic Journal*, 74: 541-547.

Kleinknecht, A. (1987), 'Measuring R&D in small firms: how much are we missing?', *Journal of Industrial Economics*, 36: 253-256.

Kleinknecht, A., T.P. Poot and J.O.N. Reijnen (1991), 'Formal and informal R&D and firm size: survey results from the Netherlands', in: Z.J. Acs and D.B. Audretsch (eds), *Innovation and Technological Change: An international comparison*, Harvester, New York.

Kleinknecht, A. and J.O.N. Reijnen (1992), 'Why do firms cooperate in R&D ? An empirical study', *Research Policy*, 21: 347-360.

Klevorick, A., R.C. Levin, R.R. Nelson and S.G. Winter (1995), 'On the sources and significance of interindustry differences in technological opportunities', *Research Policy*, 24: 185-205.

Krugman, P. (1991), 'Increasing returns and economic geography', *Journal of Political Economy*, 99: 483-500.

Krugman, P. (1995), 'Technological change in international trade', in: P. Stoneman (ed.), *Handbook of the Economics of Innovation and Technological Change*, Blackwell, Oxford and Cambridge, Mass., pp. 342-365.

Krugman, P. (1996), 'What economists can learn from evolutionary theorists – and vice versa', invited lecture at the EAEPE 1996 Conference on 'Work, Unemployment and Need', Antwerp, November 1996.

Kumar, V. and S. Magun (1995), 'The role of R&D consortia in technology development', Industry Canada, Occasional Paper, 3.

Kuznets, S. (1930), *Secular Movements in Production and Prices*, Houghton Mifflin, Boston.

Laursen, K. and J.L. Christensen (1996), 'The creation, distribution and use of knowledge - a pilot study of the Danish innovation system', Danish Agency for Trade and Industry, Copenhagen.

Lebrun, M., M. Bruwier, J. Dhondt and G. Hansotte (1979), *Essai sur la Révolution Industrielle en Belgique, 1770-1847*, Palais des Académies, Brussels.

Levin, R. and P. Reiss (1988), 'Cost reducing and demand creating R&D with spillovers', *Rand Journal of Economics*, 19: 538-556.

Lichtenberg, F. (1996), 'The European Strategic Program for Research in Information technologies (ESPRIT): an ex-post analysis', presented at the CEPR/WZB Conference 'Does Europe Have an Industrial Policy?', Berlin, 19-20 April.

Lichtenberg, F. and B. van Pottelsberghe de la Potterie (1996), 'International R&D spillovers: a re-examination', *NBER Working Paper* N° 5668.

List, F. (1883), *Das Nationale System der Politische Ökonomie*, 7th ed., Cotta, Stuttgart.

Lucas, R.E. (1988), 'On the mechanics of development planning', *Journal of Monetary Economics*, 22: 3-42.

Lundvall, B.-Å. (1988), 'Innovation as an interactive process: from user-producer interaction to the national system of innovation', in: G. Dosi *et al.* (eds), *Technical Change and Economic Theory*, Pinter Publishers, London and New York, pp. 349-369.

Lundvall, B.-Å. (ed.) (1992), *National Systems of Innovation: towards a Theory of Innovation and Interactive Learning*, Pinter Publishers, London and New York.

Maddison, A. (1982), *Phases of Capitalist Development*, Oxford University Press, Oxford.

Mansfield, E. (1964), 'Industrial research and development expenditures: determinants, prospects and relation of size of firm and inventive output', *Journal of Political Economy*, 72: 319-340.

Mansfield, E. (1988), 'Industrial R&D in Japan and in the United-States: a comparative study', *American Economic Review*, 78: 223-228.

Mansfield, E. *et al.* (1977), *The Production and Application of New Industrial Technology*, Norton, New York.

Marengo, L. and A. Sterlacchini (1990), 'Intersectoral technology flows. Methodological aspects and empirical applications', *Metroeconomica*, 41: 19-39.

Meeusen, W. and L. Cuyvers (1985), 'The interaction between interlocking directorships and the economic behaviour of companies', in: F.N. Stokman, R. Ziegler and J. Scott (eds), *Networks of Corporate Power*, Basil Blackwell, Oxford, pp. 45-72.

Meeusen, W. and M. Dumont (1997a), 'Some results on the graph-theoretical identification of micro-clusters in the Belgian Innovation System', presented at the OECD/DSTI-workshop on 'Cluster-analysis and Cluster-based Policies', Amsterdam, October 1997.

Meeusen, W. and M. Dumont (1997b), 'The network of subsidized and spontaneous R&D co-operation between Belgian and foreign firms, research institutes and universities: a graph-theoretical approach', presented at the Conference 'Uncertainty, Knowledge and Skill', Hasselt, 6-8 November 1997.

Meeusen, W. and M. Dumont (1998), 'Samenwerking in O&O tussen actoren van het 'VINS', deel 1', *VTO-paper* 9, IWT, Brussels.

Meeusen, W. and G. Rayp (1995), 'Sociale zekerheid en concurrentievermogen', in: M. Despontin and M. Jegers (eds), *De Sociale Zekerheid Verzekerd?*, VUBPress, Brussels, pp. 179-222.

Meeusen, W. and G. Rayp (1998a), 'The determinants of competitiveness of OECD-countries and the relevance of some simple S&T indicators as proxies for product quality and marketing efforts', *CESIT paper* 98-02, University of Antwerp - RUCA, Antwerp.

Meeusen, W. and G. Rayp (1998b), 'Patents and trademarks as indicators of international competitiveness: the VAR versus the hysteresis approach', *CESIT-paper* 98-04, University of Antwerp - RUCA, Antwerp.

MERIT-CATI (1998), *The Cooperative Agreements and Technology Indicators (CATI) Information System*, MERIT, University of Maastricht.

Metcalfe, S. (1995), 'The economic foundations of technology policy: equilibrium and evolutionary perspectives', in: P. Stoneman (ed.), *Handbook of the Economics of Innovation and Technological Change*, Blackwell, Oxford and Cambridge, Mass., pp. 409-512.

Meyer zu Schlochtern, F.M.J. and J.L. Meyer zu Schlochtern (1994), 'An international sectoral data base for fourteen OECD countries (2nd ed.)', *Economics Department Working Papers*, 145, OECD, Paris.

Meyer-Krahmer, F. (1997), 'Science-based technologies and interdisciplinarity: challenges for firms and policy', in: C. Edquist (ed.), *Systems of Innovation*, Pinter, London, pp. 298-317.

Mowery, D.C., J.E. Oxley and B.S. Silverman (1996), 'Strategic alliances and interfirm knowledge transfer', *Strategic Management Journal*, 17 (Winter Special Issue): 77-91.

Mowery, D.C. and N. Rosenberg (1993), 'The U.S. national innovation system', in: R.R. Nelson (ed.), *National Systems of Innovation. A Comparative Analysis*, Oxford University Press, Oxford, pp. 29-75.

Müller, J. (1989), 'Policy options for government funding of advanced technology – the case of international collaboration in the European Telecommunication Satellite Programme', *Research Policy*, 18: 33-50.

Nelson, R.R. (1959), 'The simple economics of basic scientific research', *Journal of Political Economy*, 67: 297-306.

Nelson, R.R. (ed.) (1993), *National Systems of Innovation. A Comparative Analysis*, Oxford University Press, Oxford.

Nelson, R.R. and S. Winter (1973), 'Towards an evolutionary theory of economic capabilities', *American Economic Review*, 63: 440-449.

Nelson, R.R. and S. Winter (1982), *An Evolutionary Theory of Economic Change*, Harvard University Press, Cambridge, Mass.

Nordhaus, W.D. (1973), 'Some sceptical thoughts on the theory of induced innovation', *Quarterly Journal of Economics*, 87: 209-219.

OECD (1991), *Technology and Productivity. The Challenge for Economic Policy*, Paris.

OECD (1992), *Science and Technology Policy, Review and Outlook - 1991*, Paris.

OECD (1995), *Science and Technology Policy, Review and Outlook - 1994*, Paris.

OECD (1994), 'National innovation systems: work plan for pilot case studies', Working Group on Innovation and Technology Policy, DSTI/STP/TIP(94)16/REV1, Paris.

OECD (1996), 'National innovation systems: report on pilot case studies', Working Group on Innovation and Technology Policy, DSTI/STP/TIP(96)4, Paris.

OECD (1997), 'An empirical comparison of National Innovation Systems: various approaches and early findings', DSTI/STP/TIP(97)13, Paris.

OECD (1998a), 'National innovation systems: analytical findings', Working Group on Innovation and Technology Policy, Paris, DSTI/STP/TIP(98)6, Paris.

OECD (1998b), 'National innovation systems: policy implications', Working Group on Innovation and Technology Policy, Paris, DSTI/STP/TIP(98)7, Paris.

OECD (1998c), *Statistical Compendium 1998/2* (CD-Rom), Paris.

OECD (1999), 'Managing Innovation Systems', Working Group on Innovation and Technology Policy, DSTI/STP/TIP(99)1, Paris.

OSTC (1997), *Tasks and Activities*, Brussels.

Ouchi, W.G. and M.K. Bolton (1988), 'The logic of joint research and development', *California Management Review*, 30: 9-33.

Papanastassiou, M. and R. Pearce (1994), 'The internationalisation of research and development by Japanese enterprises', *R&D Management*, 24: 155-165.

Patel, P. and K. Pavitt (1991), 'Large firms in the production of the world's technology: an important case of non-globalization', *Journal of International Business Studies*, 22: 1-20.

Patel, P. and K. Pavitt (1995), 'Patterns of technological activity: their measurement and interpretation', in: P. Stoneman (ed.), *op. cit.*, pp. 15-51.

Pavitt, K. (1984), 'Sectoral patterns of technological change: towards a taxonomy and theory', *Research Policy*, 13: 343-374.

Pavitt, K., M. Robson and J. Townsend (1987), 'The size distribution of innovating firms in the UK: 1945-1983', *Journal of Industrial Economics*, 35: 297-316.

Peretto, P. and S. Smulders (1998), 'Specialization, knowledge dilution, and scale effects in an IO-based growth model', *Center for Economic Research paper* No. 9802, Tilburg.

Peterson, J. (1993), 'Assessing the performance of European collaborative R&D policy: the case of EUREKA', *Research Policy*, 22: 243-264.

Petrella, R. (1989), 'Globalization of technological innovation', *Technology Analysis and Strategic Management*, 1: 393-407.

Porter, M.E. (1990), *The Competitive Advantage of Nations*, Macmillan, London.

Ray, G. (1984), 'Innovation and long-term economic growth', in: C. Freeman (ed.), *Long Waves in the World Economy*, Frances Pinter, London.

Rayp, G., W. Meeusen, K. Vandewalle and L. Cuyvers (1998), 'Innovatie-inspanningen en ondernemingsgrootte', in: R. De Bondt and R. Veugelers (eds), *Informatie en Kennis in de Economie*, Proceedings of the 23rd Conference of Flemish Economists, Acco, Leuven, pp. 197-211.

Rebelo, S. (1991), 'Long-run policy analysis and long-run growth', *Journal of Political Economy*, 99: 500-521.

Romer, P.M. (1986), 'Increasing returns and long-run growth', *Journal of Political Economy*, 94: 1002-1037.

Romer, P.M. (1990), 'Endogenous technical change', *Journal of Political Economy*, 98: S71-S102.

Romer, P.M. (1994), 'The origins of endogenous growth', *Journal of Economic Perspectives*, 8: 3-22.

Rosenberg, N. (1982), *Inside the Black Box: Technology and Economics*, Cambridge University Press, Cambridge, UK.

Rostow, W.W. (1952), *The Process of Economic Growth*, Oxford University Press, Oxford.

Samuelson, P.A. (1965), 'A theory of induced innovation along Kennedy-Weizsäcker lines', *Review of Economics and Statistics*, 47: 343-356.

Scherer, F.M. (1965a), 'Firm size, market structure, opportunity and the output of patented innovations', *American Economic Review*, 55: 1097-1125.

Scherer, F.M. (1965b), 'Size of firm, oligopoly, and research: a comment', *Canadian Journal of Economic and Political Science*, 31: 256-266.

Scherer, F.M. (1967),' Market structure and the employment of scientists and engineers', *American Economic Review*, 57: 359-394.

Scherer, F.M. (1982), 'Inter-industry technology flows and productivity growth', *Review of Economics and Statistics*, 64: 627-634.

Scherer, F.M. (1991), 'Changing perspectives on the firm size problem', in: Z.J. Acs and D.B. Audretsch (eds), *Innovation and Technological Change: An International Comparison*, Harvester Wheatsheaf, New York, pp. 24-38..

Schmookler, J. (1966), *Invention and Economic Growth*, Harvard University Press, Cambridge, Mass.

Schott, T. (1994), 'Collaboration in the invention of technology: globalization, regions, and centers', *Social Sciences Research*, 23: 23-56.

Schumpeter, J. (1939), *Business Cycles: A Theoretical, Historical and Statistical Analysis of the Capitalist Process*, 2 vol., McGraw Hill, New York.

Soete, L.G. (1979), 'Firm size and inventive activity: the evidence reconsidered', *European Economic Review*, 12: 319-340.

Sprenger, C.J.A. and F.N. Stokman (1989), *GRADAP User's Manual*, Iec Pro-Gamma, Groningen.

Steurs, G. and K. Kesteloot (1991), 'Economische achtergronden van de Europese onderzoeksprogramma's', *Tijdschrift voor Economie en Management*, 36: 155-178.

Steurs, G. and V. Cortese (1993), 'The impact of EC research programmes upon science and technology in Belgium', report prepared for DG XII of the Commission of the European Communities.

Stoneman, P. (ed.) (1995), *Handbook of the Economics of Innovation and Technological Change*, Blackwell, Oxford and Cambridge, Mass.

Teece, D. (1992), 'Competition, cooperation and innovation – organizational arrangements for regimes of rapid technological progress', *Journal of Economic Behavior and Organization*, 18: 1-25.

Teirlinck, P. and W. Meeusen (1999), 'De O&O-inspanningen van de bedrijven in Vlaanderen. Een perspectief vanuit de enquête voor 1996-1997', *IWT-Observatorium Paper* 27, Brussels.

Tharakan, P.K.M., L. Soete and J. Busschaert (1978), 'Heckscher-Ohlin and Chamberlin determinants of comparative advantage', *European Economic Review*, 11: 221-239.

United Nations (1996), *International Trade Statistics Yearbook 1995*, New York.

UNCTC (1995), *World Investment Report 1995*, United Nations, New York and Geneva.

Uzawa, H. (1965), 'Optimal technical change in an aggregative model of economic growth', *International Economic Review*, 6: 18-31.

Van den Brande, L. (1995), *Het Wetenschaps- en Technologiebeleid in Vlaanderen: Beleidsprioriteiten 1995-1999*, Brussels.

Van den Brande, L. (1997, 1998), *Wetenschap, Technologie en Innovatie*, Brussels.

Van Essen, M. and B. Verspagen (1997), 'STEMMING 4: De Nederlandse technologische positie: de specialisatie in high-tech handel', MERIT-Ministerie van Economische Zaken, Maastricht.

van Pottelsberghe de la Potterie, B. (1997), 'Governments' attitudes towards globalization of economy and technology', *Hiroshima Journal of International Studies*, 3: 53-70.

Vandewalle, K. (1998), 'R&D-intensity at the firm level: the case of Belgium', *CESIT Working Paper* 98-01, University of Antwerp – RUCA, Antwerp.

Verspagen, B. (1994), 'Technology indicators and economic growth in the European area: some empirical evidence', *MERIT paper* 2/94-007.

Vervliet, G. (1999), 'De kredieten voor wetenschap, technologie en innovatie in Vlaanderen', in: IWT/AWI, *Vlaams Indicatorenboek Wetenschap, Innovatie, Technologie 1999*, Brussels, pp. 57-70.

Veugelers, R., G. Steurs and G. Janssens (1995), *Enquête naar de onderzoeksinspanningen van de bedrijven in Vlaanderen in 1992 en 1993*, Leuven, Katholieke Universiteit van Leuven.

Veugelers, R. and P. Vanden Houte (1990), 'Domestic R&D in the presence of multinational enterprises', *International Journal of Industrial Organization*, 8:1-15.

Vickery, G. (1986), 'International flows of technology - recent trends and developments', *OECD-STI Review*, no. 1, pp. 47-84.

VLIR (1999), http://www.vlir.be/statistiek/sav.html.

Walker, W. (1993), 'National innovation systems: Britain', in: R.R. Nelson (ed.), *National Systems of Innovation. A Comparative Analysis*, Oxford University Press, Oxford, pp. 158-191.

Walsh, V. (1988), 'Technology and the competitiveness of small countries: a review', in: C. Freeman and B.-Å. Lundvall (eds), *Small Countries Facing the Technological Revolution*, Pinter Publishers, London, pp. 37-66.

Winkelmann, R. and K.F. Zimmermann (1994), 'Count data models for demographic data', *Mathematical Population Studies*, 4: 205-221.

Author Index

Contributions to Economics

Druck: Strauss Offsetdruck, Mörlenbach
Verarbeitung: Schäffer, Grünstadt